Raging
PARTNERS

Raging
PARTNERS

Two Worlds, One Friendship

Ollie Smith & Diana Plater

Magabala Books

First published in 2000 by Magabala Books Aboriginal Corporation,
2/28 Saville Street, PO Box 668, Broome, Western Australia 6725
Email. magabala@tpgi.com.au

Magabala Books receives financial assistance from the Commonwealth
Government through the Australia Council, its arts funding and advisory body,
and the Aboriginal and Torres Strait Islander Commission. The State of Western
Australia has made an investment in this project through ArtsWA in association
with the Lotteries Commission.

Copyright ©   Text Ollie Smith and Diana Plater 2000
                     Song lyrics Arnold Smith
                     Photographs Diana Plater, Ollie Smith and others

Editor: Ruth Gilbert
Cover Design: Cathy Larsen
Typeset by: Red Logic Design
Typeset in Goudy 11/13pt
Printed by Lamb Print

National Library of Australia
Cataloguing-in-Publication data:

Smith, Ollie.
Raging partners : two worlds, one friendship.

ISBN 1 875641 62 9

1. Plater, Diana. 2. Smith, Ollie. 3. Aborigines,
Australian - Biography. 4. Aborigines, Australian - Social
life and customs. 5. Women journalists - Australia -
Biography. 6. Female friendship - Australia - Biography.
7. Interpersonal relations and culture - Australia -
Biography. I. Plater, Diana. II.
Title

302.34

Dedicated to Ron Plater,
Gwen Tolentino and Cindy Taylor

Contents

Caution—this book contains the names
of people who have died.

Introduction

Diana: When Ollie and I met in Broome in late 1970s, we would never have dreamed we would one day write a book together. We were raging partners, not writing partners.

Our friendship really got going five years later when we were both living in Perth. We'd both broken up with our men—mine happened to be Ollie's brother, Arnold Smith, known as Pudding. We were both working hard, and we intended to play hard too. My job as Australian Associated Press (AAP's) WA correspondent was particularly tense, especially because of some of the stories I had to cover. Ollie also had a tough one with the Department of Social Security.

After a difficult day's work we preferred to totally relax by getting stoned, listening to music and having a good laugh, rather than talking politics. But politics was never far away. It was an intensely fascinating time in Perth—locally with the land rights movement and the reports of Aboriginal deaths in custody, and internationally, with the protests against the apartheid regime in South Africa. We became extremely active although it was all pretty new for both of us. Ollie never had any doubt about her Aboriginality, but she hadn't been so political—restrained, in some ways, by her relationship with her husband and her upbringing by foster parents. This was her time to break out, meet new men, get involved politically and in the arts. A whole new world was opening up for her. And I came along at just that time. We were partners in crime!

Ollie: We clicked right away. What drew us together was our sense of fun and easygoing natures. We could talk to each other about anything. We saw the funny side of each other right away. But also we were not afraid to say if we thought something was not working in each other's lives. That's not to say that probably at times we didn't annoy each other, but we can't remember ever having a fight.

Neither of us was the type who would stay home and do housework on the weekend. Both of our homes could actually have done with a good dust! We both loved music, dancing and partying. We'd both tried hard in our relationships and had been hurt. So we were out to have a good time. But underneath all that bravado, on reflection, perhaps we were two quite lonely women—shopping for our soul mates.

For years, Diana had planned to write a book about her career as a journalist covering Aboriginal Affairs. This was to include stories about the so-called Stolen Generations. My story was particularly relevant, as I had been taken away as a small child from my mother and put in an orphanage in Broome.

In the past, Diana had written stories mentioning people that had been taken away, but she had not been working as a mainstream journalist when the Human Rights Inquiry into the Stolen Generations was held, and so she hadn't covered it. Still, we were amazed at how people were so shocked by the evidence—we thought more people knew, or should have known, about this tragic episode of Australian history.

Diana: So in 1993 I asked Ollie if I could interview her about her life. She agreed, and when I was staying with her in her half-built house outside of Broome, we began. We sat on the verandah in the late afternoon sun watching my then two-year-old daughter, Amelia, patting horses from the neighbouring property as they munched long grass. I turned on the tape recorder and Ollie started to tell her story. As long as I'd known her, I'd always known how she'd been taken away from her mother and put in an orphanage. But she had possibly blocked out thinking too hard about the true nature of the story—the cruelty involved in what happened to her.

As she spoke into the tape recorder she became angrier about the treatment she'd received. I wasn't used to this side of Ollie. I have a lot of women friends, and some hold their alcohol better than others. Like all people, some become abusive when drunk, others happy, others teary. Ollie was the happy kind. She'd dance and laugh and sing, act sexy, impersonate singers and others. She didn't normally get angry, scream at others or wax on about all the injustices that life had dealt her. Only she knew how fate and the authorities had affected her, but she didn't go on and on to the outside world about it.

For several reasons, the book about journalism and Aboriginal Affairs was abandoned, but a couple of years later Ollie told me the story of her Welfare files, of finding out about her Timorese father and then, of course, I heard all about her eventually meeting him. It was a story Ollie was determined to let the world know about. I immediately thought, there's a book here. As a journalist, I was fascinated by this slice of obscure, bizarre and tragic Australian—and Indonesian—history. And I was mesmerised by how that knowledge had changed Ollie. She would never be innocent again.

Ollie: So we had a brainwave—why don't we do a book together and use the 1993 interview as the basis or outline for it? We also thought it was important to tell the story of our friendship, because we believe it is an unusual one. It is told in the context of a growing, grassroots reconciliation movement, one that is becoming more and more popular everyday. This is linked to an urge by many non-Aboriginal Australians, and foreigners, to know more about Australia's Indigenous people—our culture, our forms of healing and our art.

Yet, when we talked together, we both found the reconciliation groups formed around the country to get blacks and whites together worthy, but kind of unnatural in their well-meaningness. We've both always believed things won't change unless people get to know each other on a grassroots level. But you can't force that. You either get on with people or you don't. In some of these groups people are scared to say the wrong thing, they don't want to been seen as racist. Yet lack of debate and hard questions in this context is a kind of inverse racism, because there's an expectation that Aboriginal people should be treated differently. In fact, it's patronising.

So we decided there would be no holy cows and nothing would be left sacred in this book. We wanted it to be a completely unromanticised and down-to-earth look at the most important issue in Australia today: racism and how it affects people. Nevertheless, it is a book of hope for a positive future. In a society that is trying to come to terms with race issues, we both feel 'whiteness' and 'blackness' can be overanalysed, leaving only guilt and distress. That is why friendship, trust and honesty is so important. We wanted to demonstrate that 'they' are just like 'us'. (And I'm talking about me here!)

We wanted to show that Aboriginal and white people, particularly women, do normal things together—working in the public service and in journalism, going out nightclubbing, getting pissed, picking up men, even attempting to pick up women.

Diana: Working on this book I saw yet another side of Ollie—as a storyteller. She comes, on her mother's side, from a tradition of oral storytelling and songs. It's natural for her to tell her story.

Urged on by Ollie's daughter, Cindy, we realised how important Ollie's brother, Arnold (Pudding's) role was in our story. He was the one who brought us together. It seemed a natural progression to include the words of his songs at the beginning of each chapter. We believe that modern Aboriginal music has lifted the lid on racism by opening up young people's attitudes to Aboriginal people. Modern Aboriginal music is 'cool' and it is difficult to be racist towards what's generally regarded as 'hip'.

Although there's still a long way to go in changing these attitudes, historically, Pudding's songs are part of a very important protest movement in Australia. Pudding has never been recognised as a foremost singer and songwriter, but we feel it's time. His side of the Stolen Generations story is an important one to tell. Very generously, he has given us permission to use his songs and tell his story.

One thing that has amazed both of us is how some people who we thought were friends didn't want to be named or written about in this book. Some had heard they were mentioned in it, others saw part of the manuscript. My husband didn't want to be named in it because he feels the book tells a part of my life before he came into the picture. I feel sad about that, but the story cannot be told without mentioning his part in it, even if his name is not used.

Ollie: Neither of us have any desire to offend people. We hope the people mentioned in the funny stories we tell will laugh along with us. We are not laughing at them. In fact, we have both revealed much more about ourselves than anybody else and, as Diana's old friend, the writer, Peg Job, who has nurtured and advised us all along on this manuscript, told us, 'You have both much more to lose than anybody else.'

Diana: For Ollie, writing the book has been cathartic. She has had to deal with her demons—her past, and her relationship with her mother. I understood about the healing nature of writing, having written a book about stillbirths and pregnancy problems after having two stillbirths of my own.

Ollie: Diana and I wanted to write something that gave a different idea of interracial friendship, a less earnest account. When you're friends with somebody from another race you don't sit around discussing it the whole time. You generally try to have some fun!

Diana: So we put together a proposal to Magabala Books in Broome, well known for their Indigenous books. When they—Bruce Sims in particular—urged us to write the book (and not just talk about it) we had no choice. Ollie came to Sydney for Sorry Day in 1998 and we worked together at the writing, at my home and at my family farm. Then I continued working for the second half of that year on her material. Our agent, Trish Lake, encouraged us with our writing—telling us very bluntly what was boring and what wasn't. She has always been prepared to ease our anxieties, probably having to cope with more emails and phone calls from us than any of her other writers. As well as the Magabala editors and staff, others who have been especially supportive and helpful with the book include Julie Lambert, Jo Hawke, Jan Mayman, Lucy de Bruce and Jill Dunkerton.

Early the following year, I flew to Broome to keep working with Ollie. I have never felt quite so devastated as when we went through the Welfare files together on Ollie, her mother, her grandmother and grandfather. It was extremely emotional for Ollie. Sitting at her kitchen table we spent a week talking into the tape recorder, filling in the gaps. We also discussed how to weave the files through the story.

Ollie: Diana kept working on the book back in Sydney, drawing the two stories further together. And in April she returned to Broome for more discussion, checking and editing. Later in the year she added newer material that came out of the April trip to Broome.

As we value each other's friendship, quite a few times while we were working we worried that the book might come between us. Collaborations can be difficult, especially when you live so far apart. We have spent a small fortune on airfares and phone calls. Thank God for fly buy points. If you're from different races in these 'politically correct' times it can be even trickier. But we both believe our friendship is worth more than any book.

Diana: We are celebrating twenty years of our friendship, and in a way, this book has been a twenty year process—collecting the experiences in order to be able to write about them, as well as actually doing the writing itself. It's taken our friendship to a different level.

Ollie: I joke that Diana's a white woman with soul. And Diana describes me as a black woman with attitude. We hope you enjoy the story of our friendship.

Diana Plater & Ollie Smith

Pudding, Photos
and Cosmetic Surgery

1.

Pudding, Photos and Cosmetic Surgery

Hear the bell in the morning
Ringing in my head
Someone come to wake us up
So we can be fed
We have to do what they say
We must go to school
We must learn to understand
And obey the rules
Obey the rules
Obey the rules

Stop ringing the submission bells
Stop ringing the submission bells
Stop ringing the submission bells
Do we have to go through your hell?
Through your hell?

Verse one, *Submission Bells*

Arnold Smith

Ollie: My brother, Pudding, and I were institutionalised as small kids. So we never grew up together. But somehow there was that bond there. We never saw a lot of each other but I always knew he was my brother, even if we weren't close.

Pudding's real name is Arnold, but he's been known as Pudding since my granny, Mimi Dora, named him that as a baby. I was more fortunate than Pudding. I had two beautiful foster parents. I had a nice home but he didn't have any of that.

At Granny's funeral in 1998 Pudding looked really sad. His shoulders were up, there was no smiling. I felt really sorry for him. I don't know if he has the opportunity to talk to anybody about what it was like for him to be taken from our mother as a six-year-old kid.

When he was with my friend, Diana, he told her some of it. But looking at him it appears to me that he hasn't had that opportunity and support to get it all out. Only through his songs. That one, *Submission Bells*, tells it all when it comes to our upbringing at Beagle Bay, a mission about 100 kilometres north of Broome, way up in the north-west of Australia, and also at the orphanage in Broome where I was in my early childhood when I was a little skinny kid.

The churchworkers in the orphanage were really strict. We responded to bells to get up from bed, for meals, to go to church. We had a bell for everything—bell to wake up, bell for our meals, bell to go to church. We got beatings with a bamboo stick if we were late for our meals, especially our evening meals. And if we were late for our showers, a nun would come down and flog us with the bamboo stick. I don't know if you've ever had a bamboo stick beat your wet, naked body. It stings! And then if you wet the bed we used to get a leather strap round our legs and round our hands.

When I was younger, I was never able to say sorry to people when somebody in the family died, or express my emotions about things like that. And it was really only when I told my friends my life story that I realised how sad it was. They would be crying their eyes out and that made me realise that it was bad. I had accepted it as the norm. Now when I tell my story I become very emotional. Diana says that she has the same problem whenever she tells people my story.

I think it's important to talk about your past and get it out, because that's all part of your healing. I've had years and years of suppressing those emotions. And now I've gone to the other extreme. I'm really affectionate, throw my arms around friends and give them a big kiss when I see them. I used to be so cold. Even with my daughter, Cindy. I didn't know how to express my feelings towards her because you didn't have role models in the orphanage. And you certainly didn't get hugs and pats.

I'm lucky because I've got friends like Diana that I can talk to. I wish Pudding had close friends he could talk to about all this, like he used to with Diana. It was Pudding that brought Diana and me together. So I've got that to be grateful for.

The first time I remember meeting Diana was when my friend, Dianne Williams, and I were at the Roebuck Hotel in Broome. She said, 'You've got to meet somebody. It's Pudding's girlfriend,' and dragged me over. I thought she must have been a mung bean—that's what we call hippies—to be going out with Pudding.

She was just Pudding's girlfriend in those days. I didn't really think anything as it was early days, and I didn't know if the relationship was going to last or not. Pudding had really only had one serious relationship before that, with Lorraine, his son Adam's mother. So through politeness I had to go and meet Diana. But then Pudding and I never had that close bonding, because of growing up mainly separated. I'd have had cheek saying, well, he can't go with this one or that one. I had no right.

Quite a while later Pudding brought Diana over to my place at Dianella in north Perth. They'd been living together in Adelaide where he was studying music, and they came through Perth on the way back from Broome, where they'd been on summer holidays. It always bugged me that Pudding had all the talent. He could play any instrument and sing, and I missed out in every way. The only time I think I can sing is when I get charged up!

After getting to know Diana I began to appreciate how lucky Pudding was having her, because she exposed him, and me later on, to a lot of culture that we probably wouldn't have got into, like going to plays, festivals, functions and more intelligent movies—not Hollywood-style ones. Like for me, going to a play was for white people. I would never have gone normally.

One night Pudding put on my purple tights and he was doing this dance for me and Cindy. I used to envy him with all the exercise he used to do—tai chi and jazz ballet. But then after Diana and I became friends we did cultural things together too.

Diana and Pudding were together for about four years, off and on. They had quite a fiery relationship, those two, and they didn't even drink in those days.

Christmas, 1984. I had been living at Dianella in that single-storey brick house for about ten years, with my first husband, Dave Taylor. He was a photographer on the *Daily News*. He and I would have been together about fifteen years when we split up. We decided that our marriage wasn't that great and we needed to have a break. Then I discovered he was having an affair. I'd say it was the influence of the Catholic religion because now, in retrospect, I wouldn't have broken up over one little affair. But when you're institutionalised and you have religion constantly, every day of your life, it's got to have an impact on you.

When I was young, I was extremely possessive and insecure—mind you, he was taking photos of beautiful women all the time. So when I found out about the affair, I gave him a week to get out of the house.

Dave and Diana had got on really well together, I guess because they were in the same industry, the media and newspapers. But this Christmas Dave wasn't there any more, just other friends and family and Cindy, of course. I'd invited Diana, Pudding and Adam, who must have been about five, and who was staying with them for Christmas Day.

This Christmas Day, Diana was driving, as usual. She had a little white Honda Civic. Pudding didn't have a licence. He finally got one only just recently. Now he drives the old bombs himself that he used to get other people to drive for him. In those days he used to get her to drive him here, there and everywhere. But this time they'd had a fight and she just left Pudding and Adam at the door. Said she couldn't stand to spend Christmas with him. When he came in, I said, 'Where's Diana?' but no answer. About half an hour later there was a phone call. It was Diana calling from some phone box. No mobiles in those days.

'Ollie, I've got nowhere to go and it's Christmas Day. Can I come back?' She was crying on the phone. She came over and spent Christmas with us, but she didn't speak to Pudding the whole day.

Diana: When Ollie and I first met I had just started going out with Pudding. I had met him at the Roebuck Hotel in Broome at the end of 1981. It was a typical mad Friday night at the wildest pub in the west, complete with swinging doors that were like something out of a Cowboys and Indians movie set.

Three thousand kilometres and half a world away from Sydney, where I came from. In the sweltering haze, dancers were really letting themselves go. Drunk, stoned, out of control. Tight, shoved together so that their wet skins touched, screaming at each other over the loud rock-and-roll from the local band. Beautiful local Aboriginal women wearing cotton pants, Balinese kebayas, sarongs, and gold chains round their ankles, danced with hippies and local boys.

I could feel Pudding staring at me as he lent against the wall. But then a boy asked me to dance and we pushed our way onto the floor. After a wriggle to some Rolling Stones we separated and I bought a drink at the bar. Pudding smiled and made a comment about alcohol being bad for you. It took me by surprise, because everybody used to drink in those days. Together we made our way through the thick crowd, out onto the verandah. It was jam-packed with people gulping in fresh air.

Sitting on the edge, our feet hanging over the side touching the carpet of broken glass from bottles and flagons, we had to slap ourselves every few minutes from the mosquitos that came from the mangrove swamps opposite.

On the other side of me a woman had her head in her hands, groaning and mumbling to herself. Further up, another woman was screaming at a man standing on shaky legs trying to argue back. 'See what grog does to you,' said Pudding. 'All these gurrajin people.'

We drove off to the sandhills together in my red Falcon ute and immediately got bogged in the red mud. So we had to stay the night there. He told me he was going to music school in Adelaide where a few other Broome musicians were also studying, including Mick Manolis and Jimmy Chi (who later would become well-known for writing *Bran Nue Dae* and *Corrugation Road*). Within about a day Pudding asked me if I would go with him. I already knew these guys pretty well. Jimmy was and still is a friend—in fact, I'd had a bit of a crush on him before meeting Pudding, but he'd told me we'd have to wait until the next life, and he obviously wasn't that interested. As I didn't really know what form I was going to come back to this world in, I took the hint!

With Pudding it was different. We were both sure we were made for each other. When his friends found out my name, they called him 'The Phantom'. They were raised on comic books. I eventually drove back to Sydney, stayed for a couple of months and then headed back to meet Pudding in Adelaide. We rented a little house together and Jimmy moved in with us. They kept me amused with broken English stand-up comedy. I got a job at the Department of Agriculture, of all places, and Pudding started college.

People didn't speak about the Stolen Generations in those days. But I knew Pudding was deeply scarred from his past. He wore a chip on his shoulder about a mile high. He always wanted everything to be different for him. He was somehow better. Cassettes in those days sold for about $7. He wanted to charge $10 for his.

He talked me into going on the wagon with him. We went to yoga and dance classes together, and I lost more than two stone in one year. For the first time since I was about thirteen, I looked good in shorts. Maybe that had something to do with the great sex as well. You know what they say about black men—well, it's not always true. But it was with him. We really did love each other.

When I met Ollie, she seemed extremely shy. I took her mother Rita, who was down from the Northern Territory, over to see her at Ollie's foster parents, Aunty Gwen and Uncle Sid's place in Broome. Pudding and I had been there once before, for a huge roast lunch when we were both extremely stoned. It had seemed surreal at the time. This time Ollie was on holidays from Perth with Dave. She was wearing tiny white shorts that showed off her lovely figure—I was jealous. She seemed pretty straight but also much more citified than the other Broome girls. I actually thought she was a bit of a snob, giving her mother a hard time for drinking beer.

It wasn't until about 1984 that we became good friends, when I moved back to Perth to work for Australian Associated Press. After living with Pudding in Adelaide for about eighteen months I'd moved back to Sydney and got a job with AAP. But Pudding hadn't wanted to live in Sydney. So I'd come to terms with the fact that it was the end of the relationship. I'd even bought a house in Ultimo, a great inner city terrace. But then I got called in by the editor one day and offered a job as AAP's WA correspondent, based in Perth. This, of course, meant getting back with Pudding.

That Christmas, our friend Donna stayed for Christmas Eve with her son at my little unit overlooking the muddy river at Rivervale, a not particularly fashionable area of Perth. The unit had '60s style swirly/paisley yellow wallpaper, orange carpet and synthetic orange curtains in the lounge room and exactly the same decor (but coloured green) in the bedrooms. But I loved the position near the river and the quiet atmosphere there. Pudding was still living some of the week in a hostel in North Perth. He hadn't moved in totally yet because, after more than a year apart, we were trying to keep our independence.

Our relationship continued to be stormy. Pudding invited Donna to spend Christmas Day with us at Ollie's place. I was worried about that as I knew Ollie had only wanted close family this time. She had enough people to cater for.

'Ring her,' I said to Pudding. 'You'd better check first.' But of course he left it to the last minute and Ollie said, 'Sorry, but not this time, Pudding.'

So then we had to tell our friend. She said, 'Well, can you take me to Fremantle?'

If you know Perth, going to Fremantle in the east from Rivervale in the west is not exactly the direct route to Dianella in the north. So by the time we got to Ollie's place we were really late and I was furious with Pudding. I thought it was very insensitive of him to have let our friend down on Christmas Day. But it was so typical. And he had made me look bad in front of his son.

I kicked him out of the car but then I had nowhere to go. And I thought, *well, Ollie's my friend too, she's not just Pudding's sister. I have a right to be there too. I'm going back.*

I spent most of that hot summer day picking at the Christmas lunch—a smorgasbord of cold chicken, ham and salads—and talking to Ollie. I tried hard to ignore Pudding as he played cricket with Adam and the others out the back.

I must have spoken to him at some stage because there is one photo of that day that I still have, and I must have taken it, because you can see my reflection in the window.

It's of Ollie, Pudding and Adam. Pudding is wearing a turquoise shirt with a red rainbow serpent painted on it. He may have made it in one of his craft classes. Only he could have got away with wearing a shirt like that.

Pudding and I split up the following year, and I didn't see him again until I came back to Perth in September '88, for Ollie's wedding to her childhood sweetheart, Kim. It was her second marriage. They'd been girlfriend and boyfriend when they were teenagers, before her Aunty Gwen had sent her to school in Perth, partly to get her away from him.

It wasn't until Ollie's first marriage had finished and Cindy was in her late teens, that she and Kim got back together again. And they decided to get married. And quite a few of her friends and relatives were also staying at her house. We joked later that they—particularly Stephen Baamba Albert—came for the wedding but stayed for the honeymoon, hanging around for ages afterwards. Pudding played in the band at the reception and we chatted. I was still feeling bad about what I had done to Ollie's dress that afternoon. But if there is one thing I love about Ollie it's the way she is so super cool. She never lets anything phase her.

There she was in the shower getting ready for the wedding, and there I was ironing her wedding dress. She'd had this beautiful orange satin dress made, and a matching hat with lace that came down over her face. I was thinking how she must be the only person in the world to trust me ironing something for them when I realised my worst nightmare. I'd burnt it.

'Oh shit!' I was so upset and so angry with myself that I was scared to tell her. 'Uh, Ollie,' I knocked on the bathroom door. She had a towel around her body and another round her hair. 'You're going to hate me.'

'Why, what did you do?'

'I burnt your dress.'

'Oh, who gives!' was her answer. 'I'll cover it up somehow.' And we cracked open a bottle of champagne and took photos outside. She had not told me until that morning that she wanted me to be her matron of honour. As it was an evening wedding, I'd bought a black skirt to wear and was borrowing one of her black blouses.

'Can you be a matron of honour in black?' I said. 'It's a wedding, not a funeral.'

But I guess it was different. And it did kind of match her burnt orange dress.

Ollie: I have lots of photos of myself at the wedding and before it. A good friend, Leanne, drove us to the church, but we were a bit early so we stopped at a bottle shop around the corner. When we told the shop attendant that we wanted a bottle of champagne, he put the glasses on a silver tray and brought them out to the car for us. He told us we could keep the glasses! We were early, so we drove down to the river and had a few charges.

I'd never seen a photo of myself as a small child so I always wondered what I was like. I had nobody really to ask. Working for government, in some of their social occasions they'd have things like baby photo competitions. You'd bring your photographs in and everybody had to pick who people were. I would have stood out a mile because I would have been the only black one there. But I wasn't able to participate, because I never had any photos. (There is one photo only of when Pudding and I went up to the Northern Territory to stay with our mother. I would have been ten going on eleven. I was doing the limbo and I think Pudding was holding the broom.)

So I was surprised when I went to the Holy Child Orphanage reunion in Broome a few years back, where a display of photos was set up. There I was in one of the photos, on the back of a truck with the other girls. We must have been going to Riddell Beach for a picnic, and I was wearing a red dress with my hair in pigtails with white ribbons.

Riddell Beach—on the other side of the lighthouse from Cable Beach—was our beach. Well, it was the orphanage's. We had a dormitory out there, so that's where we used to spend our holidays. A little further up the beach we used to call that place Fatimah, where the nuns used to have a house. They'd go there for their retreat and their holidays. They'd swim on the beach there because we weren't allowed to see them in their bathers.

When we used to go to Riddell Beach us kids would jump straight off the truck to get bush tucker. We had names for all the rocks. We had one we used to call diving rock that slanted down, so when it was high tide we could run down and dive. There were all these different shaped rocks. One was shaped like a boat, we used to sit in there. We used to make our own fun. Riddell is really a special place for the orphanage girls.

One particular time we were out there, me and Lena Hunter and a few other orphanage kids were walking along the beach and on the edge of the beach near the cliffs there we saw a dinghy. So we thought, *oh well, we'll go and take this dinghy down, we'll go and take it into the water*. So we pushed the dinghy all the way across the sand into the water and then everybody saw us with this dinghy. So then all the orphanage kids piled in.

There was some big girls and us little kids. I don't know how old we would have been, maybe six or maybe younger. We all piled into this boat and we had no oars or nothing, and apparently this dinghy had a hole in it. There was water coming in, but not a big pile. As we moved we were bailing the water out and we had a big stick and one of the girls was pushing us out. And as we got further and further out one of the big girls jumped out.

We were going out too far and couldn't turn the boat around, and then everybody panicked and jumped out and the boat capsized. But I remember what I did. Sophie Phillips, one of the bigger girls, was able to swim, so when I jumped off I grabbed hold of her round the neck. There I was hanging onto Sophie's neck, I think I was choking her too, but I wasn't going to let go. That's how I got taken to shore. But in the process, because my tiny little legs were on her back I lost my jowidj—what we call underpants—so I come out of the water with no jowidj, but I didn't care.

Still, some of the girls like Rosie Albert, Lorraine Dixon and Bella, they were all drowning. There was a nun standing up on the cliff there praying. The girl that saved us was Sylvia Everett, who kept swimming in, dragging one kid out, swimming in, dragging another kid out. And then later on I heard that dinghy belonged to Jacob Caesar. We got into trouble for that, because Jacob told the bishop he had to pay for the dinghy we'd stolen. I don't think we got punished, though. I think the whole ordeal was enough punishment for us.

After that we had no fear of the water, we were able to swim. But at that time we were young and could only do dog paddle.

In the display at the reunion I found another photo of me. I was wearing the same red dress as in the Riddell Beach photo. I was on a merry-go-round with the other kids in the kindergarten. The nun in the pictures was Sister Pat, who is now the Dean of Notre Dame University in Broome. And I'm on the university's board, so I asked her if we could have a talk sometime about my childhood. But she said she'd only been at the orphanage six months and probably couldn't remember anything.

I do have lots of photos of Cindy as a child. Well, Dave was a photographer. I couldn't get enough photos. With Cindy, I wasn't that motherly. I was never maternal, I only ever wanted one child. But there was something I always promised myself, that nobody was going to take my child away. Dave and I weren't married when I had Cindy so that was a real fear for me, but it turned out okay because we ended up getting married. She was four months old.

The wedding was at the Perth registry office, with just Dave's parents as witnesses. I had none of my family there.

I always knew who my mother was and that she was Aboriginal, of course, and even though my father had left Broome before I could remember, I knew he was a Koepanger (Timorese) pearl diver. But as orphanage kids, when we grew up and became parents ourselves we had no role models, no parenting skills. So it's good now that my daughter and I can laugh about my experience as a young mother.

I've always said to Cindy, 'One day I'd like to sit down over a coffee and have a talk with Dave. Say sorry for being such a bitch when I was young and insecure.' I realise now what I put him through.

In 1993 I managed to get my Welfare files. I also got my mother's, my grandfather's and my grandmother's. The Department of Family and Community Services can change its name that many times, but to Aboriginal people they will always be the 'Welfare'. But the story about how I came to get those files and the huge difference they made to my life comes later.

Diana: A few years ago, Ollie suggested I become a publicity or media consultant specialising in Aboriginal Affairs. I'd worked as a journalist covering these issues for twenty years, and it was becoming harder and harder to do the sort of writing I wanted to do.

'Hey, Diana, all these bastards are making a fortune out of blackfella money and they don't know nothing about the issues,' she said to me. 'Why don't you set yourself up as a consultant?' So I did.

One of my jobs was doing the PR for the National Sorry Day Committee in 1998, which organised the first National Sorry Day in commemoration of the Stolen Generations. It is one of many jobs I've had helping Aboriginal issues gain better media attention. I was very amused when I read a comment by One Nation politician Pauline Hanson in *The Sydney Morning Herald* after Sorry Day, saying it had used a well-orchestrated PR campaign to further the cause of giving compensation to the Stolen Generations. That had never been the aim.

For years, I'd known about the government and church policies that separated Aboriginal children from their families, ever since an old lady in Broome who became my friend, Nancy Francis, told me her story. She was taken from her mother around 1905 and sent to Beagle Bay mission. Almost every family in Broome had been affected by these policies.

The day had special significance for me, because of knowing Ollie and Pudding's stories about being taken away from their mother as young children. I have also known many other members of the Stolen Generations, or children of those that were taken, many of whom are good friends. Still, I found it too hard to go to the Cootamundra Girls Training Centre reunion when I was working on the Sorry Day campaign. That was where my friend Robert's mother and aunties had been sent as children. They were the first Aboriginal people I ever knew. Robert's aunty had been my cousins' maid when we were kids. It's all fine in theory.

Ollie came over from WA to work with me on this book in late May that year, and to have a holiday. The timing was great as she was here for the Sorry Day concert in Sydney, and we drove to Canberra together for the Parliament House ceremony on 26 May.

With this PR job, I had tried not to think too hard about the actual issues because it was just too emotionally confronting. I preferred to try to do a professional job. But at the ceremony it was impossible not to let the ghosts of the past take over. It was both an educational and a humbling experience.

When I came into the packed theatre in Parliament House, Ollie was already sitting in the front row next to

Audrey Kinnear, a member of the Stolen Generations, who was involved in the Canberra Sorry Day network. There was a vacant seat next to Audrey and I asked if I could sit there. She said no. And I thought, *but gee, I'm the national PR person for this thing.* So I sat in the second row. Then the woman two seats up from me asked me to shift to let another Stolen Generations person sit down. It was definitely their day. I was just an observer.

I was trying hard to concentrate as I had a bad dose of the flu and was shivering and shaking, dying to take another Panadol. The woman next to me noticed and said, 'Yes, I can feel the presence of those before us watching today, too.'

Ghosts. Plenty of them. Bobby Randall sang *Brown Skin Baby*, which is about his childhood and being taken away from Central Australia to Croker Island. I had lived in his house in Darwin in the early '80s.

In the front row was Marjorie Baldwin, whose story I had heard over twenty years before. She was a nurse with Fred Hollows' trachoma team which visited the Kimberley. With them at that time was David Broadbent, a Canberra colleague of mine, and a journalist with *The Age*. He wrote a wonderful story about Marjorie being reunited with her mother at Christmas Creek station. *The Age* ran it with a stunning photo of mother and daughter in front of the mother's humpy. When I, too, visited Christmas Creek a few years later, I met her mother and she showed me those photos.

There was an enormous sadness in the room but also a feeling of reconciliation. A great deal of tears. When it came time to hold hands Ollie and I squeezed tightly. I realised during that ceremony, as I kept thinking about Pudding and Ollie, how much those separation policies had affected me—in an indirect sort of way. They were both direct victims of an inhuman policy. But as an Australian, it is my history too. The school kids were singing *I am*,

You are, We are Australian and I joined in, feeling patriotic but also very, very angry.

As the ceremony unfolded in all its churchiness and emotion, I kept thinking about Pudding. All that wasted talent that could have really gone somewhere. I'd always imagined that he'd be the one singing the lead part in Jimmy's musicals. Pudding's the father of five kids, Adam and four apparently very polite little girls, but he hasn't held down a job in years. Ollie managed to survive those awful orphanage years. But life had been harder for him.

Yet we'd had lots of good times together. Lots of laughs. We learnt so much from each other. In the end I found it too hard to cope with his mood swings and his demands. I wonder what he did on Sorry Day.

Ollie: Before the Canberra Sorry Day ceremony, Diana and I were waiting outside Parliament House for her colleagues to turn up. We were admiring the Aboriginal and Torres Strait Islander flags flying outside for a change. When Audrey Kinnear and the others arrived, Diana went over to meet them and I stood back. Diana called me over and introduced me to them. Audrey pushed Diana aside and to my surprise gave me a warm welcome with a big hug, and then we proceeded to enter Parliament House where we had to wait in the lobby for somebody to sign us in. While there I mentioned to Audrey that I was also a victim of the Stolen Generations, so she said, 'You have to come and sit up the front with us, you're one of us.'

We went up to the ABC office and Diana and I sat in the control room while Audrey was being interviewed. This was her third main interview for the day and I was very impressed with her response to the interview. She handled it really well. It made me feel proud.

And then we went to the theatre. There were introductions and then we watched the video, and from that time and throughout most of the proceedings I think I cried the whole time. It was a really moving experience. Even though Audrey invited me to sit with her and her countrymen, I felt a little uncomfortable because I wasn't from that country. But on the other hand, I felt good as well to be there, especially when the church people handed the Sorry Books back to us.

The most moving part, though, was when Bobby Randall was singing and his daughter, Dorothea, was re-enacting a mother with her baby being taken away and left with the empty coolamon.

Later on when we came back to Sydney I read an article that Diana had written a few years before. It was a review of a book by Barbara Cummings, called *Take this Child…From Kahlin Compound to the Retta Dixon Home*. Barbara's mother was taken away from her mother to be brought up in Kahlin Compound in Darwin. When the author was born, she in turn was taken to be raised at the Retta Dixon Home. It wasn't until she started researching this book that she fully realised her mother's history. She tells how she and the other children at the home were inculcated by the missionaries with a deep fear of the 'blackfella'. They were told 'sin is black' and 'white is pure'. Yet many of the Aboriginal people on the other side of the fence were their countrymen and women, some of whom came into the Home to work in the laundry and chop wood.

It reminded me a great deal of my own story, particularly the part where it said: *The missionaries would make orphans of them because there was that sense of guilt.*

To be at the ceremony in Canberra with Diana was like a reunion from 1988, when I came over to Sydney for the Bicentennial and the protest march. It was important for me to spend Sorry Day with Diana because through all the significant events we'd been together. That includes the deaths in custody protests and land rights demonstrations.

I had to change my flight details to make sure I would be in Sydney for the Sorry Day concert at the Opera House.

Diana had said, 'You have to be here for the concert.'

At the concert, Diana worked, looking after the media and I helped out, freezing in the icy winds. Amelia, Diana's seven-year-old daughter, cuddled up to me to keep warm, with my jumper around her shoulders. It was good to see the great support despite the weather, especially from people like the Good News Week crew. Archie Roach and Ruby Hunter singing *They Took the Children Away* was really special. It was all pretty emotional, so no wonder we got drunk afterwards!

I also wanted to go to Sydney to have cosmetic surgery done on my face and liposuction on my stomach. Being in my late 40s, and after years of smoking, gravity had taken over, and I'd seen a program on TV about this new laser technique that plastic surgeons were doing. Most people have to book into a plastic surgeon weeks before they have cosmetic surgery done. But I was too busy finishing up at my last job, managing the Department of Education, Employment, Training and Youth Affairs (DEETYA) and the CES in Derby, before I came to Sydney to do that. So Diana said she'd check out her doctor contacts and see what we could do. We ended up seeing a member of the extended in-laws' family for advice. He told me I didn't have a hope in hell of seeing a plastic surgeon but there was a very good Chinese cosmetic surgeon down the road.

'If he's Chinese I'd trust him,' Diana said. And over we went to make an appointment. It was the first time they'd seen a patient arrive with a doctor's referral.

A few days later I had my upper eyelids and jowls done. The doctor couldn't take the lines off my forehead as, because of my dark skin, there might have been pigmentation. I had to wear a bandage around my face. I looked like a Moslem girl. Two days later, I thought, *what the hell, while I'm in Sydney I might as well have liposuction done on my guts as well*. So I did.

Then we went shopping for new clothes. I wanted hipster jeans and I came home with sexy black and red outfits from Newtown and Paddington. On the Monday, after the doctor gave me a clean bill of health, I got a great new haircut. I'm a new woman!

Later we went to Diana's family farm at Foxground on the south coast. It was where I had been matron of honour at her wedding. I met up again with her family who, like her, were now mothers themselves. At Diana's wedding most of her sisters and cousins didn't have children. We took Diana's son, Marco, and her nephew, Sam, on a trip to an Aboriginal camp at Jervis Bay. The Aboriginal owners had invited some of the white people who worked on Sorry Day down for the weekend. Like Audrey had at Parliament House, one of the traditional owners, who is also an old friend of Diana's, gave me a big hug and welcomed me onto her land.

I took Sam for a walk along the rocks while some of the gardiyas (white people) who were there made a fire and boiled the billy. After about an hour Diana came down to get me. 'Is that tea ready yet?' I asked her.

'No,' she said, 'the silly fella's got the billy on top of the barbeque. It'll never boil.' We went back and waited a bit longer but you know the saying—a watched billy…

'Let's go to Berry for a cappucino,' I whispered to Diana and we cracked up laughing. It was getting dark and that gardiya was calling out, 'Tea's ready,' as we drove off back to the farm, the kids almost asleep in the back, from salt, sea and fresh air. It felt a bit like driving home to Broome from Beagle Bay.

Diana: In 1999 I was again asked to work on Sorry Day, which had had its name changed to the Journey of Healing to mark the need to move on from sorrow to communal healing. It was launched at Uluru on 5 May in an amazing ceremony where the men and women of the Mutitjulu community told their story of what happened when their brothers and sisters were taken by the authorities. Uluru was chosen because, as the organisers explained, it is the 'heart' of Australia, and healing comes from the heart. The traditional owners of this most famous of Australia's icons welcomed back Stolen Children from their community and from all over Australia. It was the traditional women who ran the show, inviting both black and white women up to dance, who, all painted up and bare breasted, performed before all of us, including the TV cameras.

The next day at dawn I walked with three other non-Aboriginal women around the rock. It was still dark when we set off, so at 8am we stopped to shelter from the wind and eat our breakfast picnic in a sunny but prickly patch. We chatted away about the previous day's ceremony. One, who had danced with the other women, explained how she felt as if a river of contentment had washed over her. She felt totally accepted and welcomed and didn't even notice the cameramen and photographers.

The wounds of removal of children have gone deep in Aboriginal communities. In some traditional communities, the process of mourning included wailing and hitting oneself with a stick. Stories tell of some mothers acting out this behaviour as though their child who was taken away had actually died. I had been researching an article about traditional healing for the committee and had heard about women's song ceremonies, which were often performed to invoke healing through the power of ancestral spirits. On one level they operated in a spiritual sense, on another they drew the ailing person into the community to experience the support of others in a strong social bonding.

I was deeply sorry Ollie was unable to be at the Uluru ceremony. She was finishing up work with the WA State Department of Education, as the co-ordinator of Aboriginal education in the Kimberley.

I had met Ollie's boss when I was in Broome earlier in the year, and he had invited me back to speak at the annual school principal's conference in April. He wanted me to give both the after-dinner speech about my life as a journalist and also one on the Journey of Healing at the next day's session. The conference was held at a resort known as Eco Beach, south of Broome. It was on land subdivided from Thangoo station, land local Aboriginal people had been trying for years to get the lease for. Nevertheless, the young whitefella who came with us on the trip assured us the resort was going to hire a local Aborigine to take the tourists on bush tucker tours. How nice!

The resort was on the most beautiful turquoise bay, but the moment we got out of the car we were eaten alive by mosquitos. It was steaming hot so we decided to go for a swim. The tide was way out and we lay down in ankle-deep water gossiping about the coming night's activities.

That night I was so relieved my after-dinner speech was over that I hit the booze. The last thing I remember was: 2am, doing yoga up on a cliff overlooking the sea with Ollie and a bunch of school principals. The sky was breathtaking.

The next morning, feeling quite a bit worse for wear, I took my time getting down to breakfast. That week I had seen a quite different Ollie—one who got up early in the morning, was dressed and at work before 8am. She and her colleague had already had breakfast by the time I arrived. I wore my prescription sunglasses and sipped a cup of coffee while searching the sea for dolphins. A shirtless man sat close by doing the same thing. Then he struck up a conversation.

'I was in the bar last night and heard your speech,' he said. 'You've had a fascinating career.'

Despite being flattered, I told him I'd felt a bit disappointed with it as my jokes seemed to have fallen flat, and from the looks on people's faces, maybe it was too political. They probably thought I was a raving leftie. I was worried how I was going to sell reconciliation and Stolen

Generations history to a bunch of mostly non-Aboriginal school teachers that afternoon. After all, WA was the state where angry parents had kept their children away from school on Sorry Day because they didn't want them to have to apologise to 'those bloody boongs'. Schools in Perth had received so many obscene and racist phone calls they had them all redirected to the Director General of Education. She was shocked at the aggressive tone of the calls.

My breakfast companion explained he was a hypnotist and specialised in stress reduction. Then he offered to give me a little free hypnotherapy session. He told me to close my eyes while he whispered encouraging words. It worked wonders. I felt like a million dollars, and spent the morning swimming, walking and almost dancing on the beach. My talk that afternoon went beautifully.

Ollie's boss had told the principals that they had been privileged to have Ollie working for the department, as she had been able to explain to them on a personal level how her experiences of being taken away affected her.

Schools in the Kimberley are 90 percent black and I realised after a short time that it was unlikely that anybody at this conference was unaware of the importance of teaching the real history of this country. So I took the advice of one of the more hard-bitten principals—who had been doing yoga with us the night before—and simply asked for their help to tell the true story of the Stolen Generations.

Ollie's Early Days

2.

Ollie's Early Days

Aboriginal children
Don't have to die
To go to heaven

Some say it's a crime
When you have a good time
I believe them

Aboriginal Children

Arnold Smith

Ollie: *Dear Olive*, the letter, which was dated 25 September, read:

I would like to wish you many happy returns for your eighteenth birthday, which was on the 23rd September. I sincerely hope that your future will be bright and prosperous.

No doubt you are aware that your term as a ward expires on that date, but this does not mean that we are not interested in your future. Should you at any time feel you need our advice or assistance, do not hesitate to approach the Department. My officers, one and all, are only too willing to do anything in their power for you.

Once again I say all the best of luck for your future from your friends of the Child Welfare Department.

Whoever signed the letter, it was illegible, but it came from the director of the department. Scribbled underneath was the comment: *Yet another instance of delay! Couldn't we get the birthday letters out so that they mean something? Please advise me.*

How typical of bureaucratic inefficiency is that? (I can knock public servants, because I've been one for nearly thirty years.)

By the time this letter was sent I'd left school and was doing my nursing aide training at Shenton Park in Perth. When you're nursing you had to do a stint in Shenton Park, then you had to go to Royal Perth Hospital as part of your training. In the city there they had the old Grand Hotel which they made into nurses' quarters, and initially when I moved to the city that's where I was living, down the road from Royal Perth.

And then some other girls and I decided we were going to get a flat of our own. There was three of us Aboriginal girls and two white girls. We moved into this flat on the tenth floor in a block in Goderick Street. The two white girls ended up moving out and getting a place of their own, and then there was three of us. Then another one left and there was two of us. With the money we were getting, we were just able to pay our rent. We didn't have much money for food. We didn't have any money for buying cooking utensils and I can remember we used to cook out of anything. We used these old cake tins for pots. It's a wonder we never got tin poisoning.

I'd had my eighteenth birthday in September and a few days later there was a knock on the door of the flat. This white woman come in asking for me. She was from the Welfare office. The purpose of her visit was to tell me happy birthday, and since I turned eighteen I was no longer a ward of the state. And then she went on to tell me all the benefits I could have got while I was a ward of the state— financial assistance, clothes and all this sort of stuff. I asked her if I could get that stuff now—'I'm living on the bones of my arse.'

And she said, 'No, you're no longer a ward of the state.'

Happy birthday, you're free. You're free and you're broke. I often wondered how the hell she tracked me down. It was only when I got my files that I discovered they knew my every move.

In their reports they described me as: *Still a rather shy girl, but much more poised and is very good-looking, with dark skin and good features…Sister Baker says that Olive looks always as though she has just come on duty… Olive* (is) *very careful of her appearance and personal hygiene*. Things like that. They were having a good look and I wasn't even aware of any of this happening, except once with Father Luemmen, who was running Pallotine (where I boarded during my high school years in Perth).

After we went nursing he apparently used to pay visits to the matron of the nurses' quarters, getting reports on us. It was really funny—being a Catholic, when we started nursing we still believed we had to go to church every Sunday. So if we didn't go to morning mass, we'd go to the evening one, depending on which shift we were working. Religiously, conscientiously, we'd race down to the local church for mass. And then one day I knocked off work and bumped into the matron of the nursing quarters and she said, 'Oh, Father Luemmen came to visit and he was asking how you were.' I saw red. I thought, *how fucking dare he come up and check up on us?* From that day on I stopped going to church.

※ ※ ※

My first recollection of my very early childhood was when I was in the Holy Child Orphanage in Broome. I don't even recall being with my mother. I suppose I would have been about 30 years old when I had an opportunity to speak to my mother about my childhood. I asked, 'How old was I when I was put in the orphanage?'

And she couldn't tell me, she just said, 'You were up to my knee.'

Then I asked her, 'Why did you put me in the orphanage?'

Her response was, 'Baby, I got tired of running.'

Fortunately, I knew what she meant, because I was aware of the Aborigines Act 1905 (WA), which made the Chief Protector the legal guardian of every Aboriginal and 'half-caste' child under sixteen. This meant it was his right to make whatever decisions he wanted to on behalf of us. So if the government, or, in some cases, patrol officers and later Welfare workers thought that an Aboriginal child was being neglected he could have that child put in an orphanage. But they really didn't need a reason.

My mother was always on the run. She told me she used to run away to Derby because the local police would take the kids away from the parents. She told the sergeant here in Broome, 'You can't have my kids until they're old enough to know me.'

She ran right across the Kimberley; from Broome, to Derby, to Halls Creek, to Wyndham. She used to say, 'See, there was no social security or family allowance for Aboriginal people, so you had to work to feed yourself to survive.' She worked in pubs or as a domestic for white families, or in hospitals, and when she had no money she'd go to the rubbish dump to feed us.

I knew my father was a Koepang man who came over here for the pearling industry. He'd left Broome and gone back to where he was from, and that's about all I knew about him.

Pudding had a different father to me. In 1953, when I was about two years old, Mum and Cooney (short for Cornelius) Tolentino had Pudding. About a month later they applied to get married. They were given permission by the Commissioner of Native Affairs to get married. But they never did.

On 10 November, 1954, I was put in the Holy Child Orphanage. I was three years old. On 24 July, 1958, I was declared a destitute child and: *committed to the care of the Child Welfare Department until eighteen years of age.*

Mum was still pursued by the department to: *contribute towards the maintenance of her child*. However, the Clerk of Courts wrote back saying that, as Mum was of: *poor moral character and low intelligence*, she was not in a position to contribute towards my maintenance.

Pudding was put into Beagle Bay mission in February, 1959, because there wasn't an orphanage for boys in Broome.

In my mum's file, apart from some documents about trying to obtain her child endowment money, the very next document is a report by the Assistant District Officer, a Welfare inspector, in Halls Creek in 1960. It says she was found by the Halls Creek police outside the local hotel, trying to find a white man to take her for the night. The Welfare inspector appeared for her defence when she went to court, charged with having no lawful means of support. He told the court he would find her work locally and, if given the chance, she would refrain from getting into further trouble. She was, however, found guilty, and sentenced to one month's jail.

My mum used to drink. I'd say she was an alcoholic. But then if I was a mother and my children were taken away, I would have ended up an alcoholic.

※ ※ ※

The history of the Broome orphanage is that in 1896, Father Nicholas, with the support of St John of God nuns, started a school for Aboriginal people in Broome. It later became a boarding school and eventually the Holy Child Orphanage.

From what we've learnt later, us girls were carefully protected by the staff—much to the annoyance of the men to whom we were promised. Twice in its early years the buildings were set alight by frustrated suitors! During 1907 the boarding school closed, but with the arrival of Sister Antonio from Beagle Bay in 1908, a group of mixed-descent children were gathered under her care. In 1912 the St John of God Home for Native Girls was established. This continued until 1941, when it became known as the Holy Child Orphanage. The term orphanage is not an accurate description because the girls were not orphans, but station children removed from their families by the Aboriginal 'Protectors'. None of us were orphans. And just to use that term was untruthful. And the church and the government authorities knew that.

In March, 1942, a Japanese plane bombed Broome. The orphanage was closed and the Sister and some of the girls were evacuated to Beagle Bay. During the war years, first the army and later the air force used the orphanage buildings. In 1945 the nuns returned.

❋ ❋ ❋

When we were in the orphanage in Broome our parents were only allowed to come and see us every first Sunday of the month, but that was a really devastating experience. My mother used to come occasionally and I used to always wonder why she didn't come more often, say every month like the other mothers. But when I look back now I put myself in her shoes, because we used to go through this ritual when the mothers turned up. You see, you had these screaming kids, clinging onto their mother's legs, little tiny things they were. It was very nice to go out and spend time with your kid, but when it was time to go home there was this ritual of all these screaming kids. It was really sad. I put myself in my mum's shoes and I wouldn't come and visit my child as often because of that.

So on the first Sunday of the month my Granny, Mimi Dora, would take me out. (In Broome we call our grandmothers Mimi.) She took me to Morgan Camp, on the other side of Chinatown, where she lived. Lulu Margi, who was a relative of my father, also lived there.

Granny mentioned my father's name but never told me anything about him. My mother was the one who said Lulu Margi was a blood relative. I was very close to him, I suppose me being Koepang. He treated me like I was his granddaughter. He was like a grandfather to me. Only my Aunty Joy, Mimi Dora's youngest daughter, was left at home then. Her father was a Chinaman—I remember him too. Earlier, when Granny lived behind the picture show, she was living with him.

There was always gambling going on. I never took it up, whether horse racing or cards. And still today, if I go to the casino I'll allow myself $20 to bet with and that's it. If I lose I lose. I'd rather spend my money and have something to show for it. Mimi Dora used to play a game with sticks known as kudga kudga. There were other Asian games they'd play—cards, quince. That's a big problem in Aboriginal communities now, an influence from the Asians. There would have been opium dens in Broome, before my time. The Malay boys that came over, they would have been on drugs before drugs were popular. I'm not sure what drugs they used. They were always stoned, you just knew they were out of it. But there was no violence. When we were young we didn't know nothing about drugs.

I've got special and fond memories of my grandmother, because she used to be able to come and take me out. The parting was different when my mother came on those rare occasions, to when I said goodbye to my granny. There were these scenes where you didn't want to let her go, because you didn't know when you'd see her again.

Not one of us would say we preferred the orphanage to remaining with our mothers and families. I guess we were more fortunate than some Aboriginal people, who were forcefully taken away and taken down south, for example, and they never got to know their families and their mothers. In some ways we were fortunate—we knew who our mothers were.

Still, after a while you just accepted you were in the orphanage. Except for some, like Clare Albert, who used to run away all the time because her mother lived up the hill (at the reserve on Kennedy Hill). And every time, they'd go and pick her up and bring her back. I used to think she was so brave, cause I could never have done that.

I think initially the law was they took kids that were part-Aboriginal, but in my recollection with all the girls— it was an all girl orphanage—we had part-Aboriginal kids from Chinese, Malay, Japanese, Koepang, white man father. I think initially they thought at that time that the Aboriginal race would die out, so they'd take all these part-Aboriginal kids away and then assimilate them. But we also had a lot of Aboriginal girls in the orphanage who were full blood.

We used to call each other names. They'd call me 'Koepang bastard'. We used to say, 'You little Malay bastard, you little Chinaman bastard.' It was in jest, we didn't know what it meant. We were only kids.

I can recall being locked up in the orphanage where there was no running water, because our showers were separate to the dormitories. The temperature goes really high up in Broome. We used to have one bucket of water and that used to go for about 40 kids, and that would go in the first half-hour.

We used to go to the movies, but not very often. We had the dormitory, and all around the dormitory were these verandahs and they had wooden floors. We had chores to do, and as kids we had to polish the wooden floors on our hands and knees, with oil and rag. Someone would come and help after to shine them up—buff them up a bit. We were referred to as little girls and big girls, and we were the little girls, and sometimes we wanted to go to a certain movie, like A Town Like Alice. 'No,' we were told, 'only the big girls can go.' I remember saying to the nuns, 'Yeah, we're little girls when it comes to going to the movies but we're big girls when it comes to work.' Sometimes we used to have movies shown on a projector.

We went to the kindergarten next door to the orphanage, where non-orphanage kids went too. And then when we were a bit older we went to St Mary's school. We didn't have any shoes, and it used to be really hot running across the road to the school.

Then in 1963 the bishop closed the orphanage down and all us girls had to go out to Beagle Bay mission, over 100 kilometres away. The orphanage became a convent for the nuns. Years later, in the 1970s, the Aboriginal Medical Service had its first clinic there. Now it's just long grass, still the same trees and memories. All the girls from the orphanage are still very close, like a big family, like sisters, which is one good thing.

Beagle Bay mission was founded in 1890 to bring 'natives' in from the bush, teach them about Christianity, save their souls and perhaps their lives.

Broome at that time was a pearling port, a haven of pubs, brothels, gambling houses and 'dens of iniquity'. As the books said, Orientals mixed freely with 'natives', producing offspring of rare beauty. But the church and the government said they feared that such children were being brought up in an evil environment. According to *Bringing Them Home*, the report of the Stolen Children's inquiry, in 1906 the Pallotines at Beagle Bay requested that the police round up the Indigenous children living in and around the north-west towns, now wards of the Chief Protector, and send them to the mission. Some even came from as far away as Borroloola.

The reasons were confused and varying. Part of it was to lessen the embarrassment of the white fathers, one reason was to assimilate the children who the church and government thought had a better chance of succeeding in the white world because of their white blood. One was to make sure they had a Christian upbringing and to save them from the 'horrors' of Aboriginal customs and Laws thousands of years old. But who really knows what the thinking was in those days?

So there had been an orphanage at Beagle Bay since the turn of the century. In fact I think my grandfather, old Dick (Richard) Smith, was one of the first six boys to go to Beagle Bay in the boat. That's where my grandmother and grandfather met. He was Jaru, from Flora Downs station near Halls Creek. He was taken away from his parents and put into Beagle Bay. Mimi Dora was from Fitzroy Crossing. She was Bunuba and she was also taken away and put into Beagle Bay. Mum, her brother and one of her sisters had their early years there.

So when we arrived there they already had girls and boys living in the orphanage. On the mission itself lived three generations of Aboriginal people. Some families lived in what they used to call 'colony', a section of small stone houses set apart from the orphanage section.

People like Dianne Williams came from the Broome orphanage with me. She was seven months old when she was taken from her mother. Neenyah Charles was also at Beagle Bay, she was known as Annarella then. She reckons I had a pair of red shoes that she fell in love with, she said I gave them to her. But I can't remember that. We never had any personal possessions.

I guess when I was in Beagle Bay, that was the first time I started really thinking about my mother and why I was in an institution like that. Maybe it was because I was older— about twelve—but I started to question things and wonder about my life, like why my mum put me in the orphanage. I used to cry, and Margie Deegan, a very special person, used to come to me and comfort me. She will always be a special person in my life.

At Beagle Bay you had the girls and boys in separate dormitories. You had the nuns living in a hostel in between separating the dormitories. The school was just outside the fence line. You had the girls' dormitory, the church, the nuns' living quarters, the hospital and then the boys was on the other side. I remember my first meeting with Pudding.

When I got sent out to Beagle Bay I knew of Pudding. But that was my first meeting, he was about nine then. He was six when he was taken away. And I remember him and one of my cousins coming up to the fence from the boys' side and we met. I had two shillings or something, and I gave it to him.

All my cousins used to bully me in Beagle Bay. I don't know what the reason was. When my cousin Stella first met me she called me a 'slanty-eyed'—and that was my cousin. 'How come she's my cousin and she's slanty-eyed?' she said.

Other boys like Cassy used to beat me up. Margie used to tell me this story. She said Willie, my Aunty Betty's son, was fostered out to Mimi Rosie Victor and he was brought up by her. She said Willie Boy had this knife and we used to play these games in the sand with the knife, and she reckons that Willie said, 'This knife is for someone,' (real menacing-like). He wanted to stick me with this knife.

Apart from Pudding, I had no close family there. We were only allowed out on Sundays and it was Yvonne and Freddy Cox, and Ruby and Teddo Cox; they were the families that took me out. They're special people. I found out later they were related to my grandmother.

We'd go fishing. We used to walk everywhere. We used to carry Mimi Ruby's babies in a bingin (coolamon). I used to look forward to that. As a child it was exciting, you didn't notice the distance.

We all went to school together. In Beagle Bay you had more company with the boys and more exposure to families, like in 'colony', than you did in the Broome orphanage.

I didn't find it a particularly awful place because I guess we didn't know anything different. It was an accepted thing that we were there. All of us knew who our mothers were, but we just accepted that it was our fate to be at the mission.

We had been taken away from our family, and we had to reject our Aboriginality because of the Catholic religion. They tried to brainwash us. But the nuns didn't totally destroy that because we always knew. There were still a lot of practices, things like the Law and punishment. Even though we were in an institution, the beliefs and practices were still there. We were aware of singing, pointing the bone, initiations and stuff, though I wasn't aware of women's initiations and ceremonies at that time. But there were no ceremonies done at Beagle Bay because of the Catholics. We had to totally reject all that side, or we were pagans and heathens.

Our language was denied but we still ate our traditional food. We would go out hunting for barni (goanna) and go fishing, but it was restricted because we were institutionalised. The boys and girls were kept separate. Sometimes we'd stand at the fence, and the old people would bring tea and damper. We'd have stew for dinner. There was never enough, we were always hungry, and there were worms in the porridge.

If you weren't institutionalised or living in a town situation with your family, there was a stigma being Aboriginal. With us we were pressured to reject our Aboriginality.

As a child I used to enjoy going to church, but when I think about it now, it was because it was an outing. Mass on Sundays, and then we made our first holy communion, and then confession. I used to love going to confession. As a child you didn't have any sins to confess, but I used to love it, simply because it was an outing. It got you out of the orphanage. The same old thing: 'Bless me Father because I have sinned. It's been a week since my last confession.' We may have sworn or told lies or things like that. I mean, kids don't commit mortal sins.

I still say I'm a Catholic, but I'm not a practising one, and there's a lot of the teachings that I disagree with now since I've become an adult. I question a lot of their teachings—as a child I didn't. It was more fear than anything else.

⁂ ⁂ ⁂

Mum must have left Broome after Pudding was taken away. She went hunting crocodiles in the Northern Territory. She met her husband, Les Turley, up there. I think they were crocodile shooting, both of them. She had an interesting life. Then she had Lesley.

I spent about twelve months in Beagle Bay, and during that time my mum used to write to us from the Northern Territory. The priest used to read the letters to us. So she used to write and say she was married and she had another child, and asked if we wanted to go up there on a trial basis. And that's what happened—in early 1964 Pudding and I went over to stay with Mum and her new husband at Pine Creek. And that's how we got out of the institution. Because she was married to a white man, it was now acceptable for us to live with her.

I got on all right with Mum's husband but Pudding never got on with him. My mum was still drinking at that time, and every time she had a fight with her husband she'd be running back to Darwin and dragging Pudding and I backwards and forwards. When my mother ran away to Darwin with me, for three months I never went to school. I was up and down between Pine Creek and Darwin because she was drinking. When she had a fight with her husband she'd drag me off to Darwin and then dump me with Granny, Mimi Dora, who was up there then.

I was in Darwin and Pine Creek for about a total of six months. I thought the Welfare would come and get me again because I wasn't going to school. When she'd run away to Darwin she had to leave my baby brother, Lesley, behind. Her husband wouldn't allow her to take him. That's when they had fights.

Once, she was drinking metho with some white man, and he said something to me. I told him, 'Get fucked,' and I remember my mother giving me a flogging all the way home because I swore at her friend. That's why I can sympathise with other Aboriginal girls whose mothers hung around with these awful white men. They'd be touching up the girls and all, and the women didn't say anything.

So in the end she decided to send Pudding back—I stayed on for another three or four months. And then eventually she sent me back too, on the plane from Darwin.

When I was sent back I was too young to feel angry with my mother because my life was always controlled. I didn't have a say. What happened to me was the acceptable thing.

Pudding and I were sent back to his father. I knew Cooney wasn't my father, but I used to always call him Dad. We went to stay with Cooney and his white wife, Betty, who he'd married after he and Mum split up. She was a nurse at the hospital in Broome.

And then one day we went to this circus that came to town. It wasn't a circus at all, it was just a sideshow, but we used to call it a circus. We went down there one night. As we went towards the sideshow there, Betty Tolentino said to me, she reckoned, 'I want to talk to you.' She took me across from where the circus was and to where the Sun Pictures are, just in front where they have all the posters.

She said to me, 'I want you to stop calling Cooney Dad.' And I think I would have been eleven or twelve years old. That was really devastating for me, for here this woman was, saying, 'Don't call him Dad,' and I didn't understand why. Ever since then I could never address him. I could call him Cooney, but if I'm in his company I just say what I have to say to him. The only time I can address him is if I'm talking about him to somebody else.

But I don't think he ever knew that incident with Betty occurred, and this is the first time I've thought about mentioning it to him. I'd like to let him know how I felt, and ask him whether he noticed that all of a sudden I stopped calling him Dad.

I lost a lot of respect for Cooney later because he kicked Pudding out. He used to think the sun shone out of Pudding's arse and he had this really good bonding and relationship with his son. And this woman, Betty, seemed to be jealous of me, and she seemed to be even more jealous of Pudding. I thought she disliked Pudding and that was because he was a reminder that he was Cooney's son to another woman. But even though I don't like the woman because of what she did to Pudding, I was always civil to her.

Gwen and Sid Tolentino were always Aunty Gwen and Uncle Sid to me, because Sid was Cooney's brother. And Gwen was his wife—she was white, you see, and Gwen, Sid, Cooney and Mum had knocked around together and they were good friends.

Gwen had always been a big woman and Sid was a small man, but she still rode on the back of his motorbike. Once, they were on the motorbike and Sid felt as if it was a bit light—apparently Gwen had fallen off, she'd been left behind.

There's another story Sid tells about coming home one night, with Gwen and her mother opening the door, and Gwen was so drunk Sid just pushed her through the door. Sid was never lost for women. He left home at fifteen and even in those days there were a few nuns and novices chasing him!

So when I came back I naturally came to Cooney. But as I said, Cooney had married this white woman, Betty, and didn't want to know us, particularly Pudding.

One night I went out to a dance in the local hall. And I was sitting on the verandah and I was very, very shy, just sitting on my own on the verandah. And then Gwen walked past and she said to me, 'How would you like to come and stay with me?'

I grunted, 'Yes.' Never thought anything more, and then the next day she was round to Cooney's place to pick up me and my gear. Gwen and Sid didn't have any children of their own then.

And the only possession I had was this tiny little suitcase, like kids have for their first year of school, with all my little possessions in it. I don't recall even having clothing. I treasured my little school case. Months and months later, I was going through my suitcase and found this letter from my mum to Gwen. I said, 'Oh, here's a letter for you.'

The letter was asking Gwen to look after me. When my mum sent me back I was supposed to stay with Gwen, and she sent her this letter, see. But I went to Cooney and Betty. I always thought it was like fate that Gwen asked me to stay with her—she hadn't known that my mother had written the letter, cause she hadn't had any contact with her.

So then Gwen and Sid approached Cooney and Betty and asked if they could take Pudding in too. They flatly refused, and threatened Gwen and Sid. Said they'd get the police on to them if they interfered. As we lived pretty close by, we had a lot of contact with them, and they would have seen Pudding regularly.

Then Pudding was kicked out by Cooney and Betty and he moved around from pillar to post, to different families. He ended up being sent to the boys' hostel in Derby and I didn't see too much of him for a long time after.

When I was about thirteen or fourteen I met Kim Bin Amat. But Gwen wanted me to get an education and not just end up with a Broome boy. And then I got selected to go to high school in Perth and board at the Pallotines, the Catholic mission there.

In my day there was no high school in Broome, so many of the girls had to leave school at grade seven when they turned fourteen. The closest high school was in Derby, and you had to board at the hostel run by the Catholics. The other option was to go to the Pallotines in Perth, another Catholic institution. Or you left school and got a job.

The white kids were sent to boarding school too, or stayed with family down there. Pallotine mission was on the border of Riverton and Rossmoyne in Perth. We went to school in Victoria Park at St Joachims. The boys went to Trinity, in the city near the WACA sporting grounds. Some boys went to other schools. A couple of girls went to Mercedes College in the city. After my generation there were a few changes where they went to other schools, such as Rossmoyne High School.

One of the questions you could ask is how the brightest kids were selected to go. I don't think I considered myself a bright kid. Maybe the nuns thought I had potential, but I don't think I was bright by any means. I'd say I was an average student. Apparently my teacher recommended I go. And the reason I said, 'Yes, I'll go,' it was my way of paying back Gwen and Sid for what they'd done for me. They wanted me to go down there, so I thought it was the least I could do.

But a lot of the older girls never had the opportunity to go away to Perth. A lot of them missed out on an education and they feel inadequate. I benefited out of it, getting the chance to have an education. Just a handful of us were fortunate to get a secondary education. There was about five others who were sent to Perth at the same time as me. There were three age groups around me that had the opportunity to go away.

I stayed with Gwen and Sid until I left home to go to Perth. In those days there was no Abstudy, so Gwen and Sid paid for my education.

Academically we were behind, but it was happy times. On weekends, as a group, we might go to football and stuff. But I didn't have any family to take me out. I had three years there, and in my last year the priests were getting white families to take the kids out at weekends. And then they'd pick you up for the day or the weekend. Prior to that we stayed there in the school.

The kids of today can come home every term when they're boarding. When I was going to school you flew down there at the beginning of the year, but you didn't come home until the end of the year when school finished. So even the holidays were spent in Perth. Back in those days, too, what they call year ten today was Junior. Your TEA was your leaving certificate. I didn't do my leaving. I was in school in Perth from 1966 to 1968. In 1969 I left school and started nursing. It wasn't really my choice, but at that time I didn't know what to do or be. There was a few things like being an air hostess or a hairdresser. Because there were some other girls going into nursing I decided to do that.

Really, my first job was when I came home from holidays—in Broome, with Streeter and Male (then the main shop in town). I was what they call today a sales attendant in the haberdashery and manchester section. That was good, because I was getting paid good money.

Gwen and Sid, they had no children, despite trying desperately. They didn't seem to be able to have children of their own. They fostered me. When I was sent to Perth to go to boarding school they ended up having a child, Bradley. I think he was about ten weeks old when I left. I always considered Bradley as my brother. When I used to come home on school holidays Gwen used to work, so I had to babysit Bradley. He was always like my own child, and we're still very close. He's married to Bernie now, with four kids of his own. Three boys and one little girl. And the little girl is my godchild. I felt really privileged that Bernie and Brad asked me to be godmum. But I love all the kids the same, they're beautiful kids. Bernie's also a beautiful person and I love her very much. They're my family.

Then another time I came home for holidays. I was married to Dave, and we spent our holidays in Broome. Every second year we'd come up to Broome. And I remember one time coming to Broome and my foster mum was sick. And just before I left I said jokingly, 'You've got all these symptoms of being pregnant.' And at this time she was 40. When I went home about a month later she rang to say she was six months pregnant! Adrian's about 23 now. He's the younger brother and he's a really special person.

My mother's family live in Broome and I guess they can't understand why I'm so close to my foster family. But to me they're strangers, I've never had anything to do with them.

Sid and Gwen are my father and mother, who I love very much. I consider myself very lucky to have had wonderful parents like them. I grew up in a loving family with a beautiful home. Sid worked on the train for the Harbour and Lights Department and played sport on the weekend. Later he drove machinery for the shire council.

My foster mum used to shower me with gifts, and I remember when she was working in Streeter's, she'd come home every afternoon after work. I'd never be home, so she'd come up the back and start yelling out for me and I'd come racing home. She had this huge big voice and I used to feel shamed, she'd be singing out for me and the whole town would hear. So I'd make sure I'd sprint home so she wouldn't yell out too many times. And then when I got close and when she saw me, she'd say she had a present for me. She'd leave it on my bed and I'd go racing in. Yeah, I was spoilt. Little things like that were really important to me.

I remember once they bought me a bike for Christmas. Not having parents and being institutionalised, it was the first time I had a Christmas present, so I wasn't able to express myself or show any emotions like love, affection. What we used to do was go to midnight mass. I used to like going to midnight mass, because then I could come home and open my presents. And this particular Christmas my foster mum said, 'Close your eyes,' and walked me into the lounge room, and there under the Christmas tree was my bike. And I remember I was so stunned, I wasn't able to say thank you, or put my arms around her and tell her that I loved her.

It was only years later when I started nursing that I used to write letters to Gwen to try and make it up to her. But the letters used to sound really mushy. I'd screw them up and throw them in the bin. Finally, one day I sat down and wrote a letter, saying what I thought about her, telling her I loved her and apologising for the way I couldn't express my feelings. And I used that bike as an example. I could imagine her getting the letter and just crying. I finally decided to post it off, and it went off and I felt really good that I was finally able to tell her how much I cared for her and how much I loved her.

I didn't finish my nursing training because I ended up pregnant with my daughter Cindy. I'd met her father, Dave, not long after I started nursing. Cindy was born in January, in Broome. I spent the last couple of months of my pregnancy back home because I wanted to have her there. Dave and I got married that May. Dave was twenty-one, I was nineteen.

In Broome when I was growing up, it was accepted as normal behaviour that you flogged your wife. That was the 'culture' in those days. Growing up in Broome you saw it, you saw the men bashing their wives and I thought that was not for me. I wasn't going to be flogged. I thought, in my teens, *I'm not going to marry some bloke who is going to bash me*, and that is why I married Dave, a white man, a good man who was not going to touch me. Not for me gambling, drinking and bash your wife.

Traditionally women weren't beaten, because they had their Laws and they had to abide by those Laws, even though older men had younger wives and they'd have several wives. Women traditionally gathered, men hunted and they all had their roles, like teaching the little ones. With child-rearing, they were not just brought up by the mother, but by all the women. You had to marry your proper skin. You were promised to your proper skin and there was no jealousy.

I guess there were some cases where two people fell in love and they were from the wrong skin, and they persisted—and so then they were banished. But I think the bashing and jealousy came after with the alcohol.

And I think too, when white men came, that's how the white man treated the Aboriginal people—the beatings, the cruelty—and then consequently the Aboriginal men did that to their women, they became the abusers. There were Aboriginal pearl divers in the beginning, in Broome. They did free diving. They had to go down to the sea bottom to get the shells. You hear stories that if they didn't come up with shells they'd be bashed, and made to stay down there. They even used to make Aboriginal women in their last months of pregnancy dive.

Then there was horrific stuff that happened on the stations to Aboriginal workers. At one infamous station, the station owner used to get the blackfellas to sit up on the hot tin roof all day, for hours and hours, as their punishment. You can just imagine the extreme temperatures.

So anyway, I wanted to get married to Cindy's dad. I was making inquiries about marrying Dave. I don't know who gave me this bloke's number in some government department. But he said, 'Because you're under twenty-one you have to get permission to get married from your mother. You're under-age.'

And again I got a bit angry for that. I said, 'Why should I get permission from my mother? I've got foster parents in Broome. They look after me. I've only spent six months with my mother. She's got no right.'

He said, 'If your mother's unreasonable, you can go to the court. The magistrate will have to give you permission.' I ended up getting the papers from him. I think she did complete it and send it back, that's how I got married.

Gwen and Sid had not met Dave. They met him after we got married. They fell in love with him.

Our problems later on weren't really anything to do with him being white. I mean some of my best friends—like Diana—are white people. I don't stereotype people, I take people as they come. With my real friends, sometimes we don't see each other for years, but we're still friends even though we're living a long distance apart. Aboriginal people take people in but people use and abuse them for their own means. Aboriginal people are human. We laugh a lot about things that have happened to us. It's survival instinct, I guess.

Despite my marriage with Dave though, I was craving for affection and love. But he had been smothered and suffocated by his mother as a child, so he shunned that sort of thing. So we were a funny couple, there I was craving for it, and he didn't want it because he had too much of it. I would say, 'Give me a cuddle,' and because he couldn't bring himself to do it, he used to make a joke out of it. He'd stand there and put his arm around me and say, 'One two three four five six seven eight nine ten,' then he'd laugh.

I put a lot of pressure on Dave too, because I wanted a parent's love, a father's love as well as a husband's love. I was craving that.

I've told people since those days that my life's been complicated, and I think that's true.

Diana's Early Days

3.

Diana's Early Days

Well I used to be a good time girl
I suppose you'd have to say
I used to go out and play
every night and every day

Good Time Girl

Diana Plater

Diana: St Vincent's Church in Redfern was cold and dimly lit. It had suffered hail damage in the wild storm of 14 April, 1999, and was still to be repaired. Pews, badly in need of a few nails, had been moved around into the alcove, and a lone candle was lit in front of the altar. As the Who's Who of the Aboriginal world filled the congregation, a nun wearing a raincoat hit the button on a tinny tape recorder and the church filled with the sound of a hymn.

It was pouring with rain outside as we took part in a Thanksgiving service to celebrate the life of John Newfong, the Aboriginal journalist and activist. The whole congregation gasped when a friend of John's, a woman from Zimbabwe, spoke these words: 'I was so glad when I woke up this morning and found it was raining. You know, in Africa we have a superstition or belief that when a great person passes away, if it rains on the day of their burial service it is a sign that the gods are welcoming this great person into their world.'

Speaker after speaker told of their admiration and respect—and frequent fiery arguments—with John. One young man had been the first Aboriginal school captain at his school, and told how John helped him write his maiden speech. The audience was totally knocked out, he said, by this erudite, articulate and charming black man. And John had got a kick out of it, despite getting no credit for his brilliant speech writing. His sister, Judy, told how their parents had brought the family up to always be well-dressed, carry ironed handkerchiefs and wear starched shirts. John had always been a bit different to the other Aboriginal people in Brisbane. He'd take Judy to his favourite symphony orchestra concerts, while she would have preferred a rock-and-roll gig.

Another friend told how they had worked at the ABC in Brisbane together at their first jobs out of high school. Even then John had enormous presence and a beautiful, round, mellifluous voice. One of the snootier presenters, cigarette-holder in one hand, asked him about his background. When he got to the bit about growing up on Stradbroke Island she said, 'Oh, I'd lose that part.'

John Newfong was one of the first Aboriginal people I ever met. More correctly, he was one of my first Aboriginal friends. He was also, I'm pretty sure, one of the first gay men I came to know well. John was the first Aboriginal person employed as a journalist in mainstream print media. In 1967 he was hired by *The Australian*. I met him around 1977. I had been working in Canberra on an exchange scheme with *The Canberra Times*, and later went to work in the press gallery office of *The Sydney Morning Herald*.

John was a good mate of my friend, Shubha Slee, a wonderful Indian journalist who lived in Paddington in Sydney and who also died far too young. They had met at the Aboriginal Tent Embassy, on the front lawns of Parliament House in Canberra, in 1972. His experience as a foreign correspondent and his international contacts were invaluable to John when he took up the role of an ambassador or spokesman for the Tent Embassy. As he later pointed out, 'This protest was to prove a major milestone in the history of the Aboriginal movement.'

A fellow Tent Embassy participant, Gary Foley, told me when I was working on John's obituary that the major reason the Embassy was a success was because of the way they were able to portray themselves to journalists, and John, understanding exactly how the media worked, played a crucial role in this.

John was one of the first people in the Aboriginal movement to realise the importance of international pressure on the Australian government—particularly from the African nations and from the media. He had contacts with diplomats, royalty and influential people from Russia to Ethiopia and was a frequent name on the guest list of diplomatic cocktail parties in Canberra.

Both John and Shubha were party animals. So I think I must have actually met John in Sydney at one of Shubha's great parties. But I do remember frequent nights out on the Canberra nightclub scene as well.

John was ahead of his time in many ways. We clicked right away and he asked me to write some articles for *Identity*, the national Indigenous full colour magazine. But his standards were too high for me. I'd been used to most of my stories getting a run in the *Herald* or *The Canberra Times*. He, however, wasn't so impressed by one article I wrote about Borroloola, an Aboriginal community in the Northern Territory. I had tried to introduce some 'colour' to the story by making a reference to the sack cloth curtain around the shower, and the cake of soap on a bit of wood at the town camp I stayed at. He jibed me about my use of bad grammar and rejected the article. I was pretty stunned, thinking I was quite the experienced journalist at that stage, and to add insult to injury, *Identity* wasn't even paying for its articles.

At that rainy Redfern service I smiled remembering those times. Thinking about John also reinforced what a long struggle it has been, and is, to educate the media about Aboriginal issues. Most of all though, I felt a deep sense of loss for my past, and for the friends who have died or I have simply lost touch with. Although we'd spoken on the phone, I had only seen John once in the past ten years or so. So I couldn't vow to be a great friend of his, although we'd certainly been good friends at one stage of my life—John had lots of dear friends. As somebody at John's service said, 'Old friends are precious.' And, as I said to Shubha's two daughters, who were at the service and remembered John from when they were very young, it was an earlier and very different era.

So I'd have to say my life's been adventurous and interesting, but unlike Ollie's, I wouldn't say it's been complicated. Also unlike Ollie, I doubt if I was ever shy, and I was probably not that well-groomed either. Sometimes I wonder how we can relate so well and how I can feel so much closer to her, whose background is so different to my own, than most of the girls I went to school with in Sydney.

I was one of those kids that was attracted to trouble or maybe just couldn't stand to have an easy life. Later my Aboriginal friends, particularly Dianne Williams from Broome, were always telling me to take it easy, or slow down.

I was only about thirteen when I started hanging out with the cast of *Hair*. We'd go to Centennial Park on Sundays, smoke dope and look at the sun through balloons. 'It blows your mind, man.' One evening we all went back to a rambling old house in Woollahra, where half the cast were living, for a party. My girlfriends and I were having a great old time—I distinctly remember my cousin on a swing in the garden, surrounded by guys with hair to their shoulders and wearing flares—when my mother turned up. Seems one of my friends had called her mother to say she'd be late and gave her the address. Well, how embarrassing was that for a budding weekend hippie?

Later I helped out on one of the stalls at the flea market in Kings Cross, selling T-shirts with slogans like 'I feel good—feel me' to American soldiers on leave from Vietnam. It was the days of the R and R—rest and relaxation. The black guys would go wild over the pendants, posters and shirts. 'Gee, blows my mind. Must buy them to show the folks back in 'Nam.' I was only interested in the black ones with their afro haircuts, of course. They were cool.

As long as I can remember I was interested in social issues, even if the people I mixed with weren't particularly political—more anti-establishment, I guess.

Although I was vice captain of my school, Sydney Girls' High, I wasn't the typical Miss Prim Prefect. The school was close to Surry Hills, Paddington and Kings Cross, and we grew up very much aware of alternative lifestyles and the counter-culture. Some of my friends' mothers were part of that scene. My mother wasn't an alternative type at all, but she was adventurous herself and gave me a great deal of freedom. The Aquarius festival was held at Nimbin in the north of NSW, and a family we were friendly with moved there. Once, two friends and I hitched to Byron Bay for our school holidays and visited them. I didn't tell Mum we were hitchhiking though, so when she dropped us off at the train station and discovered there was no train to Byron Bay she hit the roof. Finally she just told me to go, which we did.

A few of us were also involved in the Australian Theatre for Young People and did holiday workshops with them. At school, with no help from teachers, a group of us put on plays such as 'A Macbeth' (I was a witch) and 'Marat Sade' (which the headmistress banned after the first night).

Most of all I wanted to become a journalist and I'd scribbled since I could remember. I guess I got my grounding in journalism and PR at my father's office. It was a public relations consultancy, where my mother also worked. I would go there every afternoon after school and pretend I was a secretary, making cups of coffee for the people who worked there. I wrote and edited little newsletter rags that I printed off there. My first was when I was about eleven, in fifth grade at primary school. It was two pieces of paper stapled together. I flogged it around the playground to pubescent reluctant readers, furious with anybody who would rather spend their five cents on a buttered fingerbun than my answer to the *Washington Post*.

In high school I became more interested in writing about social issues. In my last two years I edited 'Write-Off'—the unofficial school magazine that I started—and earned the Headmistress's ire by going straight to the P and C with a funding request, thus bypassing her. No teachers were involved in these first attempts at journalism.

When I heard the news in late 1974 that I had been selected as a copy girl with the promise of a cadetship with *The Sydney Sun*, it was like all my dreams had been answered. I remember talking on the telephone upstairs outside my bedroom with Fairfax's cadet counsellor (they call them training executive or something these days). It turned out that I was to be one of four copy girls that were promised cadetships.

It's kind of funny that making cups of coffee was my first job in journalism. It was as a copy girl in the subs room at *The Sydney Sun*. A smoke-filled hole, it was dominated by a large wooden table and a group of pallid looking men who sat around it, bending over bits of copy paper. No computers in those days and no women subeditors. I used to think 'sub' stood for subhuman.

At the top of the table sat the Chief Sub. He was a pretty unremarkable sort of character. He didn't wear an eye shade but he was almost as old-fashioned as those editors you saw on midday black and white movies. He had a big job, getting five editions of the paper out each day. And copy people were just cogs in the wheel—there to be yelled at if something was going wrong. He drank his coffee white with two sugars. I knew all the subs by how they drank their coffee. Black, two sugars, white, none. But it was a problem if they moved seats!

Those were 'hot metal' days. Our main job was taking the stories typed on copy paper out of the out basket and shoving them down a metal chute to the fourth floor, where the compositors picked them up to work on. They were used to the copy people being known as 'boy'. They would call, 'Boy' or 'chute' when something landed in the out basket. When us girls arrived, they had to change the command to, 'Chute, please.'

It was an unusual year when we joined the *Sun* as it was the first time that Fairfax had actually taken on more female cadets (or copy people) than male ones. Some of us were promised that we would get cadetships, but we first had to work as copy people until a vacancy came up. We were to be the non-official affirmative action cadets.

My dad had done his cadetship on the *Sun* after the war. At the time it was owned by Associated Newspapers. He had a great photo of himself in the newsroom, fast asleep on one of the desks, surrounded by his journo mates. The newsroom didn't seem to have changed that much. Up one end were rows of desks that belonged to the *Sun*, and down the other end were rows of desks that belonged to the *Herald*, its sister morning paper.

Eventually I moved into the police rounds room where my job as copy girl was to monitor the police, ambulance and fire radios. If anything sounded exciting I had to call the station involved and find out what was going on. Of course, as it was illegal to be listening in to these radios, I had to pretend somebody had called us with a news tip. Nudge, nudge, wink, wink.

In mid year I gained my cadetship, but not on the *Sun*. It was on the Sun's big sister, *The Sydney Morning Herald*. After a stint on 'police rounds', I was sent for my penance to the women's section, known in those days as Look! For half the week I worked with the then editor of *The Sun Herald* Women's section, Margaret Vaile, who taught me more about journalism than possibly anybody since.

From interviewing, to reporting, to subediting, she was a real pro—but most importantly, she taught me how to have a thick hide.

But even she got tricked by a rather silly, but devastating, joke played on me by a senior journalist. Possibly the most important part of my job was covering the social rounds—going to functions with a photographer and finding at least five eligible candidates for 'social pics'.

Her strict rules insisted that I ask somebody whose photo we might use whether she was single, married or divorced, so we knew whether to refer to her as Miss Jane Smith, Mrs John Smith or Mrs Jane Smith. That certainly taught me not to be afraid of asking absurd or awkward questions.

At one such function—the Black and White Ball, or something like that—we took a photo of a woman and a man, who I did not know. The woman gave me her name as Prudence Bookbinder, which I thought was a bit odd, and even odder when she said her necklace was given to her by the Emperor of Ethiopia. (We always needed a little item about their dress to make the caption more interesting.) But being pretty young and scared of looking a total fool, I didn't say, 'But that can't be your real name, surely.'

It wasn't until after the picture was printed in the Sunday paper that we learnt that Miss Bookbinder was really the then deputy editor of the *Women's Weekly*. When Margaret, or Maggie (as she hated to be called) heard of the mistake via a radio disc jockey—'These social columnists who don't know who's who'—she refused to allow me to take the blame and published a correction the following week. You can imagine who then looked the silliest. Anyway, I received a bouquet of roses from Miss Bookbinder soon after.

Maggie taught me that even if something looked deadly boring, there was always a story in it somewhere. Once, on returning from a press conference, I told her there was no story. She looked me straight in the eye and asked, 'Do you really want to be a journalist?'

Conservative politically, on election day she'd hang blue and white ribbons around the area where we worked, on the printers' floor. But she didn't let her personal opinions prevent her carrying unusual stories, particularly about strong, capable women, in her pages. In fact, I think the best stories in the paper were often in her pages. And it was in her pages that the first interview I did with an Indigenous woman, Margaret Valadian, was published. That was in 1977, and many of her comments, particularly about health issues, are still valid today. But when I asked her about her past, she insisted she didn't want a 'bleeding heart' story written about her.

Around this time I started to write feature articles in my own time, as a way of doing stories I was especially interested in. I sold one feature to Guy Morrison, who was then the features editor at the *Herald*. It was run in the Saturday section. A few nights later I was standing at the bar in the Australian (the *Herald's* pub in Broadway) when Guy complimented me on the story and offered to buy me a drink. He was a tall, handsome man, who looked a good twenty years younger than his then 59 years.

I was pretty stunned when he invited me out to dinner that night, and actually thought he was being kind, or at a loose end or something. We drove in his funny old Holden to a restaurant in Paddington. As we got out of the car he apologised that it was bourgeois, and then I said my line that at the time I thought was so clever: 'Well, it's the bourgeoisie who make the revolutions, isn't it?'

It took a good two years before I became disenchanted. From the moment we went back to his house, full of beautiful paintings and ornaments, and I learnt that not only had he been a member of the Communist Party in the 1930s and '40s, he'd also gone out with a woman who'd been Leonard Cohen's lover, I was totally infatuated.

It wasn't my first journalist love affair by any means, but it was the first one which became a relationship. We were an odd couple. He, the respected features editor and layout man (he designed the original *Australian* newspaper), me the naive cadet. But we had great parties, complete with Guy's vegetarian cooking and a great deal of drunken dancing. I met Shubha through Guy and then later through Shubha I met John.

Having Guy as a boyfriend may not have hugely helped my career at the *Herald* but he taught me an enormous amount about feature writing. Of course, there were those who suggested my stories were only published because of my relationship with him.

Perhaps as a way to have a break, and also as an opportunity to see what covering Federal politics was like, I applied for a three month cadet exchange scheme with *The Canberra Times*. I cried as I drove off, waving him goodbye, but it didn't take too long before my sights were set on further goals.

Half my time was spent in *The Canberra Times* press gallery office in the old Parliament House, and half in the main office, then downtown. It was an introduction to a whole new world of politicians, politics and very late night drinking in the non-members bar. All great fun for a party loving twenty-one year-old.

The journey of my involvement with Aboriginal people probably began later that year—1977—when I went to the tiny settlement of Borroloola (in the Gulf of Carpentaria in the Northern Territory) to cover the first land claim under the Aboriginal Land Rights (Northern Territory) Act 1976.

In Canberra, it had not taken too long to become involved with another man, a journalist, Jack Waterford, who was moving to Alice Springs for a year to work for an Aboriginal health organisation. I decided I would follow him, at my own invitation, and have a holiday in the NT. It was he who introduced me to Aboriginal Affairs, as he had worked with the trachoma program under Fred Hollows. He had covered the Tent Embassy and the associated police violence in 1972 for *The Canberra Times,* and had great contacts with the burgeoning modern Aboriginal political movement.

Jack had suggested I go to Darwin first, and call the Northern Land Council (NLC) to see if there were any stories I could cover.

So I did—having absolutely no idea what the NLC was. They told me the Borroloola people's land claim case was being held in Darwin. The Land Rights Act was passed by the Fraser Liberal government after being introduced by the Whitlam government. This claim for about 500 square miles was by 600 people living at and around Borroloola. They were also claiming fifteen square miles of proposed Robinson River reserve and the Sir Edward Pellew group of islands.

I wandered down to the courthouse, and at the end of the day went up to the lawyer and asked him if he was working for the Northern Land Council, which was representing the traditional owners in this claim. 'No,' he said. 'I work for the CLC.'

What the hell is that? was my first thought. But I soon learnt it was the Central Land Council, based in Alice Springs, which represented the Aboriginal people of Central Australia.

That afternoon a few people who were involved in the claim and I got together at the Darwin Hotel for a drink. We discussed how we were going to get to Borroloola in the Gulf country for the land claim hearings that were to be held there. And I decided to rent a car and drive there with an Aboriginal woman, Marie Bennett, who I met that day. It was only 1,000 kilometres, about ten hours drive!

I had a wonderful week covering the land claim, fishing, hunting and spending time with the women.

Each day, before the Land Commissioner in the township's school hall, the traditional owners gave evidence about their land, the feared impact of a mine proposed for the area and the history of white contact there. It had been a violent history, and some were hesitant to give evidence because they feared white reaction. One old woman asked me in relation to the claim, 'Whitefella use tomahawk?'

I was deeply honoured to be invited to an important ceremony. I will never forget sitting in the dust under the stars, surrounded by the women chanting and dancing until the early hours of the morning.

Feeling on top of the world after being so warmly welcomed by these people, I joined Jack in Alice Springs. I stayed a short time, then caught a plane back to Darwin and continued my adventures. I did a trip out to what later became Kakadu National Park. We bumped over sandy roads with buffalo hunters, and I later met up with museum staff and was shown ancient rock paintings, climbing high in the escarpment as eagles flew around my head.

My feature about Borroloola was run, but the subeditor later told me I should be more careful about wearing my heart on my sleeve. This was a comment I didn't exactly welcome, but years later came to respect. I'll never forget the irrational comment I was given by one deputy editor of a magazine when I offered them a story on the crazy town of Alice Springs. Just before that I'd done a freelance job, editing the Central Land Council's newsletter. He said that there was a conflict of interest for me to write such an article because I had been working for an Aboriginal organisation. There never seemed to be conflicts of interest if you were working for a mining company or something like that. When I started working for AAP in 1983 it was several months before I wrote a story on Aboriginal people. I wanted to prove I could write about anything first. Then I got a pretty free run. Other journalists who have covered this area told me they have had to use similar tactics.

After my stint in Canberra and my holiday in the NT, I ended up back in Sydney working in state rounds at Sydney's Parliament House, when Neville Wran was Premier. I loved the job and was particularly interested in prisoners action and the reform movement. I was also involved in covering the outcome of the Nagle Royal Commission into prisons. My highlight was getting drunk with a couple of prison officers who gave me an extremely critical report about a recent prison riot at Long Bay Jail. The story led the paper, but back in those days by-lines were only given out to journalists who had 'earnt' them, and apparently my scoop wasn't enough for one. So I was overjoyed when the then state political correspondent took me outside the office and told me the Herald was sending me to Canberra to cover social welfare issues.

I was the only woman in the *Herald*'s press gallery office, apart from the secretary. At that stage there were about half a dozen women journalists in the press gallery. So I informed them pretty quickly that I was not there to make them cups of coffee or to remove the sour milk that was left in the office for days. They couldn't hear me, anyway, over the cricket broadcasts that were constantly on TV (when a match was on). When one of my colleagues left with a contingent of young reporters to work for Murdoch in New York I finally got my beloved Aboriginal Affairs round.

In mid 1978 the story that was developing at the time, and turned into my biggest of the year, was the negotiations over the Ranger uranium mine with the Northern Land Council, led by Galarrwuy Yunupingu. These days it's quite fashionable to be critical of the NLC's role, especially with the focus on the proposed Jabiluka uranium mine and the NLC's agreement to mine it. But if you knew the full story of how the NLC came to sign the Ranger agreement, it would be easier to understand the reasons why there are uranium mines on Aboriginal land today.

The government had been putting a great deal of pressure on Galarrwuy and the NLC to sign the Ranger agreement as, with the passing of the NT Land Rights Act, it was the first time a mining company had had to negotiate with an Aboriginal organisation. The government, with its pro-uranium mining stance, was determined the deal would go through with no more delays. (The Federal government was an equal partner with Peko-Wallsend Ltd and EZ Industries Ltd in the Ranger project.)

I had met Galarrwuy a few months before when he came to Canberra with his American adviser, Stephen Zorn, who spoke at the National Press Club about his involvement in the Ranger negotiations. Zorn was a New York lawyer famous for managing to get royalties of up to 25 percent for Native American groups he had represented in mining negotiations.

Later that afternoon, obviously on a high, Galarrwuy dropped round to my office in the press gallery with Zorn. Handsome, young (in his late twenties) and charming, he sat on my desk and, laughing, told me this story. He'd just been in the then deputy Prime Minister, Doug Anthony's office. Anthony had joked about the NLC holding up the negotiations by trying to get a higher royalty rate. But it was obvious he was deadly serious. Galarrwuy picked up a silver cigarette case on the desk and said, in a take on the old blankets and beads for land trick, 'Well, I'll take this cigarette case and I'll give you an agreement.' Anthony, surprised at the move, agreed.

In September of that year, I begged my news editor to let me go to Darwin to cover the final negotiations. It was suicide season and it was tense. The pressure was mounting on the NLC to get this agreement happening. In fact, the NLC had fallen victim to the then Prime Minister Malcolm Fraser's politics. Galarrwuy told me years later, 'The aggressiveness of politics was in full swing. It all happened in the name of development, but Aboriginal people suffered.' The 'little shit' politics of the Northern Territory became big news.

At the time the NLC was still negotiating to get a better deal than the 4.25 percent royalties on the total mining income of the project that Ranger had so far agreed to. But it had virtually reached the end, and Zorn advised that they could not argue for more payments. It was the best they could get. At the same time, Aboriginal opposition to the agreement seemed to be steadily growing.

The Labor Party, particularly Bob Collins, then the NT Labor representative for Arnhem, was very vocal against the mine. The Liberal government was getting desperate. There were traditional owners on one side and people influenced by politicians on the other. Then there were the greenies doing their bit, and the land council was caught in the middle. The issue was splitting the council in half.

It wasn't the first time the Gagadju people had been under enormous pressure. They had already faced the crocodile and buffalo shooters, the missionaries, the Welfare and the police. They were also no strangers to mining. Not far from the Oenpelli escarpment area, uranium had been mined at El Sharana, and gold at Pine Creek. There'd been a mission and Welfare compound at Oenpelli, near the mouth of the East Alligator River. Traditional owners such as Big Bill Neidjie remembered it all. But now they were worried about the effect the mine would have on the environment, the fact it was slap bang inside Kakadu National Park, and about mining uranium, the most dangerous of all minerals, in a very sensitive landscape. The Ranger negotiations were taking pressure put on Aborigines to a new height.

Around that time, Galarrwuy received a letter from a Labor Federal member, Doug Everingham. Because of the Labor Party's non uranium policy in those days, he didn't want the NLC to sign the agreement. Galarrwuy, normally a Labor man, was so fed up with this sort of well-meaning manipulation that he sent the letter to Ian Viner, then the Aboriginal Affairs Minister, and authorised him to use it in whatever way he saw fit. You can imagine how fast copies of that letter landed in the press gallery boxes.

As negotiations stalled while the NLC team held out for a higher royalty rate, and ultimatums were passed saying the government was going to use the 'national interest' provisions of the Land Rights Act to override Aboriginal lack of consent, the politicians from Canberra hit Darwin. Viner, a wiry little man from WA, and the deputy Prime Minister, Doug Anthony, sealed off Galarrwuy on his own in a room at the Travel Lodge and applied a blowtorch to the belly. Over cups of tea, they said if he didn't sign they would go ahead with the uranium mine under those 'national interest' provisions, regardless of the consequences.

Anthony was also the Minister for Minerals and Energy, and Galarrwuy didn't want him influencing the decision, but he said Fraser insisted he be there. Their main threat was one of closing down the NLC and changing the Land Rights Act if it didn't sign the agreement. Galarrwuy told them he'd make sure the agreement was signed if they lifted the pressure on him and the NLC. He, almost alone, realised that economically and socially, the Gagadju had no choice but to adapt. But then he had to sell the sell-out to the council members.

And this is when the cloak and dagger activities began.

A crucial meeting was scheduled for Bamyili near Katherine. Silas Maranulungula, council chairman of the Oenpelli community in the Ranger basin where uranium was to be mined, declared he would fight with everything possible. And on the eve of these final talks, council delegates Leo Finlay from Borroloola, and Harry Wilson from Peppimenarti, said they would move for the election of a new chairman.

With my friend Marie, who I had travelled to Borroloola with the year before, and a gang of journos, including David Broadbent from *The Age* and David Trounce from the *NT News*, I left Darwin and headed for Katherine, where we booked into a motel run by a buxom blonde—Sylvia someone—who headed the local 'Rights for Whites' organisation. At 4pm I came out with the other journos for a scheduled press conference. When we were stopped from getting in at the community gates by uniformed NT police, we thought it was taking secrecy a bit far. The police had a note from Galarrwuy: *No news, go back, will call.*

The only whites who were allowed at the meeting were Viner, the NLC Manager Alex Bishaw, a lawyer and two secretaries. But even they were kept out of much of it.

We all went back to Katherine and wrote stories about tense meetings in the bush, with very little information in them.

But that evening there was a knock on the door of my motel room. It was a totally worn out Galarrwuy. 'We better not talk here,' I suggested. 'Let's go for a drive. How about Katherine Gorge?'

Well, I don't know whether we were too drunk or tired or what, but instead of the gorge all we found were donkeys, as we got more and more lost driving along dirt roads in the middle of the night.

Years later I saw Galarrwuy at the bar at the Aboriginal Reconciliation Convention in Melbourne and his only remark was, 'Donkeys. We were the donkeys that night. A blackfella can't even find Katherine Gorge.'

After two days of talks at Bamyili, the NLC agreed to ratify the agreement subject to the approval of the traditional owners at Oenpelli. The NLC executive and Viner flew to Oenpelli, and two hours later, the agreement was signed by Galarrwuy and Viner as silver pens were handed around. David Broadbent and a NSW film crew were the only media allowed at that meeting, although

Viner tried to stop them. But when Viner held a press conference in Darwin that afternoon he told us: 'I have done my job and the NLC has been treated as an independent Aboriginal body. The agreement has the unanimous endorsement of the NLC and the traditional owners.'

He then savagely attacked David Trounce's report in that day's *NT News* of leadership challenges at Bamyili. But we all knew his story was true. With tears rolling down my cheeks, I phoned through my page one story to the *Herald*, from my room at the Darwin Hotel.

The Ranger uranium mine was given the long-awaited go ahead yesterday following the signing of the Ranger agreement in the Aboriginal settlement of Oenpelli, I wrote.

The next morning I flew to Goulburn Island to interview members of the NLC as to why they had agreed to sign. We were all still trying to piece the story together. I hadn't wanted to write a feature until I could do this, but when I got back to Darwin there was an anxious message from the features editor, demanding a story for the next day's paper. I wrote what I could but I knew it wasn't enough. David Broadbent's story pulling the whole thing together didn't appear until a week later, because he was given the time to do it.

I met Galarrwuy the next day at a hotel, wearing my best cream and turquoise dress. I wanted to know more about why he'd succumbed to the government's pressure. Instead, he gave me a scoop. He'd sacked Stephen Zorn by telegram after Zorn had released a letter to the media saying the agreement was not as good as it could have been. Galarrwuy found this particularly galling after he had wanted to hold out longer for better royalties—and Zorn had recommended they accept the 4.25 percent.

Now Galarrwuy says: 'In my heart I did my best for the deal I was trying to pull for the people for the first time, and I felt I didn't do badly, regardless of all the hardship we went through.

If I would have let it go we would have had a terrible deal—if government had gone ahead and signed it—it would have set a different picture of the land council's credibility, and jeopardised the land council's future. I was happy to do what I did because I showed my strength and determination as a leader. The land council had to stand on its own feet and do what it had to do.'

Now the NLC is big business, employing more than 80 people, and is the de facto political opposition in the NT. A uranium mine in Kakadu was part of that deal. The following year Galarrwuy was made Australian of the Year (AM). These days he describes that as tokenism. His brother, Mandawuy, also received the Australian of the Year for his work with his band, Yothu Yindi. Galarrwuy is involved with the band but says his brother deserved the award more than he did.

'They never gave me a knighthood,' he said. 'The Fraser government offered me an MBE and I chucked it away. I didn't like it, that bloody Queen's shit. I wanted an AM, to be community recognised. I met Fraser at the Governor General's in 1988, he said, "Hullo, long time, no see."'

When I returned to Canberra there was a memo from the news editor waiting for me, referring to the feature I wrote. It accused me of being unable to divorce my personal attitudes from my work. I was 'too emotionally involved'.

I was extremely upset about this memo, particularly after all the hard work I had done trying to get the facts behind the signing of the agreement (not to mention my scoops), and wrote one straight back, with the help of David Broadbent. I guess the news editor thought I was a young, greenie, leftie that needed to be brought into line. It was actually more that I was pro-Aboriginal and still wanted to tell their various sides of the sad story. Reading the memo now, I can see what he was getting at. But, at the time, all it did was successfully dampen any desire I had to keep working for *The Sydney Morning Herald*—then a much more conservative newspaper than it appears to be today.

It took a few more months, but at that point I decided I was leaving Canberra, the press gallery and the *Herald*. I would drive back to the NT via the Kimberley region of Western Australia and work where I really wanted to—the coalface of journalism!

※ ※ ※

A few years after my school days, my old friend, Frances Peters, was growing up in Birchgrove—next to Balmain—as one of a handful of Aboriginal families in the area. For a large portion of the year she would be sent to stay with her mother's relatives in western New South Wales. The daughter of singer Jimmy Little, she grew up in a world of pop music hysteria and extended Aboriginal family and friends. One of the catalysts for her parents' move from Redfern to Birchgrove in the early '60s had been the fact that two Aboriginal people (one an Islander) played rugby league for Balmain.

Once, we were sitting in a pizza place in Glebe having a conversation, and in the background the phone continued to ring with pizza orders. Despite the noise, we managed to get into a discussion about love for land and loss of land and the heated question, what is identity? Frances believed I could never really identify with the Australian land because I am white. My ancestors were the oppressors. I can 'love the land' but it is not the same as Aboriginal feeling towards the land. I argued that non-Aboriginal people were not incapable of feeling towards the land. Our relationship with land was different. When I sat up on a hill overlooking the Foxground valley, where my family has a farm, I could feel part of that land. We are all human beings, after all—surely we still had some of that so-called 'primitive instinct' for the land. I don't go for that argument that some races are somehow superior to other races, but I do understand the concept that most of us from the West have moved so far from nature that we have lost the plot. Frances' and my discussion became an argument about guilt, or lack of guilt, and whether there was any possibility of mutual understanding.

It's an argument that goes to the heart of both the Aboriginal and non-Aboriginal relationship with this country—the difference between being black and white, Indigenous and coloniser. Frances also believes that more white people than have ever realised it have Aboriginal ancestors. And that one reason we whites haven't come to terms with our soul in this country is because we haven't identified this, or indeed, come to terms with our past.

'Bennelong's children survived, as did a lot of Aboriginal people's children,' Frances told me. 'They survived. But they were told they were no longer Aboriginal because they didn't live in a certain way. And because they no longer came from where the new boundaries said they came from, they were then told they were no longer Aboriginal.

There's a lot of people around who are descendants of Aboriginal people, whose families denied their Aboriginality going back generations. That's been the process of genocide. It's being told you're not what you are. They're around, they're everywhere.'

As a journalist covering Aboriginal affairs, these are issues I've tried to come to terms with, but not particularly successfully. Although many white people tragically still only meet Aboriginal people through the media, it wasn't always so. The relationships between the two groups have been and will be a great deal closer than most realise. And the relationship between Aboriginal people and those in authority hasn't always been a one-sided one. There have been links through the union movement, the Communist Party, the Labor Party and the churches.

The relationship has not only been between the 'left' and Aborigines. There are also strong connections on the 'right' of politics. Over the years a motley gathering of political groups and organisations have lent support to the Aboriginal cause. And although Aboriginal organisations have often preferred to control their leadership, a number of non-Aboriginal individuals have been involved.

Some politicians have been deeply influenced by their contact with Aboriginal groups and individuals. For example, several Ministers for Aboriginal Affairs and state premiers have received their grounding as lawyers when they worked for the Aboriginal Legal Service. These include Robert Tickner, Peter Dowding, Wayne Goss and Fred Chaney.

And some politicians have had Aboriginal spouses, such as Peter Dowding, John Dawkins, Peter Cook and Bob Collins. Many others have had Aboriginal lovers. In some cases, there is resentment by Aboriginal people towards some of these people, who feel they were used and then dropped along the way. There's probably some resentment coming from the other direction too!

Just as journalists' relationships with politicians are often more multidimensional than is perceived, so too has been our contact with Aboriginal people. Since the days of the British Colony's first newspapers, there have been journalists who have been sympathetic to the plight of Aborigines. In fact, I discovered years later, my and others interest in reporting Aboriginal affairs was following a historical lineage of journalism about Indigenous issues.

In the late 1820s, the voice of humanitarian critics began to appear in Sydney's first newspaper, the *Sydney Gazette*. These sentiments were strengthened with the arrival of free settlers, missionaries and Aboriginal protectors after 1820, some of whom were shocked by the bloodshed and outraged by the easy acceptance of racial violence. Many of these were aware of, or involved in, the new humanitarian movement in Britain—a movement that culminated with the anti-slavery movement in Britain from 1820 to 1830.

In the mid 1920s one of the first Indigenous political organisations, the Australian Aboriginal Progressive Association (the AAPA's) most active white supporter was JJ Moloney, the editor of the *Voice of the North*, the Newcastle newspaper. From the 1960s on, Aboriginal people became more sophisticated in their use of the media, and journalists such as Graham Williams, Shaun McIlwraith, Alan Ashbolt, Caroline Jones and Oliver Hogue often wrote stories that publicised their cause. These days journalists tend to be given more respect for their work in Aboriginal affairs, although it is still not a popular subject to write about.

Although my mother used to call me a do-gooder, and quite a few other people have used even less kind terms, I believe that as a 'white woman' journalist writing about race issues I have worked during some of the most interesting times you could imagine. Despite all the difficulties over the years, I have been greatly enriched by my friendships with Aboriginal people, particularly the women, like Ollie.

I guess you could say I was 'bitten' during that first visit to Borroloola. But it wasn't until after I'd actually lived in the Kimberley in 1979 that I read JRB Love's book: *Stone-Age Bushmen of Today, Life and Adventure among a Tribe of Savages in North-Western Australia*, published in 1936, and realised that my mother's side of the family had connections with this part of the world, and with Aboriginal people. This JRB Love was my great-uncle, Bob Love, a Presbyterian missionary working in the Kimberley earlier this century. Yet I knew nothing of him until I discovered his book in my parents' bookshelves.

I became fascinated by this family history. I'd always known a lot more about my father's side of the family than my mother's good, strong Presbyterian stock from Ireland.

That's because she never spoke about them. I had found it pretty strange that I never met my grandfather until after my grandmother died, when I was about ten or eleven years old. We used to visit Grandma at her home in Woollahra and she would give us whatever small change she could find on her bedside table. She'd been an orphan who went into nursing. When Grandma was in her twenties she started dabbling on the stock exchange with whatever was left over from her wages at the end of the week. She made a modest fortune and married George Love, a wool merchant, in her late thirties. Apparently she used to sit up the back of shareholders' meetings and yell out confronting questions about the performance of the company.

Once, at her house, I caught sight of a man downstairs and asked my mother who he was. 'Just your grandfather,' she said. When he died a few years later and I was crying (well, you're meant to cry when people die, aren't you?) she told me to dry my tears.

'Do you know what our Sunday afternoon entertainment was?' she asked. 'Driving to the wool stores where my father worked as a wool merchant, and sitting in the car while he worked inside.' She could be quite cutting, my mother.

'I was dux of my school. But while I was studying for my leaving certificate he told me not to bother, I'd only become a waitress, anyway.'

She had two brothers, who I also hardly knew. One, Uncle Brian, died a couple of years before her. He was an alcoholic and lived in a nursing home. The other, Uncle Greggar, lives in Newcastle. We went to visit him not long after I finished working on The Festival of the Dreaming in 1997.

Greggar had lived alone in his little timber house for years. He'd go off wandering the streets and the police, who knew him, would bring him home. But then one day they decided to put him into the local mental institution. He'd called Dad and, in Dad's words, had said the most coherent thing he'd muttered in years: 'Get me out of here.' So we were going up to see what we could do.

Both Greggar and Brian had been intelligent boys. We found Greek and Russian dictionaries, as well as a Russian newspaper he subscribed to, in Greggar's house. But my grandfather's cruelty had led both of them to have nervous breakdowns, and possibly, to Greggar's schizophrenia. My mother, an extremely intelligent and charming, but often moody woman, had got out just in time when she married Dad. I have a lovely photo of the three of them, taken in a studio, when they were small children. They looked so angelic, with Mum holding a toy. So innocent of the future.

I'd had a bad year with some depression, and later when I watched Uncle Greggar in his grey tracksuit pants that finished halfway down his calves, hopping up and down in pleasure at seeing Dad, I suddenly thought, *maybe his mental condition is genetic. God, maybe I've inherited it.*

Uncle Greggar loved my mother very much, and was heartbroken, as we all were, when she died at the age of 67 from lymphoma. But he provided the only comic relief at her cremation. Some of the younger members of the family spoke about her at the service to the background noise of Uncle Greggar muttering to himself.

'Is Uncle Greggar going to speak next?' my husband whispered to me, and I suddenly got a bad case of the giggles.

So it was pretty remarkable for me, back in the late '70s, to find not only a quite normal relative on my mother's side (Uncle Bob was Grandpa's brother), but a famous one. It was also extremely weird to discover, after seeing the ill effects of missions, that I had a missionary in the family.

'Uncle Bob was the only member of the Loves that my mother could stand,' my mum told me, when I asked her all about him. 'When he came to visit he'd tell us wonderful stories about his time in the bush.'

He was a missionary, but I nicknamed him the 'revolutionary missionary' because, although he wanted to spread Christianity, he apparently did not want to destroy Aboriginal culture and Law. He was a linguist—during his time at Kunmunya mission on the wild north coast of the Kimberley, with the help of his Aboriginal translation team, translated the gospels of John and Mark into Worora. Later he worked at Ernabella in South Australia and translated the Gospel of St Mark into Pitjantjatjara.

He was 25 years old when he first went to the Kimberley in 1914, and had possibly seen more of the Australian continent than any other white man alive at that time. Two years before, the Presbyterian Board of Missions decided it should be taking some responsibility for Aboriginal welfare, as the Catholics and Lutherans had for quite some time. So it asked Uncle Bob to undertake an expedition 'for the purpose of enquiring into the conditions of life among the Aborigines of the interior'. During the next two years he travelled thousands of miles, mainly on horseback, visiting remote Aboriginal communities.

Uncle Bob ran Kunmunya at a time when the usual policy was to take 'part-Aboriginal' children away from their tribal backgrounds and put them into missions (as had happened with Ollie's grandparents just a few years previously). I don't know how Uncle Bob felt about this, but I understand he was determined not to interfere with tribal custom and he didn't tolerate paternalism. He found remarkable similarities between Worora and Christian rituals, including the rites of the Last Supper, baptism and the laying-on of hands.

All (these rituals) *were here, practiced in the spirit of the deepest reverence and awe by naked savages in north-western Australia,* he wrote in his book. *And there are those who will say that the Australian blackfellow can not understand Christianity.*

Despite my largely agnostic upbringing—and my use of different language—I felt a strong feeling of affinity with Uncle Bob. He may not have been perfect, but I still feel for his time that his thinking appears to have been fairly unusual. He had been 'bitten' by the Kimberley and Kimberley people and so had I. Although it wasn't until 1927 that he returned to Worora country, he had never stopped thinking about the place. He had the feeling of coming home, this time with his wife and family, and stayed there until 1940.

One steamy afternoon in the late '80s I was sitting under a mango tree in Jimmy Chi's garden in Broome, sipping tea talking with him and his partner, Glennys. My husband and I had just done an amazing trip into Worora country to my Uncle Bob's former mission, Kunmunya. Jimmy believes, as a sort of inheritance from his mix of Aboriginal and Christian upbringing, in dreams, positive thinking and a bit of pop psychology. It was from him that I first heard the term 'creative visualisation'. He had been the first Aboriginal university student in Western Australia. But he had a traumatic car accident and spent a long time in hospital. He told me he became bitter about the world. Quite a long time later when he was back in the Kimberley, he went to Derby and met Albert Barunga. Here was a man who had seen plenty of white brutality towards his tribe, and yet he held no bitterness. When Jimmy asked him if he wanted a beer, he replied that he'd prefer a soft drink. For Jimmy that was a real eye-opener at the time. All blackfellas drank, he had thought.

Jimmy believes it was the way Albert Barunga had been able to combine his Aboriginal beliefs and his Christianity that had made him what he was. Uncle Bob had been Albert Barunga's teacher (in the white man's way), and in his turn, he had taught Uncle Bob about Aboriginal culture and language. Albert Barunga had helped Jimmy, who has helped me, and, he told me, I'd helped him. And the strangest thing was that I first went to the Kimberley knowing nothing of my great-uncle.

'You came to the Kimberley because your great-uncle had been here and you had to write about him,' he told me. When other people speak New Age mumbo jumbo I feel like screaming. With Jimmy, it sounds like pearls of wisdom.

Mimi Dora, Relations and Noonkanbah

4.

Mimi Dora, Relations and Noonkanbah

You came from the Dreaming before time began
The sun was agleaming on you, early man
You came so far in time
It's no nursery rhyme

Hey Jacky
They don't want you around here any more
Hey Jacky
They don't want you around here any more
No more

You fought with your weapons
But they had the gun
The Crown was ascheming on you
Early man
They came from across the seas
You were in harmony

Hey Jacky
They don't want you around here any more
Hey Jacky
They don't want you around here any more
No more

Verses one and two, *Hey Jacky*

Arnold Smith

Ollie: My Mimi Dora knew who her mother was. She was a Bunuba woman, from round near Fitzroy Crossing. The Bunuba area goes across to the north or Gibb River side of Fitzroy Crossing. The famous Aboriginal hero, Pigeon, or Jandamarra, was Bunuba.

In her Native Affairs file it says Granny's mother was known as Gypsy, although that obviously wasn't her Aboriginal name. Granny's full name was Teresa Dora Smith. Her father was a white man, Jim Leaky. Her date of birth is listed as 8 November, 1912.

What always amazed me about my granny was that she was multilingual. She must have got an education at Beagle Bay, where she was taken as a small child, but probably only up to primary. Still, she could speak the Asian languages. She could speak Bunuba, her own native tongue. She could speak Derby lingo, Broome lingo, and communicate in Indonesian. And here I am, educated, and I'm battling with English! She was a gutsy lady and a hard worker. She worked as a cook, a laundress and anything else that would pay.

Being institutionalised, and then in a foster home, we never had the contacts with the family to sit down and discuss family history and these issues. When I was young I suppose I wasn't interested, because the same thing happened to me—being taken away—and it was accepted as the norm. But when I was in Darwin in 1981 I tried to talk to Granny about her background. It was like some of it she couldn't remember, but some of it she didn't want to talk about. She died in 1997, when she was about 90 years old.

But then when I read her file there was quite a bit of information that she never told us. There's also lots of gaps that I guess I'll never be able to fill in now. She got married to Richard (Dick) Smith at Beagle Bay in May, 1926. His mother was listed as Dinah (full blood) and father as Bill Smith (white man).

Mimi Dora had six children altogether, five girls and one boy. My grandfather, Dick Smith, was the father of the three older kids; Rita (my mum), Dick and Mona. Later she had Lena, Betty and Joy. After they had these children my grandfather went droving down in Wiluna and later back doing stockwork on stations around Halls Creek. In my grandfather's file are all these letters from my grandmother wanting to reunite with him. But he kept fobbing her off.

She'd been back and forth, constantly writing to her husband through the authorities so they could reunite and live as a family.

One letter, written in 1935 from Beagle Bay, when she hadn't seen him for three years, said: *And the other thing is I see for myself it's no use stopping here. It's better for me to go somewhere, why, the reason is this, he knows quite well the mission is keeping us up alive with food and so on, and now he thinks he hasn't to worry so far, as long as the children are not starving for want of tucker. But my thinking is to go away and let him see that it isn't right at all in the first place.*

One of his answers read: *I have written her stating that she could join me in three months time, when I hope to be able to make some arrangements to keep her and the children with me. Although I have been in constant work, my job takes me away from home, and at such times Dora would have to have company as she will not stay alone. My present employers will not allow women near the main camp, but are willing to provide quarters out on the run. But as this arrangement will not suit Dora, I will have to find other employment, if possible, where I can be home every day. This may be hard to find as I cannot keep her on ordinary station wages. If I could get exemption from the Aborigines Act, I could get a small block of land where there would be neighbours.*

The authorities were trying to help her get back with her husband and I think at one stage she actually did make it to Wiluna. All these letters were begging him to join up again with her. And then something bad must have happened between them when she did join him. So she ended up going to Broome and back to Beagle Bay. That's when she had Lena (whose father was a full blood from around Beagle Bay). And I guess my grandfather didn't want somebody else's kid, and his last letter to the authorities said: *I have told you in one of my letters some time ago that I didn't intend to take my wife back again.*

I can understand Granny going from bloke to bloke after that. She had three kids for him, and then he didn't want her. What a bastard he was.

My grandfather went to Alice Springs after Wiluna and Halls Creek. And when I went to Alice I found out he lived with a woman over there but they never had any children together. She was in a nursing home there but I never went to visit her. That's before he headed off to Queensland. My uncle Dick also went to live in Queensland, and his children got to know our grandfather better than we did. Uncle Dick's son, Eddy, moved to Broome. I never actually met my grandfather. I think the old boy died in Queensland, in 1968. Uncle Dick was at Granny's funeral with the rest of Mimi Dora's children.

After Lena, Mimi Dora had Betty, whose father, William Kada, was a Koepang, and then later she had Joy, who had a Chinaman father. According to the file his name was Look Yew. I knew him when I was a kid because Granny was living with him then.

Mimi Dora went through hell after she had Betty. She was seen as a 'sinner', because she was the mother of an illegitimate child, but also because Betty's father was a Koepang from Portuguese Timor. She was living with William Kada and the baby when the house was raided in 1941 and he was arrested.

William Kada was warned to stay away from Granny. He was a bosun on a pearling lugger and transferred to Darwin. Aunty Betty found out he died when she was thirteen. The lugger he was on capsized during a cyclone and she heard the news on the radio. She hadn't even seen him since she was a baby.

The government wanted to make an example of Granny and the other women to discourage interracial relationships. They didn't want the Asiatics and the 'half-castes' mixing and having children. They were removed under Section Twelve of the Native Administration Act 1905–40. The memo from the Commissioner of Native Affairs to the Commissioner of Police says: *For a great many years the Broome native situation has caused this Department great concern, and it is now felt that some definite steps must be taken to rectify matters. The half-caste women have adopted the attitude that they are able to associate with the indentured Asiatic crews ad lib., and that no action will be taken against them.*

They were to be taken by mission truck and warned that they could not leave the mission until the warrant placed on them was removed. If they tried to escape they would be taken back to the mission. Despite this, the church was not so happy at being told they had to take the women and children for an 'indefinite period', as they would have preferred them housed in Broome.

So Granny and three other mothers of Asiatic children were sent back to Beagle Bay and made to live in the former leprosarium. On the way to Beagle Bay, Betty said that they were so hungry that Granny had to steal from army trucks to feed them.

They were shunned by the other women at Beagle Bay and their children were not allowed to play with the other mission children. At the inquiry Betty told how she wasn't allowed to associate with the other kids because she and the other 'Asiatic' kids 'were the sins of the Asiatic people'. She regretted that her mother couldn't mix with other people because they had branded her as a sinful woman.

Mimi Dora was not at all happy about it either but apparently she tried to be on her best behaviour while she was there. She wrote several letters to the Commissioner of

Native Affairs, and reading them, you can feel her frustration at her imprisonment. The first one was written one year and four months after they were sent to the mission: *Please could you kindly let me know about my baby Elizabeth and myself, as we are anxious to go home again. Anyhow I am very much worried about my house. I suppose by the time I go back the white ants will be so plentiful.*

William Kada had bought a house for Granny and Betty but she was never able to take ownership of it.

The Commissioner told Granny that, as the war was on, she must: *remain at Beagle Bay mission until world affairs are once again back to normal... When you lived in Broome previously your conduct was unsatisfactory and it is my firm intention to prevent such conduct in the future.*

In October, 1944, when she was five years old, Aunty Betty was put in the orphanage in Broome where she said she learnt to cook, sew, make her own soap, tend the garden and do men's jobs. Around that time, Mimi Dora learnt that her warrant had been cancelled but that she still had to stay at the mission. In 1945 she applied for a job as station cook at Noonkanbah station, near Fitzroy Crossing (back near her tribal country). Mum, who was sixteen at the time and living in the girls' dormitory at Beagle Bay, went with her, even though there are letters in the file from the Acting Commissioner of Native Affairs saying Granny was not a suitable person to have control of her daughter. The sisters at Beagle Bay said Mum had a heart condition, but they believed the job at Noonkanbah would do her good. Apparently Mum and Mimi Dora were 'happy and contented' at Noonkanbah, probably, I think now, because they had all their relatives around them. They were even allowed to have a holiday in Broome after being at Noonkanbah for a while, and flew by small plane to Broome. Later Granny went to work for Mrs Kimberley Male at Roebuck Plains station, as she was not allowed to work back in Broome at that time.

Later in the file there's Granny's application for a certificate of exemption from the Native Administration Act. She said she was applying for exemption to 'try to get a better position and give my children a better chance'. She finally got what we call the dog tag card in 1954. I asked her what happened to it, because I thought I'd use it when I was teaching my cross-cultural awareness courses. She said after the 1967 referendum, when she and other Aboriginal people got citizenship, she went and ripped up her 'dog tag' and threw it away.

The last entry in Mimi Dora's file is a sad little notice—a report of death for Kevin Smith, Granny's premature baby, who only lived 36 hours. He was born in Wyndham Native Hospital on 30 January, 1963 (after I was born) and buried at Wyndham Native Cemetery. The burial was authorised at contract rates and cost 30 pounds.

Diana: Whenever I think about the Kimberley I think about roads and driving. And whenever I think about Noonkanbah I think of the sweep of that dusty track, just before it leads down the hill, across the plains to the homestead. That's where you come across a clump of boab trees like a group of old women, their hands on their hips, gossiping.

Beyond them in the dry and enveloping stillness way over on the horizon is the blue escarpment. But there amidst the smell of dry grass, cockatoos and crimson-winged galahs fly from branch to branch screeching their messages.

White men caught and chained Aboriginal people, and in the great Australian tradition, turned the bottle-shaped trees into prisons. Old Man Boab, whose wise, graceful branches once reached out to protect the people of this land in his embrace, was used to cramp them in black, airless space. But, like the people of Noonkanbah, the trees have withstood the invasion. So strong in their strangeness, they belong there.

And every time I think of Noonkanbah I think of that first meeting I went to, where I met Dicky Skinner, now known as Dicky Cox, the chairman of the community.

I was travelling with Phil Vincent, an Aboriginal Legal Service lawyer, and we'd left Derby (about 250 kilometres to the west) when it was still dark. But dawn had turned to bright sunshine and the heat mingled with the red dust, which streamed in through every crack of the four-wheel drive. I had only known Phil a short time, but there's nothing like long outback trips bumping over rough dirt roads to get you better acquainted.

While steering the Toyota, Phil spoke about a case he was working on in Fitzroy Crossing. It seems some Aboriginal stockmen from Christmas Creek station had been in town with the station manager. They'd been drinking at the pub—the stockmen in the black bar and the manager in the white bar. As a 'joke', the manager had poured a bag of flour that he'd bought at the store over the men, saying he'd make them white. On the drive home he stopped the Toyota and assaulted some of the men. They went home and organised the whole community to walk off the station. They established a community closer to the highway, and it was years before they went back to Christmas Creek to work. Phil was going to court for them, as they'd decided to take out an assault case against the manager. It was previously unheard of for Aboriginal stockmen to take that sort of action.

He had seemed happy enough to take me to Noonkanbah when I asked. I had wanted to write a story about an Aboriginal-run cattle station, and at Noonkanbah the people had been running cattle for a couple of years since they moved back to the station. As he was going there for a meeting between the community and Amax, the American oil company that wanted to explore on their land, it seemed like a good time for me to visit.

Ollie on the back of the orphanage truck (in red dress).
About three years old.

Ollie at kindergarten, orphanage in background.

Diana, sitting on her mother Erica Plater's back at the beach.
About three years old.

Diana (middle), with her mother, brother Ian and
sisters Lindy (left) and Antoinette (right).

Diana, Pudding and The Red Terror in South Australia.

Diana and Pudding.

Diana and Pudding in Perth.

Ollie and Diana at Ollie's wedding.

Pudding, Ollie and Adam in Perth. Diana in reflection of door.

Nancy Francis.

Diana and Ollie, waking up at Lady Macquarie's Chair on
the day of the '88 march.

Diana, Rita, Lesley and
Mimi Dora at Pine Creek.

The Noonkanbah gate.

After a few more miles the road scattered into a series of tracks that opened out into a wide red road, which I realised was the airstrip. We drove off it through some thick bush over a dry creek crossing and came out onto a flat, dry plain. Bits of bracken were sweeping across it, and a willy-willy was blowing up in the distance as we drove past the sheds and yards to the homestead.

Dicky, the chairman of the Yungnora community, was standing on the verandah of the colonial building. He was splendid in a ringer's outfit—boots, jeans, held up with a well-worn leather belt, a checked shirt and faded felt hat. He grinned as we climbed out.

'You two fellas hungry? There's beef over there.' He pointed with his lips to a carcass of blood-red meat swarming with flies. Sauntering over, he swept the flies away with one brush of his arm and cut two big slabs with a sharp knife.

'You got bread?' We nodded. 'Well, make yourself at home,' he grinned again as he handed us the meat. After making a billy of tea we had a good breakfast, sheltering from the hot wind inside the corrugated iron shed next to the homestead.

The meeting was held in the bough shelter in front of the homestead. A trellis of timber was covered in spinifex branches to give an open shade. All the men were on one side and the women sat in a group in the dust on the other side, whispering to each other and glancing shyly from the corners of their eyes.

We heard a small plane buzz overhead, carrying the mining company men. Soon after Dicky arrived, driving the Toyota with two passengers who looked pretty uncomfortable. They were dressed in typical mining gear— khaki shorts, socks, solid boots, terry towelling hats and bright red faces. One man—the fat one—kept getting his hanky out to wipe his face. The sweat stuck like puddles in the big creases around his neck.

The other one was thin and muscular. His eyes focused more on the women than anything else. The fat man started talking, politely. 'We would like to talk to you people about exploring on this station.'

'Excuse me,' Dicky interrupted. 'But the community doesn't agree with cutting or drilling land. Another mining company came here. They said they were going to look for diamonds.'

'Oh no, we're not like that.'

Dicky put his hands on his hips and looked straight at him. 'Well, what are you looking for then?'

'Oil, mainly,' the fat man replied. 'We're looking all over the Kimberley. We drill holes, small pits are dug. If nothing is there, we go away again.'

'The sacred area is important to old people. It's hard for white people to understand.'

'Well, we're interested in the area we flew over by helicopter.'

'All places are important. Noonkanbah is pastoral country, but more important, it's cultural background.'

'We always go and talk to the managers. We like people to know what we're doing. This happens all over the world. Sometimes it's not nice to dig up the ground, but it's necessary for the benefits. We have a mine at Bougainville. That's in New Guinea, you know. The people know there are benefits, so they let it go and work on it.'

'Listen,' Dicky interrupted again. 'Where were you born?'

The fat man looked surprised, but he kept smiling. 'South-east Australia—Melbourne, actually.'

'I was born just here,' Dicky said. 'People took the land from Aborigines once. Now it's happening all over again. They come in, drilling holes and not worrying about tribal people again.'

'But some Aborigines don't mind mining,' the fat man said.

'We trying to get back onto land. The community is trying to establish itself, on land. Trying to keep away from trouble with grog.'

'Those east Kimberley people don't mind. We dug holes and filled them in again.'

'But you can't say the government owns the land,' Dicky ignored the miner's last point. 'It doesn't know what that tree is. Our Law came from under the ground. Who put the government and your company's name on the oil?'

The fat man didn't answer. He thought the company's mineral claims had been registered. 'Bill,' he turned to the man with him. 'Could you check on that?'

His assistant went and looked through some papers in his briefcase. 'No,' he said, when he came back. 'They've only been recommended.'

Phil looked up. 'A report is now being prepared on this area by the state museum and is pending. Therefore I think we should be more careful.'

'That's why we're here at a meeting,' the fat man began to look agitated. He bought out his packet of cigarettes and lit one.

'And how much money are you getting for that oil?' Dicky asked.

'We haven't found any yet. No money is being made. If we did find any we'd obey the laws and pay taxes. The government uses the money as it sees fit. That's where you get money for the Department of Aboriginal Affairs.'

'But who put the oil in the ground—you or the government?'

'I don't know. They've been here longer than us.'

'Well, from the tribal side you can't say it's your company's or the government's. If you dig up the ground or mess up the ground you get punished in the tribal way. As police punish by arrest, these people have agreement that we arrest anybody who disturbs sacred sites, and punish them.'

'Well, ah,' the fat man coughed and looked uncomfortable. Then the other fella piped up.

'Well, actually, you don't own this land under the law, you just have a grazing lease.' The fat man glared at his colleague, trying to tell him to shut up. But Dicky had already got the message and was growing angry.

'Look, we're sick of this talk about white man law,' he paused, and everybody waited in silence. 'How would you like to live out in the bush for a while?'

The fat man laughed and said he wouldn't mind a bit of a holiday.

'Yeah, but would you like to live out in the bush—with no food and no clothes?' Dicky asked once again.

The fat man's face was turning redder and his colleague began to twitch.

'Are you threatening me?' he asked.

'No, we're not threatening you,' Dicky spoke slowly.

Then one of the old men stood up. He looked angry as his voice grew in intensity. 'Who was here for thousands of years?' he asked. 'White or black?'

The fat man took another cigarette out of his pocket. 'Look, we know this, but it's happened.' He put the cigarette in his mouth.

'What do you think of us?' the old man asked.

'We're all Australians. We don't want to hurt Aborigines.'

Dicky stood up and walked around in a circle. He arrived in front of the fat man and stopped. 'Look,' he spoke emphatically. 'People here don't want any more talk, meetings or drilling. No more talk, no more mining. If people come we will punish them in Law. Also if drilling, same thing. We set up new Law here to say we mean it. Government laws are no good because they don't help us.'

'We'll be in touch.' The fat man started shoving papers into his briefcase. He looked at his watch.

'Well, that pilot must be getting hungry. Better be off.

Ah, thank you, Dicky. Well, ah, see you next time.' He glanced at the group and then for the first time looked at me, managing an embarrassed smile.

Dicky talked to one of the younger men, who stood up and led the mining company men to the Toyota.

The people laughed as the miners drove off—from relief, I suppose. But I heard one woman sigh and say, 'I wish those miners would go away and leave us alone,' before she drifted away to her camp.

Dicky led Phil and me into the homestead kitchen. It was a large mud brick room with wood stoves on one side. It looked as if it hadn't changed much since the pioneer days. A big woman in a floral shift sat cross-legged on the huge wooden table in the centre of the room. She was peeling potatoes. Another woman was standing over an enormous pot of stew of home-grown beef, carrots, onions and potatoes.

The women looked up and smiled as Dicky explained they were making lunch for the school children. He handed us some cups of steaming black tea from a burnt billy stewing on the wood stove, then led us back into the cool corridors of the homestead.

On the wall of the homestead was pinned a notice with the names of the community members divided up into jobs—stockcamp yard work, fence work, school teachers, preschool storytellers, school workers, home and house workers, laundry, store, clinic, workshop and cleaning round the house. The community decided who did what. Dicky, a traditional doctor, also acted as the community health worker.

After a short talk with Phil about some legal problems with the community's cattle contracts, he offered to show us around the station. His Toyota was sitting next to the bough shelter with the key in it. On the way across the flat plain, Dicky explained how the station was run.

The men worked in a co-operative way to muster the cattle, brand them and send them to the meatworks. Even the young boys helped in the stockcamps. Everybody had their role, women and men, and all took turns in different areas, from looking after the kindergarten children to mending fences. Most people lived in separate family camps, some near the homestead, others in the shearing sheds near the school.

The people had worked on Noonkanbah when it was a sheep station, but in 1971 they had walked off because of what they described as bad living conditions. This basically meant being treated like animals. They moved into Fitzroy Crossing, where they became fringe dwellers. From there, led by spokesman Friday Mulla, they fought to get their land back. In 1976, after years of agitation, letter-writing, visits by politicians and squats on a neighbouring station, the Aboriginal Land Fund Commission bought the lease to the station. The community, who ran it as a cattle station, then refused to have a white manager. So it was run by a management committee made up of members of the community and chaired by Dicky, who represented the tribal elders. The station received assistance from the Department of Aboriginal Affairs and advice from the Departments of Agriculture and Community Welfare.

Cars and four-wheel drive vehicles were forever coming and going at Noonkanbah—carrying people to town to shop or attend meetings, to go to stockcamps or on hunting trips.

Dicky took us to one of the stockcamps to get a closer idea of how the station was run. As he changed gears turning corners around the soft dirt tracks through scrub cropped short by bullocks and cows, I could see a cloud of dust in the distance. As we got closer the dust became men on horseback rounding up the cattle, who were bellowing in anger.

A couple of the men and a young boy had one calf down on the ground with a lasso around its ankle. The calf let out a surprised and mournful moan as one of the men brought the iron down onto its back. They let it go and it jumped up with a start and hopped around the yard, before finding the gate and freedom.

What a show they can put on. The cattle were herded together in one yard, all waiting their turn for the brand. The men were riding behind the other bullocks, forcing them into the yard. There was much yelling and screaming and carrying on.

Dicky and Phil climbed up onto the fence and I climbed up behind them. 'Hey, Dicky,' one of the older stockmen yelled as he approached us. He was wearing a crumpled hat pushed over his eyes and held on with a piece of elastic under his chin. It looked as if he had worn it and slept in it for the past twenty years. I couldn't help smiling. 'Who that girl with you?'

'This is Diana. She came out here for that meeting, you know, about that mining mob.'

As we chatted, the stockman explained to me that the community at Noonkanbah was made up of two groups— the Nyikina, who had occupied the country for millenia, and the Walmajarri who came from the south.

When we visited the shearing shed that had been converted into a school, the children were busy in every corner: reading, doing lessons and writing. The old women were taking the kindergarten. After reading stories they sang songs in Walmajarri and the children clapped along.

The year before, the people had decided to set up their own government school. Not able to get government funds, they employed two white teachers with 'chuck-in' money, and help from the people at Strelley, another Aboriginal-owned station near Port Hedland.

The community had decided they did not want their children sent away for education any more. Everything could be taught at Noonkanbah. So two of their old men taught traditional skills and culture and the white teachers taught basic literacy and numeracy.

'We decided the children should learn the language,' Dicky said. 'We fought for our community school, but the government wouldn't listen. There were promises, but nothing. We paid our own teachers, black and white, for one year from a community chuck-in. Our children began to learn the language; they began to belong to the land again.'

That night some of the old men and women sat round the fire singing songs of their country. The children snuggled close, wrapped in blankets, and hummed along. The sound of loud country music from a cassette player drifted over from one of the camps.

'We want the children to learn about the old ways,' an old man, Nipper, told me. 'We teach them the songs and the dances.'

Another old man nudged me as he gazed with liquid eyes at the children dancing with their mothers. 'You know, we just want our children back, half-castes and all. Those missionaries and policemen took them away from us. But we want them back.'

⁂

I'd arrived in the Kimberley only a week or so before this. I'd driven via the Nullabor and Perth, where I'd had a great night with Bob Marley and the Wailers! After a couple of nights in Broome, I drove on my birthday to Derby. The then chairman of the Kimberley Land Council, Jimmy Bieundurry, had kindly allowed me to use his and the ALS office as a base. It was a pretty tiny organisation in those days—just Jimmy and Sarah, a young, white anthropologist, who was helping with administrative work. She and I became good friends.

The cluttered office, in a timber building surrounded by a verandah behind the YWCA, doubled as that of the National Aboriginal Conference. Jimmy was the first member for the west Kimberley. Jimmy was a wonderful man who was forever writing letters, making phone calls, lobbying to have the idea of land rights recognised as a serious notion.

Although a young man, he was an elder of the Walmajarri people. The short white history in this region is illustrated by the fact that it was not until he was about ten, when his family came into the Balgo mission out of the Great Sandy Desert between the Pilbara and the Kimberley, that Jimmy saw his first white person. Once, a plane flew over them and he was frightened, thinking it was a spirit come to get them.

Once in contact with white people, Jimmy became a drover and would take cattle down the Canning Stock Route from Halls Creek. Unable to read and write, he decided to go to school at Fitzroy Crossing when he was in his twenties. He married Olive, a talented translator and interpreter of Aboriginal languages, and had a big family. For a while they worked as missionaries in Papua New Guinea. Although a traditional man he was able to blend his Aboriginal beliefs with his Christianity.

The KLC began in 1978 as a voice for Aboriginal people, when mining companies were exploring this last untouched country. Jimmy turned the KLC into an organisation which gained the respect and confidence of communities in dealing with mining companies and government.

He had the instinctive knowledge of a tribal man—the capability to track animals, to know food sources, to tell whose human footprints were left in the sand. Once, when I was at a meeting down by the river at Noonkanbah, Jimmy arrived with Sarah.

'Diana's already here,' Jimmy told Sarah as they climbed down the sandhill to the riverbank.

'How do you know?' she asked.

'Those are her footprints,' he said, as he pointed to mine.

Phil agreed that it was incredible, the way Jimmy managed to mix this background and his strong tribal cultural heritage, with political activism and an understanding of the benefits of white society. He said Jimmy was one of the real Aboriginal statesmen. He would probably be described as a leader, but that term is pretty meaningless in Aboriginal culture where decisions are made by the group.

The issue over mining on a sacred site at Noonkanbah became a test case for land rights, supported by huge protests around the country in 1980. Steve Hawke's book, *Noonkanbah*, goes into lengthy detail about the whole story. I reported on much of the first year of the dispute for papers in WA and in the eastern states.

We worked out of Fitzroy Crossing's community welfare office, where the staff were extremely sympathetic to the plight of the Yungnora community. In fact, people like Stan Davey and his wife, Jan Richardson, had helped the Yungnora community move back to Noonkanbah. I'd use their telex machines to send my stories and there'd be telex tape winding out through the door as I tried to work out the machine. I'd stay with the Welfare staff or the kindy teachers. It was an exciting time for everybody involved. We felt as if we were caught up in a fight for justice. Couldn't these people just have some time to be left alone to get the station working and heal the community? But that seemed too much to ask, for some.

Eventually, the state government forced the American oil company, Amax, to drill on the sacred site, after manning an oil rig with 'black' labour and driving it right up the WA coast to Noonkanbah. At the turn-off to the station scores of people were arrested. They held hands so tightly it took several policemen to pull each protester apart.

Although the public perception is that Aboriginal people are always against mining, this is not always true. In recent times some Aboriginal people have in fact been miners themselves. Back in the late 1940s, after taking part in the Pilbara stockmen's strike, Aboriginal people banded together with Don McLeod, a white prospector, to form the Northern Development and Mining Company. It bought Yandeearra station and three others from mining profits, then in 1970 took over Strelley station.

Strelley was an inspiration for other Aboriginal groups, who gradually were able to buy back stations such as Noonkanbah with funds from the Federal government.

Since the early 1980s, after all the fuss had died down over Amax, the people of Noonkanbah actually did make several agreements with mining companies, and so have other Aboriginal communities across the country, in those places where they have the right to negotiate with these companies. But where the miners mine is crucial.

Another trip to Noonkanbah in 1979, to write stories for the *Perth Daily News* and *The Age*. My car was loaded with women and children when we went on a fishing trip to a beautiful spot on the Fitzroy River. We bumped past Pea Hill, close to Bundarra, where Amax had set its site for its exploratory well.

'This is the song for this country,' Lucy Cubby, one of the women, said. And they all joined in singing of the time when the goannas were on Pea Hill. They went underground and travelled round, coming up at stages to lay eggs, which became rocks. Lucy explained it was a male ceremonial ground and women could not go there.

Noonkanbah, with all its troubles, had become famous. The walls of the homestead had a new addition. Each day Ivan McPhee, the community's secretary, pinned up newspaper clippings and photographs about the proposed mining and drilling. One of the men had written a story about it, illustrated by Polaroid photos.

And the gate to this once open community had been locked and chained to stop the Amax people coming in. The gate was draped by an Aboriginal flag.

Ollie: When you drive into Fitzroy Crossing your first impression may be that the town has lost its way. There's a sprawl and a maze of dirt roads that confuse the visitor. Started in the 1880s as a town for the west Kimberley stations, it takes its name from the narrow part of the river, which is passable in the dry season. The river flows down from Geikie Gorge, a crystal clear pool between sheer cliffs of granite. The whitefellas built, huddled together, a post office, hospital and police station. On the other side of the winding crossing was the hotel and store, with a caravan park perched next to it.

In the old days this placing led to a convenient situation for the drinkers—for when the rain came the river would become impassable. The police were marooned on the other side to the hotel, so the drinkers—a motley bunch of stockmen, squatters and travellers—would drink on regardless into the early hours of the morning without threat of arrest or harassment. Further away was the mission and its store.

It used to be only the missionaries who bothered with the welfare of blackfellas—and, of course, Native Affairs. But modern times emerged and so, too, had the Department of Community Welfare. A Welfare office was established, a new hospital built, and a white section of the town grew up to house the new white public servants. The police were moved to a swanking new police station and jail—complete with guard towers and barbed wire fence—to cope with all the charges of 'drunk and disorderly'. And running in between the river and the old section and the new section was, of all things, a golf course.

At the petrol station on the highway there's always a stream of blackfella kids buying sweets and cool drinks. Cars, caravans and Toyotas are usually parked higgledy piggledy around the driveway. Men lean on them yarning to each other. Truckies unload gear, while others sit in a group drinking beer.

There's a song by the Warumpi Band about going back to Fitzroy Crossing. It's got a bit of a country style about it, and it certainly makes you homesick for the place. Fitzroy is where Mimi Dora came from. I've got relatives there, and I'm just gradually finding out who they are.

Every time I went through Fitzroy with work I would ask if they knew my Granny, and would ask who she was related to and which area she was from. I didn't have any success for many, many visits. I used to always ask Joe Ross. Joe used to say, 'Go and see my mum.' A couple of times I didn't go, and then on two occasions I finally got up the courage to go to her place—because I don't like going uninvited. But she was away. The second time I went she'd gone fishing and it'd gone dark. I thought, *getting dark, she must be coming home soon*. So I waited. Mimi Yvonne Cox was there, so I sat there talking to her. I thought, *I better go, it's getting late*. And I missed her again. She has died since then, so it's sad I didn't meet her, because she's a cousin or something to Granny. I never ever got to meet her, and now she's gone.

Then one day I went to Muludja Aboriginal community at Fossil Downs station and met up with Edna Shaw. Edna was taken away and put into Beagle Bay. I must have left Beagle Bay when Edna came there.

She rattled on with all these names of people that I was related to. That was really exciting. It was lovely to meet Edna. It was like finding my roots. Edna told me all the mob I was related to in Fitzroy. She told me about Olive Bieundurry, that she was a relation. I'd only just met Olive then. I went to this meeting in Bayulu and Olive was there. She's a beautiful woman. I heard this woman talking, a really articulate lady. I had to go up to her. I said, 'My girlfriend, Diana Plater, she knows you, and she used to talk about you all the time so I had to meet you. I heard so much about you.' Olive reckons I call her Aunty.

For my work, I go out to Wangkatjunga community at Christmas Creek and there, Sharon, Olive's daughter, knew who I was. It's really nice now going out there, and I said to the girl travelling with me from the education department, 'Hey, this is my relation.'

She says, 'Ollie, you got relations everywhere.'

I said, 'No, this is proper relation.'

I've worked with Marmingee Hand, the chairperson of the Kimberley Education Council, for many years since I came back to Broome—and just last year she tells me I'm related to her. I was the executive officer of the council. Marmingee is a Fitzroy girl. Kununurra was our first meeting place, then the second meeting was at Fitzroy Crossing. Marmingee said to me, 'I'm your relation, you call me Aunty.' I'm meeting people all the time. It's interesting finding all this out. I guess Granny and my mum knew all this but they didn't tell me.

When people say I'm related to this one and that one, I need to know how and why. Is it out of respect or is it a real relation? We often call somebody Aunty as a respect thing because she is a friend of the family. It was interesting for Cindy when she stayed with me, she got some work with ATSIC. She went out to Fitzroy Crossing and was introduced to all her relations. That was really good for her.

Cindy was with me for Granny's funeral. Olive came too. At first Cindy didn't want to go. She said to me, 'Mum, I don't want to go to the funeral.'

I said, 'That's all right, bub, you don't have to, do whatever you want to do.'

Then she thought about it and she said, 'No, I'll come, Mum.' And it was good too, because when we got back we started to talk. I had to tell her the relations—from my knowledge. Blackfella way, some of them are sisters, but we're actually first cousins. But my sisters and brothers are Cindy's mothers and fathers too.

I'm even related to kids I was in the orphanage with, as well as people who looked after me at Beagle Bay, like Yvonne and Mimi Ruby. Yvonne's mum lives at Noonkanbah and she's working in the clinic there. When me and Pudding had no family in Beagle Bay those two used to take it in turns to take me and Pudding out. They're our family. But even today I don't know how they're related to my granny.

For me it was a sense of relief when I met Edna. I finally found my roots and my identity.

I was given this little cut-out from the newspaper and it was from this person in Melbourne, Mrs Smith, who wanted to have contact with anybody who knew Dick Smith, or were relations of Dick Smith, in Fitzroy Crossing. Unfortunately, I lost the cut-out with the phone number, so I couldn't make contact with Mrs Smith. That was a pity.

To me, learning my Mimi Dora's story puts the political scene in the Kimberley into some kind of historical context. Recently I met Carolyn Davey, who was a teacher at Noonkanbah and whose mother-in-law is apparently a cousin of my granny. She told me the tribal people all knew EXACTLY which children were taken away, who they were related to, and where they came from.

It's a story of how bureaucracy and government laws controlled our lives, our every movement. In the late 1970s, when the trouble at Noonkanbah happened, the government was still trying to control our lives, trying to stop blackfellas owning land, and if they did own land, stop them having some rights or control over it. I wish I'd known more about Granny's life at that time and I wish I could have asked her what it was like living at Noonkanbah in the war years.

Noonkanbah, Broome
and the 'Coloured' People.

5.

Noonkanbah, Broome and the 'Coloured' People.

They took all your powers
Which give them their life
The Law is abeaming on you
Early man
If you go back into the Dream
People will cry and scream

Hey Jacky, they don't want you around here any more
They don't want your Law

Verse three, *Hey Jacky*

Arnold Smith

Diana: The last time I saw Nancy Francis was in June, 1993. She was almost a skeleton dressed in a floral shift, lying in her narrow bed in a Homeswest house in Broome. She was in her late eighties. Nobody was quite sure of her exact age, but I remember her telling me she was about five years old when she was taken to Beagle Bay in 1911.

She was obviously dying, for only a few years before she had been sprightly, walking everywhere around town. But despite her illness she still remained the matriarch of her large family.

Nancy must have been beautiful once. I'd seen some early photos of her, with her long, dark hair, her golden olive skin and slim body. Her father had been an Italian gold prospector and she had perhaps inherited some of that Botticelli beauty from him. Her mother was a traditional woman from Turkey Creek. Nancy only ever saw her mother again once after the police came to take her away, and by then she was too old to appear to appreciate the gap their parting had made to her life.

Despite her frail frame and almost inaudible voice, Nancy was just as alert and was overjoyed to meet Amelia, who was then two, for the first time. Amelia jumped on the other bed for most of the visit and Nancy laughed. 'She's very clever, very clever,' she kept saying.

Nancy loved children. She'd brought up her own three and scores of others—including grandchildren and great-grandchildren. They all called her Nana. 'They'd just leave them at the gate,' she'd told me. 'So what could I do?'

I considered Nancy a sort of adopted grandmother. I think she considered me a friend. Once, she came to stay with me when I was living in Darwin. There had been an intruder a few nights before and in the middle of the night we thought we heard somebody.

'I'll scare him,' she said, grabbing a kitchen knife. And I think she might have, wandering through the house with her long, white hair flowing over her frilly nightgown, as she held the weapon.

I met Nancy in 1979 on my first trip to the Kimberley. When I was living in Derby I'd go down to Broome for weekend trips. But this time—close to the end of the dry season—I decided to go for a bit longer, before I headed up to Darwin.

I got waylaid. I was asked by Geoff, an artist, if I would help him write some submissions for funding for his Broome Arts Group—a bunch of local unemployed kids doing silk screening and odd jobs around town. He had had his funds cut off due to both his inability to deal with the bureaucracy and the bureaucracy's inability to deal with a young man's way of doing things. Both didn't seem to have been able to come to any kind of compromise on a scheme to give young people employment in a town that had one of the biggest unemployment rates of the country.

Eventually I also ended up editing the *Broome News*, at the time a few roneoed sheets stapled together at the corner.

Geoff invited me to stay at his place, a ramshackle former pearling master's house, cool and dark inside with wide verandahs, shuttered windows and huge mango trees in the garden. In such a house even the rubbish looked artistic. He introduced me to people around town, and one day took me round to Nancy's place—I think initially to use her washing machine.

Nancy was sitting out the front on a bench under a blossoming rain tree when we pulled up in Geoff's beaten-up Dodge truck. There were a couple of wrecked cars in various states of disrepair in the garden. In one corner a tent was pitched and I could see the outline of a man lying on a swag.

Two little girls—their hair like cobwebs, and teeth rotten from eating lollies—were playing next to her in the dirt as she muttered to herself in distinctive Broome English. 'You kids so dirty. Making humbug. I'm always the one left to look after them. These people don't give their children love.' Seeing us, she stopped growling and invited us inside.

Hers was one of the older commission houses—weatherboard, on small stumps, with three wooden steps leading to a small verandah, which led into a kitchen. The three bedrooms, piled high with clothes from the many children that lived there, were off to the left of the kitchen. A bathroom was off the back verandah. The kitchen was dominated by a laminex-topped table covered in breakfast bowls and cooking scraps.

On top of the stove, which was black with grease, a big pot was simmering. Nancy ladled some stew into a plastic bowl and added some rice to it from another pot before offering it to me. I said, 'No, thanks,' thinking I would be taking food from her family. But she insisted, saying there was plenty to go round.

Meanwhile, a boy and a girl in orange school uniforms arrived, helped themselves to lunch and sat down at the table with us. Another woman, who I later learnt was Nancy's daughter, appeared out of the bathroom. Her hair wet and combed, she also helped herself to two plates of stew, giving them a quizzical look before taking them back down to the tent. The kettle's steam filled the room.

'Tea there,' Nancy pointed with her lips to a table next to the sideboard, which was filled with old bottles and jars, bandages, ointment for boils and used Sunshine milk cans. Tinned milk, tea bags and sugar were on the table, the pannikins were next to the sink. I made myself and Nancy a cup, making sure to stir hard before the milk went lumpy.

'These people don't know how hard life can be,' Nancy mumbled as she took a sip of tea. 'I won't be here to look after them for ever. They don't know what it was like to grow up at the mission in the old days.'

Gradually her story emerged. It was the first time I had ever heard about the Stolen Children, not that she described herself in this way. And it came as quite a shock.

'It was the law then. They took away all the half-caste children to Beagle Bay so the nuns could look after them. My people tried to hide me but the police found me. Other kids' mothers painted their faces black with charcoal so they'd look like full bloods. They took the children in a dray pulled by bullocks to Wyndham. We huddled together, frightened, you know. We went by lugger across to Broome and then again by bullock dray to Beagle Bay.

The German nuns and priests looked after us there. They were very strict and sometimes they would get bad tempered with us. We didn't understand them, but they must have been so hot and uncomfortable in their heavy habits. They taught us to sew and to cook. We'd work in the vegetable gardens and out in the stockcamps. Now church has left, and they don't even have vegetable gardens any more. That place is rubbish now.'

It wasn't until a few weeks later that I visited Beagle Bay again. Earlier in the year I had gone on a trip with Jimmy Bieundurry to One Arm Point, stopping in at Beagle Bay on the way. That was when I met Dottie Cox, who was renowned for having one of the best shell collections around. A widow in her early forties and mother of six children, like Nancy, she had brought up several others. The death of her husband, a respected member of the community, had devastated her.

But after a long period of mourning, without caring about the scandal, she gave up her house and headed off to Darwin. We became better friends up there, where she became known for her flamboyant red dresses and dancing all night at discos. She had come to the conclusion that she deserved a life and she was going to make the most of being single again.

This time I went with Nancy, Geoff and his mate Peter, a jolly older Aboriginal man who always wore stubby shorts and an open shirt, revealing the biggest stomach and a huge purple scar from an operation that, according to him, 'had taken half his guts out'.

Peter was Nancy's nephew and was forever playing practical jokes and telling silly stories. An insomniac and a former truck driver (who, according to him, held the record for the fastest trip from Broome to Kununurra), he'd spend half the night driving around town spying on the romantic comings and goings of the young population—to see who was 'covered in pindan dust or beach sand'. He seemed to know who was pregnant even before they did, and was extremely judgemental about the notion of teenage sex.

He would spend most of the day under the bonnet of one of his or Geoff's trucks, driving Nancy crazy with exasperation, because all she wanted was somebody to take her on a holiday to visit her grandchildren in Halls Creek or a lift somewhere. No wonder she ended up walking around town! (There was no public transport in Broome, and every corner had a shortcut engraved into the grass.)

Finally she got so fed up she decided to catch a plane to Halls Creek. So she went and booked herself a ticket when her pension cheque came. Peter took her to the airport. She had wanted to take some fish with her but the only thing she had to carry it in was an old cloth guitar case. She looked like 'the singing nana' walking out to the plane with that guitar case sagging at the end with the weight of all the fish!

Nancy's granddaughter, Dianne Williams, also came on the Beagle Bay trip. She and I had been knocking about together since we met one night at the Roebuck Hotel.

She was staring at me, holding half a glass of beer and leaning against the wall. I'd just bought a drink and was watching the band, a group of local boys bashing out great rock-and-roll. I smiled at her. She smiled back. 'What kind, jija?' I looked at my watch, and thinking she'd said, 'What time?' answered that it was nine thirty. She laughed, then took another sip of her drink.

'Not what time? What kind—how are you?' she explained the Broome slang.

'Oh! Fine. Hot in here,' I said feebly, trying to make conversation. Nobody said anything for a while.

'You're new in town, aye?' she said. I was a bit surprised that she'd noticed.

It turned out that she'd been working as an assistant at the kindy in Derby, where I'd been based for the past nine months. She was in Broome this time, running away from her white boyfriend who used to give her a hard time.

As I came to know Dianne I discovered she was one of the best bush mechanics around. She was a strong woman, great at changing tyres, talented with car engines (and we had lots of opportunities for this, travelling in my station wagon and later my old red ute). But strangely, she didn't have a driver's licence. There was no doubt she was good with children and at her job, but I reckon she should have been a mechanic.

Once, we were in Darwin and she was sleeping on the floor of a friend, David's house. David owned a big black dog called Jingo. He arrived home late at night, quite drunk, and saw Dianne. 'Out, Jingo, out!' he shouted, kicking at the figure on the ground, until he realised his mistake. From then on, we sometimes used to call her Jingo as an 'in' joke. She'd just tell us to shut up.

Another time, also in a Darwin bar, we were sitting with some friends, including Neenyah Charles. Neenyah, who is very dark and slight, could pass as Indian. She was working as a croupier in the Darwin casino at the time, and she was telling us this story. Somebody chatting her up had asked her how long she'd been in Australia. She answered, 'Oh, only about 40,000 years.'

Then a white man, who had been listening to us talk, came up to Dianne and said, 'Gee, you speak English well.'

'Course I do,' she answered in her deadpan way. 'I'm an edumacated Aborigidiginee.'

Dianne was not only funny, she was wise. She had a permanent half-smile at the carrying-ons of whitefellas, who, she thought, always seemed to be rushing around madly, especially in the heat of the day when you were meant to lie down and do nothing. 'They make me laugh, even if sometimes they make me sorry,' she'd say. Her other expression, usually aimed at me, was, 'Take it easy, girl.'

Dianne's explanation for Broome's 'coloured' population was put in her singsong way, a mixture of English and expressions from Malay, other Asian, and Aboriginal languages of the area, known as Broome English.

'See, us 'coloured' people are Aboriginal, but many of us got some other type of blood in us too—white, Malay, Chinese, Japanese, Koepang, Filipino. See, all those Asiatic people were brought out here as pearl divers. They used Aboriginal labour first, although they never tell you that in them tourist brochures. This town is kinda like one big family, really.'

Dianne was always around Geoff's place when she was in Broome. And she and I helped Geoff with the Aboriginal Week dance he organised at the Civic Centre. Sitting on the outside steps in the sun, we painted decorations and later decorated the hall with the screen-prints of turtles and other animals. We laid the tables with sprigs of bougainvillea and hibiscus. Others made curry and rice for supper. The local community welfare officer was running the bar. He was also secretary of the local Labor Party branch, and planned to use the takings for the campaign fund. It was the best night, although the band didn't start until 10pm. Apparently Peter had had to drive all round town to bludge sound equipment because the boys couldn't afford it.

They started with good, old country and western. Then came the rock-and-roll. As the night wore on all the old Broome musicians jumped on the stage to jam with the band, singing and playing guitar and harmonica. The finale was when Stephen Baamba Albert, who used to play with the Broome Beats before he went to Canberra to head the National Aboriginal Education Committee, appeared. Doing a bit of a wiggle, he grabbed the microphone as his knees wobbled to the rhythm. We danced to the point of exhaustion.

I remember once, a photographer staying at our place was surprised by the outcomes of another wild night. He remarked, 'Broome reeks of sex.'

'Well,' as Dianne said, 'there wouldn't be any coloured people if it wasn't for sex.'

There was certainly something extremely sensual about the place and the people. Maybe it was the tropical climate, maybe it was more to do with a relaxed attitude to sex, despite the attempts by the church to repress it. Many people lost their virginity before they reached their mid-teens. Girls had babies very young.

Listen to the words of Jimmy Chi or Mick Manolis's bawdy songs. Even the name of their band, Kuckles, a local word for a type of cockleshell, has deliberate sexual connotations. And affectionate slang words Broome locals use for each other derive from private parts of the body.

Ollie: It's funny—and sad—how the Catholic missions like Beagle Bay, Kalumburu and Port Keats in the Northern Territory, are the most screwed up. Some of the young men are very unsure of their sexuality. At some institutions in WA there have been allegations emerging of molestation and rape. The church was the authority, and there was no guidance from the community elders. And some older Aborginal people who grew up there are so pro-Catholic they aren't able to deal with this or question it. Those actions committed are now coming full-circle—sometimes the abused become the abusers.

Now, at Port Keats, it seems there's no community feeling whatsover. It should be called Fort Knox, with barbed wire all around the houses. I had to drive down there once and I was scared they might stop me and take the car.

Beagle Bay is really fucked up now because of the child molesting that apparently went on. They call it 'poofter's paradise' now. These days the boys who were in the mission are all mixed up about their sexuality. The truth about a lot of the molesting and abuse that went on in the missions still hasn't come out. A number of the victims are the people who have now become the abusers.

The Catholic religion has done a lot of damage to Aboriginal culture. Traditionally, with the skins groups, you had to marry the right way—but they've destroyed that, because you had all these people from different areas plonked into the one place. A lot of them married wrong way. And now look at Beagle Bay and Broome. The people are all intermarried and somewhere along the line we're all related, whereas traditionally that didn't happen. That's caused a lot of social problems.

Because of these problems and alcohol, people don't have as much respect for their elders. Beagle Bay is a sad place, and that's a community where they can't get it together now because you have all this infighting and jealousy. And Aboriginal people can be their own worst critics.

I don't think the church recognised that they caused a lot of these problems. Perhaps only some individuals did.

In the mid 1970s the Whitlam government gave us our independence, so that the administration of the missions was no longer in the hands of the church, but run by an elected council. But now old people feel that what they still call 'mission' has gone to rack and ruin, and that this is the community's fault. Beagle Bay won't go ahead until the people there, and the church, come to terms with this history.

Diana: The road to Beagle Bay is soft red dust with corrugations, bumps and sandy patches that countless cars have got bogged in. It becomes a river in the wet season. It turns off the main bitumen road from Broome to Derby and heads north, passing through cattle stations and Aboriginal reserve land.

Narrow tracks lead off through the scrub to tidal creeks and the sea—and some of the best fishing spots. They're all part of cattle stations but the owners don't usually stop people going there. Big stretches of saltwater creek are surrounded by mangroves. When the tide goes out it leaves strips of sandbank. Sandhills on the other side lead across to enormous beaches with wide rolling waves. Nobody for miles, just seagulls diving for bait on the end of your line. And in the 1970s there were no crocodiles.

This country, however, had not escaped the pressures of mining and exploration. The oil company that was working in this area in the late 1970s was prepared to negotiate directly with the Aboriginal community at Beagle Bay. As many of the people there were not traditional owners, but had been brought there by the church and state, they felt less anxious about the land being explored and further drilled. They saw that there were advantages in negotiating with the oil company, which agreed to employ some of the youth, build fences, dig bores and make better roads. But the state government, then led by Liberal Premier Charlie Court, had insisted that mining companies were not to pay royalties to individual communities. In fact, it said they risked forfeiture of leases if they talked directly to communities. It was a catch 22 situation, but some companies ignored it.

As we drove in I remembered the stories people had told me about why they were sent to Beagle Bay. One old lady, of Chinese, Malay and Aboriginal background, who was taken there around the same time as Nancy, grinned, showing her toothless gums as she commented, 'They moved us all up here to try and get rid of the half-castes. But it didn't work, we're still here.'

A lonely-looking sign pointing to the sky at a fork in the road was the only indication that we were almost there. After about ten kilometres the track rounded the corner and a church steeple emerged out of nowhere. A few yards on a broken gate formed the entrance to the former mission. The steeple became a church looking down on a cluster of stone houses and timber buildings. A hundred dirt tracks led off in all directions. Horses, mules and cattle grazed and roamed the paddocks surrounding the community. It was quiet, so quiet not even the dogs were barking.

As Geoff stopped outside one of the tiny stone houses to have a conversation about the fishing, Dianne took me to see the church, described as the most beautiful building in the north of WA. It was hard to believe my eyes as she pushed open the heavy doors—the altar was a magnificent display of pearls, shells, coloured stones and mother-of-pearl. Dianne explained that Nancy and the other mission kids were really proud because they had helped the nuns collect all the material and build the altar.

Walking across the oval on the way back, Dianne explained that she was brought to Beagle Bay when she was about seven years old. (She and Ollie had been at the Broome orphanage before going to Beagle Bay. I didn't know Ollie at this stage.)

'There was about 70 of us orphan kids. That's what they called us, even though most of us did have parents. Fifty children came from stations over near the NT border for education. All the children who had parents at Beagle Bay then lived with them in 'colony', that's what we called the area where the coloured people lived. There was about 80 of them. Early times, before Father Kearney come, all the children did grow up in dormitories. They did take them from their families when they started school. Their mothers and fathers could only visit them weekends. Then Father Kearney came here and he said the children should be with their parents. So that just left us 'orphan kids'. It was okay. We had some fun, riding the mules and all. But that was just weekends. Every day after school we did work round the garden, raking leaves from nun's quarters down. By the time I finished school there weren't that many of us. They don't take kids away that much any more like they used to, they end up staying with their aunties or their grandmothers, usually if their mothers can't look after them. Like Nana—she grew most of us mob up, except for me.'

We bought some fresh, white crusty bread from the bakery, and walked down to pick up Nancy from the priests' quarters. With one grandchild on her lap and the other at her feet, she was having a cup of tea with Father Francis, a German priest in his 80s, who had stayed on at Beagle Bay after the community was given independence. He took the Sunday masses, married couples, christened babies and took the young people through communion.

He stood up when he saw us at the door and shook my hand when Dianne introduced me.

'Isn't our church beautiful?' he asked in a strong German accent. 'You know, everything here was built from what we could find—the dormitories, the butcher shop, the bakery, saddle shed. All the roofs were made of paperbark. When it was wet we cut them into big sheets and brought them in. Each roof would be prepared at the beginning of each wet season. The cupboards and the benches in the church were hewn from the red wood with a big circular saw.'

Father Francis's eyes grew misty as he spoke. 'The mission killed all its own meat. Goats gave milk, the hens gave eggs. We had two big vegetable gardens. And we had the cattle. All the clothes were made on the mission, except for the khaki pants and shorts.'

'Yes, Father,' Nancy stood up to shake his hand. 'I helped build the church. I was about ten then. All us children collected the shells and the stones on the beach and carried them back. The nuns took us down in a horse and cart. They showed us what to do and we did the work. But mission's all rubbish now, too much drinking, people too lazy. Too many young boys on the council, no old men. It was so much better when the church was here. It should never have left.'

Dianne didn't say anything, she just looked at me.

Later, after a day of fishing and dragnetting at a beach where calm, deep blue water met sky on the horizon, we sat around the fire enjoying a dinner of fish and tea. 'Don't you ever feel resentful about what happened to you as a child?' I asked Nancy.

'Oh, no,' she said. 'We got an education. We learnt to read and write. We grew up as Catholics. The nuns were poor, too. They didn't have any money. I don't like people saying things against them. Things were really bad for them too, but they tried to help us. I keep saying these people will never get anywhere without the church.'

We slept on the back of the truck that night, Nancy, Dianne and myself, still talking as we lay under the blankets. The bedding reminded Dianne of the dormitories at Beagle Bay. 'Lights out at eight every night and no talking. Nuns locked the doors, but some girls did climb out the windows to see their boyfriends,' she said.

Nancy tut-tutted. 'Not when I was young. We didn't make humbug. When we grew up we all got husbands from the mission boys. The nuns let the married ones live in the old houses then. My husband was from around this way, he was a native. We came into Broome after the war. I worked as a maid at old Mrs Heynes' house. They gave me a bed and tucker. I fished from the old jetty and sold the fish. I never did come empty handed. That gave me a little money for children. Now I'm still stuck with them. I'm the only one who would ever take them to church. Now the girls will be having babies soon.'

'Children, children,' she muttered as she fell off to sleep.

⁂

Once, when I visited Broome, there were no sympathy cards left in the grocery store and newsagent in Chinatown. There had been so many deaths and funerals, they'd all sold out.

And everytime I call Ollie she tells me about another person who has died. Of course, many are old people, but also some not so old such as, sadly, Peter and Dianne's father, Frank.

But it's the premature deaths of the young people through alcoholism, car accidents, suicide and curable disease that seem so senseless. A well known musician, former footballer and generally well regarded person died when I was last there. He was in his late thirties and had five children. Two of his brothers had also died prematurely. He was about the twentieth young person from Broome I knew personally who had died prematurely in the past ten years. One friend told me recently that Broome just wasn't the same without him around.

Many deaths are from suicide. One young man, who had been a schoolteacher, was also well regarded and respected. Whether it was splitting up with the mother of his children or something else, he couldn't take life any more. He hung himself. Even at the funeral there were inter family squabbles and resentment.

The mothers are the ones who keep going, who keep the families together. One woman I know has lost two sons to suicide.

There's a morbid fascination by some in telling all the details of the burial, the coffin, the embalming. Death, to use the cliche, is a way of life.

It's no wonder that there's also a large number of 'mad' people in Broome—schizophrenics and others with mental illnesses. They wander from house to house, drop in for a five-minute chat then wander off again. The locals just seem to take it for granted. They call them 'meter readers', and nobody introduces them when they walk through the door. Maybe they're just more visible in Broome. Perhaps it's the dope or the alcohol, or the pressures of life in a place that's meant to be Paradise, but is, at times, a tragic and ghostly facsimile.

One pressure is overcrowding. Some old people who have lived in the town all their lives still do not have anywhere permanent to live. Young couples with children live with their extended families. Homeswest workers used to run the place. And although it has escalated its building program, there is still a long wait for public housing. People are told that if they complain too much their names will go to the bottom of the list.

Another pressure is the one to perform, to make it in the white man's world. Some of those pressures and tensions come out on the football field. In Broome during the dry season the Aussie Rules football match is a weekly get together, a much looked forward to social occasion. But it's also a chance for some people to air their real feelings, and an informative way of learning about Broome politics, hierarchy and family feuds.

In the days I used to watch it, the late '70s and early '80s, the barefoot Beagle Bay team didn't train during the week. They were too busy throwing bullocks around at stockcamp. They came to town on the back of a truck, and after a thorough session at the pub were driven back home. In their black and red jumpers they ran fast and wild, kicking goal after goal. But some of the town players looked down on them, describing them as 'bush blackfellas' and 'gurrajins', or drunks, and took pleasure in jumping on their bare feet with their spiked football boots.

During the game children climbed all over everybody, begging for money for ice creams and drinks. People yelled at each other to get out of the way. Swearing filled the air, particularly at the 'empire'. Trucks swayed from side to side as the portly mothers of the players jumped up and down in the excitement.

'You might be called Saints, but you're not virgin soldiers,' one woman yelled in the course of one game between the Beagle Bay team and Saints, one of the town teams. 'Yeah, you—you got my youngest daughter boogajin (pregnant)! You pretend you're white but you're black, black as the ace of spades, just like me.'

Many managed to overcome their fear of conflict and trouble to take part in the protest at the Broome turn-off waiting for the oil rig that was headed for Noonkanbah in mid 1980. A group of the town's musicians performed on the back of a truck. They sang *Bran Nue Dae*, Jimmy Chi's song that has become Broome's anthem.

Many had matured in their political thinking. Their songs reflected this, as they gradually added words with a political influence to a mixture of West Indian reggae beat and Aboriginal traditional rhythms, to their repertoire of country and western and rock love songs.

It was a day of intense emotional feelings in an almost festive atmosphere, because for most of the 200 local people there, it wasn't just a protest, it was a reaffirmation of their Aboriginality. 'I have to be here,' said one old lady, who was taken to Beagle Bay as a child. 'Noonkanbah's my country, the place where I was born, my mother's country, never mind they took me mission. I must support them blackfellas. They're my people.'

Then, in the late afternoon, as the loud noise of the convoy approached led by police cars with sirens blaring and blue lights flashing, the crowd chanted, 'Off Noonkanbah now, off Noonkanbah now,' throwing stones and gravel at the blacklisted trucks and drivers as they passed.

Noonkanbah was a time when people had to decide whether they were 'coloured', Aboriginal or white. Earlier that year many had put their energy into getting the Labor candidates for the local seats elected—Ernie Bridge, an Aboriginal pastoralist from Halls Creek, who later became Minister for Aboriginal Affairs, and Peter Dowding, who later became WA Premier for a brief time.

But the events that had surrounded the attempts by Amax to drill on the station had rocked their beliefs in the democratic system to the core. If you were a 'coloured' person, who had grown up in the area, it wasn't a remote happening you heard about on the radio. They were events that forced people to make decisions about where they stood, and more importantly, who they were.

For some, it was an easy decision that didn't require much soul searching. For others, particularly the Beagle Bay people, it was the hardest, most frightening decision they had ever made.

Many were scared. Many understood white culture—or religion—more than Aboriginal culture, because of the influence of the church. Other people didn't believe they had the right to speak for other people's country—or in this case, to join a protest.

Nancy supported the protest. Although a devout Catholic, Nancy had an instinctive feeling for her people and the Law. She once proudly told me that Purnululu (the Bungle Bungles) in the east Kimberley was her country, her sacred sites.

Dianne, too, always a bit of a rebel, was sure of her Aboriginal identity. It had never been in doubt, Christian indoctrination or not. But people like Peter couldn't see the point of the protest. Worrying about Aboriginal Law and sacred sites wasn't going to help anybody. It was better to beat the white man in his own world. The Noonkanbah people were just making it impossible for other 'coloured' people and blackfellas to get their own land.

Ollie: Noonkanbah had a big impact on a lot of 'coloured' people, finding themselves and their identity. It was the turning point for people to get involved in marches and politics and all that. I used to watch the news in Perth when Noonkanbah was happening and I was so proud, really proud of how the people stood up to the authorities. A lot of Broome people were at the protests and roadblocks. I was surprised to see them because I knew some of these people when they didn't identify as Aboriginal. Broome people were always referred to as 'coloured'. If you weren't institutionalised but lived in a town situation with your family, there was a stigma being Aboriginal. A lot didn't identify as Aboriginal because of the stigma. Some used to say, 'I'm not a blackfella, I'm Japanese,' or some other nationality. But everybody knew.

In Broome there were real colour bars—usually European fathers never recognised their 'illegitimate half-caste children'. People go on about the wonderful racial harmony of Broome, but there's always been a hierarchy there and of course the Aborigines are at the bottom. Among the Asians, the hierarchy went like this: the Japanese were the top of the scale, then you had Chinese and Malays, and then the Koepangs were on the bottom of the ladder.

Aboriginal people had been pearl divers since the 1860s. They were really good at tracking down pearl shell and were strong divers. But they hated the helmet suits that were brought in. Around the 1870s Asian labour was brought to Broome to work as pearl divers, because legislation had been passed to improve working conditions for Aborigines on the pearling beds. But the Aboriginal divers still worked the pearl shell beds with the Asians, who were not covered by the Australian laws, so the pearlers could get away with hazardous working conditions. Chartered schooners transported divers from Koepang to Broome. With the White Australia Policy, Asian women weren't allowed to come here, and the only ones were those who'd come late last century—old Japanese prostitutes, for example.

The Japanese and the Koepangers didn't get on at all. And there was no love lost between the Filipinos, Malays and the Japanese. The Japanese resented that the Koepangers accepted lower wages, which stopped the migration of more of their countrymen. There were riots in 1914 over this.

When the Japanese had wars they used to chase the Malays and the Koepangs. One story an old white lady told me was, they'd be sitting at the dinner table and then some Japanese would come in chasing the Malay through their house, in the door and out the back. If the Japanese caught the Malays they'd tie them to a mangrove tree and wait for the tide to come in so they would drown.

It's sad to say, but some local people who used to always call themselves 'coloured', or even Japanese, or something else became Aboriginal because of the financial benefits, things such as housing loans and enterprise loans. But really there were only a few people who were black for the money side. A lot were caught in between. They had an identity crisis.

In Derby some people still call themselves half-caste, and you still see media reports about 'part-Aborigines'. I would have thought that terminology had hit the dust. Even during the Sorry Day reporting there was a story in the *Melbourne Herald Sun* that described Polly Farmer as 'part-Aboriginal'. And Troy Cassar-Daley, whose mother is Aboriginal and father is Maltese, is described as 'part-Aboriginal'. But when you think about it, the terminology has changed a lot.

We sometimes use the term blackfellas, and it's not meant to be derogatory. I believe that our traditional Aboriginal people accept us. My black family has always accepted me. My grandmother, Mimi Dora, and my mother, who was fair with green eyes, have always been accepted by black people. Being brought up in the Kimberley, I can't see that people don't accept you. We're part of a big extended family.

Some of the Noongars, Yamaji and the Wongis of Southern WA take offence to the terminology of being called blackfellas. In Darwin many still refer to themselves as 'coloured' people. In Queensland they call themselves Murris. Step across the border and it's different. In the Kimberley we're proud, we're all blackfellas. We don't take offence, in fact we call ourselves blackfellas, as there are too many language groups in the Kimberley to be specific all the time. In Broome area alone there's Yawuru, Nyulnyul, Bardi, Nyikina and others.

Then there's all the Asian groups. With Malaysian names, the naming is different too. Kim's parents' names were Mamid Bin Amat and Rosa. His brother was Duttu Bin Amat, but the girls got Mamid as their last name. Kim went by Mamid until he found his birth certificate and it was Bin Amat. A lot of Asians, they take the father's first name, and some take the last name.

While working in the Perth area I was often asked by Aboriginal people if I was a Noongar. My response would be, 'Yes, I'm Aboriginal but no, I'm not a Noongar.'

It can be difficult getting into the Noongar scene because you can be seen to be an outsider, even though you're Aboriginal. And even going to Perth to high school there was that distinction—you're a Norwester or a Souwester. And the groups stuck together. A lot of people could single you out as a Broome person because of the Asian look.

In South Australia, it's difficult too. When Pudding was in Adelaide he found it hard to get in with the Nungas. In 1987 I went to Adelaide to sit a test for SAIT. After the test we went to the tavern, and there was three Nunga guys standing in a circle. As I walked past, one of them said, 'I've got a nine-inch dick.' At first I thought, *no, ignore it*, and as I was walking away I thought, *no, I'm not going to let him get away with it*, so I confronted the bloke who said it. I went really close up, I said in a loud voice so the others could hear: 'If you've got a nine-inch dick, why don't you shove it up your arse and fuck yourself!' He was embarrassed because he didn't expect that response. They've got that attitude that you're going to jump in the cot with them.

Although Aboriginal issues have become more popular for some, particularly in Sydney and Melbourne, in WA Aboriginal people still have to face a great deal of racism.

And in WA we've got the family feuding and factions still. I know it's everywhere, but blackfellas have got to learn to unite and put all these things behind them. That's what the white people like, to see people divided. Divide and rule, divide and conquer.

For the 'coloureds', being called black used to be derogatory, then it became trendy. Being called black is like an influence from the Black Americans—where black is beautiful. Or then there's coffee-coloured people, the big 'melting pot'. The important part is being able to call yourself what you want to be called.

Then there's derogatory terminology like 'boongs', 'boori' (in WA) and 'coons'. I think it's even more offensive to be described as a quadroon, quarter-caste or whatever. The dictionary says this means: *quarter-blooded, offspring of mulatto and white*.

In my file I was described as a 'quadroon'. My grandmother and grandfather were both half-white (white fathers), so my mother would have been described as 'quadroon'. But in my mother's file they refer to her as a 'native' woman. They also refer to 'natives in law', whatever the hell that means. How much Aboriginal blood you had in you determined which department was meant to look after you. I don't know how they worked out I was a 'quadroon'. Whoever the mathematician was who did my file got it wrong!

This whole subject of naming Aboriginal people became a big issue in the Kimberley during the Noonkanbah dispute. But even at Noonkanbah there was some racism. There was a white woman teacher living with an Aboriginal man and some people were complaining because their children would be 'part-Aboriginal'.

Diana: It seemed kind of incongruous that while the events of Noonkanbah unfolded, some of the 'coloured' women of Broome were more excited by the opportunity of having new white men in town, captains looking for 'black velvet' who would buy them drinks and bring them presents. For women who were often single mothers on pensions, these men were an important part of the local economy.

Their usual boyfriends were the white main roads guys who were working on the highway, bituminising the road to Port Hedland. They lived in main roads camps and came into town each weekend to spend their cheques. They would stay at the Roebuck Hotel and the women would go to their rooms after closing time to drink, yarn and laugh with them.

When a ship came in carrying its crew of sailors the women would go out to New Jetty to see them, hoping they would shout them drinks and give them a good time.

The oil and mining companies brought a range of new men with more money to spend. On quiet nights the 'coloured' women would search the town for them. On raging nights they would plant themselves near the jukebox in the main bar of the Roebuck and drink Bacardi and Cokes until the men arrived. They'd have an eagle eye on who came in and out of that door. And if anybody else went off with the man they wanted there would be trouble.

Typical of the contradictions of this town, this behaviour didn't necessarily mean they weren't proud of their Aboriginality and believed the Noonkanbah people should be supported.

It seemed the old saying that the only people who were interested in blackfellas were missionaries, mercenaries and misfits had been true. But then you could add to that the miners and the white women who were coming to town—barmaids, nurses, journalists. We had no preconceived idea that we shouldn't be mixing with the local boys, and found their happy-go-lucky natures, innate intelligence and sense of humour tantalising.

We'd go to the Roebuck and out to parties at Cable

Beach where they'd sing around the campfire. On the way one night, Dianne Williams and I and a group of locals stopped at the drive-in bottle shop. They asked for beer. I asked for a flagon of riesling. 'A bottle of flagon of rustling,' they said.

But not everybody approved. Often we were described as 'do-gooders', 'boong lovers' or 'southern stirrers'. Once, a nun commented to me that Aboriginal people despised white women who went with black men. Perhaps she would have approved if a 'coloured' woman had a white husband—then they would be going up in the world. Some such as Peter believed that 'coloured' women who lived with 'Asiatics' were much more house proud and better cooks (even though in these cases it was often the men who did the cooking).

Somebody told me a story about a white girl who had been living with one of the boys at Beagle Bay. They split up and one night she went to a beach party after the Roebuck closed. Some local boys were sitting in their car watching her. And just as she got to her car they grabbed her and raped her. Some say it was because she had been living with an Aboriginal boy. They thought she was easy game.

'If a white woman shows interest in 'coloured' boys then all the boys in town want to have first stab at her,' Dianne once told me. 'It's a novelty, something different. But not that many white women used to go for the boys. That's changing now. It used to be the white man always after the black woman. Now it's the white woman after the black man. Most 'coloured' people may seem friendly on the surface, but deep down they don't think they're good enough for whitefellas.'

Another friend put it this way: 'The problem is, some of us 'coloured' women had enough of chocolate boys. See, we grew up with them all. We're looking for some new spice. We don't want to be treated like one of the boys and we don't like their jealousy. They don't trust us even speaking to somebody else. See, we want to be treated properly. We want money spent on us. But maybe if I could find a good 'coloured' man I'd stay with him, cause I know he would understand my ways more than any white man could.'

Ollie: At the time of Noonkanbah I was just starting to mix with Noongar people. Prior to that my life was sheltered. I didn't mix with many people, just my family and other workers within the private sector—only non-Aboriginal people.

I felt pretty isolated living in Perth. I didn't have any family or old friends there. I used to come home every year but I got married and Dave's job was in Perth. Sometimes relatives from Broome would come to stay.

I started work again when Cindy was a baby, looking after geriatrics in nursing homes. In 1978–9 I worked for the Department of Social Security as a trainee, and in 1980 started with the education department in the Aboriginal early childhood section.

I started to have contact with Aboriginal people and co-workers. I became politicised but, more importantly, I found my identity. Without that, you wouldn't have any political consciousness. I always knew I was Aboriginal but I guess I'd been fairly sheltered prior to then, not really aware of the issues.

In 1978 I did twelve months working for Social Security, and it was the first time I'd heard of NAIDOC and National Aboriginal Day—and it was from a white man. He said, 'Ollie, it's your day today.' We used to joke about it. With friends we can joke about blackfellas and make fun. But with other people it would be offensive. I used to say, 'We'd never pass the EEO.'

The job with Aboriginal early childhood was my first real job with government and getting exposure to Aboriginal issues and on a personal note, finding out what my rights were. Among the staff, one young girl was taken away. There was an older Aboriginal woman, Oriel, who is a friend. I don't know what happened with her. There was a young girl who lived with her parents. Shirley Stack was brought up on Wandering mission. The rest of the staff were non-Aboriginal.

Because I was very young, I was totally dependent on my husband Dave, socially and financially, even though he never really had to support me. I didn't even know how to pay bills. I used to cling to him and he used to say to me, 'You're an individual.'

We had our circle of friends. But he'd say, 'You need to have your own friends, too.' But then I gradually began to find my individuality. I started to think for myself, without having anyone think for me or make decisions for me.

Dave and I are really good friends now. We have something in common and that's our daughter. I just pick up the phone and he does things for me. He sent me a beautiful photo of Tina Turner's last concert, and a photo of Shirley Bassey.

I did have problems with Dave's mother. I wasn't married when I was pregnant. She used to corner me on my own. I wasn't assertive. She'd ask, 'What will the neighbours think? What colour will the kid come out?' I didn't tell Dave for five years. Later I tried to make up with her. I told her why I disliked her. She denied it. I never turned my daughter against her, but when she became an adult she made her own judgement, although she still loved her as a grandmother.

Despite his mother, Dave had a really good attitude. He wouldn't have been married to me otherwise. As a photographer he worked with journalists who were sympathetic. Dave was a very, very wise man beyond his years as far as those issues go. Now there's all this stuff today about the republic and the royal family, he was talking about that back then. Saying we didn't need the monarchy.

I didn't understand it all then. He was sensitive, compassionate and empathetic because he, too, used to cover stories, going to the Kimberley quite regularly. If they sent somebody from Perth to the Kimberley he'd be the one.

I remember him going to Broome once and coming back and saying how racist Broome was. I said, 'I was born in Broome and it's not racist.' I realise now that when you're white they assume you're racist, and they're open about their attitudes. Diana came across this, like if you drink in the white bars they'll go on about the 'boongs' to you as if you have the same attitude. And if you challenge and disagree with them, then they clam up. Broome only had a very small white population then. The people I grew up with in the town were racist. It was quite a shock to hear that. Dave wasn't involved in politics at all but he did have his own prejudices. He was Church of England, so he hated Catholics. But he married one!

Diana: The first time I'd heard about Beagle Bay was when I was in Canberra—some architects approached me to write a story about bureaucratic bungling over the building of a windmill and houses there. Seems all this money got poured in for totally inappropriate buildings and the result was a windmill that never worked.

But even after visiting the place, and living in Broome, it was a long time before I really understood why the community at Beagle Bay had so many problems. For a year I listened to accounts blaming the people for everything that had gone wrong there. So when a priest who many had spoken of with some praise, Father Kearney, was passing through town I went to interview him for the *Broome News*.

Father Kearney was a tall, slim man in his late forties. He was straightforward and sincere about helping the people. He first came to Beagle Bay in the 1940s as a young priest, then returned in the early 1960s to be superintendent of the mission—when Pudding and Ollie were there. He began by describing the mission in the 1940s as a strong one with 300 people, a mixture of full bloods and mixed-bloods. Of these, about twenty were working men and 30 or 40 pensioners.

'There was a pride in the place,' he said. 'Women were now staying in the homes. Before they had been in the workforce, working in the stockcamps. The children lived in the dormitory as soon as they started school. The church felt the parents couldn't cope with cooking ordinary meals, so before World War II everybody ate in a common dining room. Later they established little homes.'

He explained that as Aborigines weren't then counted as citizens, there was no unemployment benefit. But the orphans were allowed a small allowance under the Department of Native Affairs. Every child that came from a station was adopted into a family. Then in the '60s Beagle Bay was one of the first places to provide pensions.

'The old people were paid cheques. Half went to the mission to cover food, lighting, water and rent. The other half we gave to the people as cash and they paid for some clothes. It was quite a change.'

Father Kearney explained he had wanted to be able to make the mission self-sufficient. They tried making tailor-made shirts and children's clothes but it was costing too much, as the factories could do it cheaper. They sold firewood and vegetables in Broome.

Then he thought of the idea of a soft drink factory. There was fluoride in the water and it was a twelve month market. 'We bought a machine that moved the bottles along, for 50 pounds,' he said. 'We used beer bottles and we found there was a real demand for the soft drink. It was fifteen cents a bottle. An Aboriginal artist did the design— a glass standing on a mother-of-pearl shell floating through the bay. We had the factory for a few years, but in the end we concluded that cattle was the best future for Beagle Bay.'

Father Kearney was trying to get the people more involved in the administration. The hard part was to get each group to accept the other group although everybody did band together at certain times, such as when they designed new housing.

Because of the '60s assimilation policies, the WA government was pressuring communities to move into town. But when the Federal Labor government came in, it believed Aboriginal people should develop their own place. During these years Father Kearney had tried to give the people there more responsibility in running the mission but he left in 1969. There was a series of different priests—and things, including the vegetable garden, went downhill.

'A big move came by the Labor government in 1975 that all the missions be handed over to Aborigines. I was afraid the government would take over. Practically every man voted for the missionaries to stay. There was a strong personal relationship as the missionaries were the only ones who had cared for them over the years.

The government gave funding and the community took over in 1977. But it was two years too late. The place had run down by then and the people on the Aboriginal council had not been prepared for independence. The different groups had not been prepared to work with each other.

You can't blame the people there for the present circumstances. It was sort of inevitable that people would lose hope, they were faced with too difficult a prospect.'

Ollie: There's only about 300 people living at Beagle Bay now but there's still a great deal of infighting, internal politics and factions. It's still also got problems with a lack of housing and bad living conditions.

Housing for the aged and for young, single people is inadequate in a lot of communities. This is where you get the overcrowding. You've got a family, they've got teenage kids that's living with them. They end up getting married and having children and they remain there, because they don't have housing. And they're not catering for those two extreme groups—the aged and the young, single people, ones just getting into relationships. That really hasn't been addressed in a lot of the communities.

But gradually the identity problems are being overcome through the out-station or homeland movement, with different family groups moving out of the settlements. At the former Lombadina mission, now known as Djarindjin, people have also set up out-stations. At one out-station at Disaster Bay, a family group have set up commercial barramundi fishing and oyster farming.

Others want to set up tourist ventures. If you're going to run tourist ventures, you've got to be professional. Some communities are working on the principles that they don't want 'handouts' any more. They're trying to break a cycle.

But I have mixed feelings about the CDEP program (or working for the dole), which I used to work on. We've got to look at generating income and cutting the welfare ties. But at the same time, I wonder why should communities have to do that too. It's imposing values and standards and trying to assimilate them in another form. It's another form of control.

Communities should be given the training and the skills to run themselves.

They've been talking about self-management and self-determination for how many years now? And from my observation there's some communities within Australia that are achieving self-determination and self-management, and what happens then is that ATSIC cuts the purse strings. They want people to remain dependent because the government has got very vested interests, and they've got their jobs.

I feel Aboriginal people can do as much good working in a government organisation as an Aboriginal organisation.

We can have an input into policy changes and the administrative side, into decision making.

But I'm not happy with the present ATSIC set up. It's like they've thrown a bone in and all the blackfellas are fighting for it. That's basically what it is.

The money was distributed more equally before ATSIC. With the regional council you've got representatives from each area. But if they're not articulate and they're not assertive their community misses out. They haven't got any skills in lobbying properly.

It would be against my principles to work for ATSIC. In DAA time it was mainly tokenism, you know, the black people there. They have had some really good people in DAA, but they've become disillusioned and frustrated because they weren't in positions of decision making. So they've lost a lot of good people.

There's thousands of dollars being spent on the administration, on salaries, for people working in ATSIC. I would prefer to see that money spent, and it would probably be more productive, if it was distributed directly to the communities, rather than having ATSIC as a middleman. And then of course, with ATSIC, you have all the different personalities within, and if they don't like a particular community, they can be penalised too by cutting the purse strings. ATSIC is dependency in another form.

Diana: With the demise of pearling, Broome became a sleepy, insular place, the total population dwindling to 4,000. When the bitumen stopped at Port Hedland, about 600 kilometres to the south, only the locals, the more intrepid travellers and latter-day hippies made their way there.

The hippies—or mung beans as they were known locally—were happy in the knowledge that while the ranger was not around they had the sandhills overlooking the beach to themselves. Also, their dole cheques were helping prop up the local economy.

Then the road from Port Hedland to Broome was finally sealed and the local hotel and caravan park owners geared up for the rush. It didn't come the first year, but the next season the word had got around about this tropical paradise in the north and the invasion started, helped along later by package deals and direct flights from Sydney via Alice Springs.

Now the population swells during the peak tourist season, from April to October. Each year the town is inundated with tourists for the Shinju Matsuri or Festival of the Pearl, which also celebrates the Chinese feast of Hung Ting and the Malayan Merdeka.

The local council began to recognise the merit of preserving Broome's unique and colourful past for the sake of tourism—hence a tarted-up but sanitised version of Chinatown, where once there were brothels and opium dens on every corner.

And then along came Lord Alistair McAlpine, of West Green, near London.

McAlpine, who had owned property in Perth since the early '60s, 'discovered' Broome with his lawyer, John Adams, in 1981. The landscape of the Kimberley—wide open spaces, wild rivers, mangrove swamps, huge tides and palm-fringed gorges—reminded McAlpine of Kenya, where he would have bought a house 'if things hadn't been so troubled in Africa'.

Two months later they returned to Broome with McAlpine's wife, Romilly. Within a few hours of inspecting the town, they had bought a house—the gracious but dilapidated home of Jean Haynes, a matriarch of one of the town's oldest pearling families—and the neglected, open air Sun Pictures theatre in Chinatown.

McAlpine moved in, complete with his own vision for the north-west as Australia's new population centre, closer to Europe and Asia. For a few years he spent up big and seemed at one stage to be the defacto town council. Broome became Australia's fastest growing tourist area.

But times changed, economies faltered and apart from the occasional visit, McAlpine seemed to grow bored with Broome. Now even his Pearl Coast zoo has moved to the Northern Territory.

But he left a legacy. The old-style operations, which tended to have little regard for the history and style of the town, could no longer go on as they had—running roughshod over everything in their way. Aboriginal and community organisations did okay as well. McAlpine gave out thousands of dollars and now even has a sports field named after him.

Still, people complained about the effect of the rapid escalation of tourist developments and the boom or bust mentality. One was that the infrastructure hadn't kept up with the growth. Some said that the tourism workforce put increased pressure on existing facilities like housing, while the longer term residents were being pushed further back into the periphery.

Since those heady days of Noonkanbah, there's been a great deal of change in Broome. As Aboriginal organisations have developed around the country and Aboriginal art, culture and music has become reinvigorated elsewhere, so too has it in Broome.

It's always the same energetic people involved, such as some of Nancy's granddaughters, who quietly, consistently and for little financial benefit, have worked on getting these organisations up and running.

Few would deny that Noonkanbah and the Kimberley land rights movement were an integral and importance influence on these developments. But these days Broome people rarely call themselves 'coloured'—certainly not the younger generations. It's seen as an assimilationist term used to divide people.

Stephen Albert, who now concentrates on acting and singing, starring in Jimmy's musicals, put it this way: 'Calling yourself 'coloured' is like being a mule. A good stockman knows if you work a mule it's just as good a stock animal as a horse, but it's still not one thing or the other. It's not a donkey, it's not a horse, but it's still a good work animal. As far as I'm concerned I'm Aboriginal and so are most people in this town, whether they've got Chinese, Japanese or Inuit blood.

You know, once I got real angry with this man in a pub in Darwin. He kept saying, "Don't call me Aboriginal, I'm coloured."

And I said to him, 'You're nothing, mate. You're just a coconut, black outside, white inside and all the rest water.'

Pudding's Story

6.

Pudding's Story

She was suffering from an illness of an experience
He was weathering the stormy tests of time
They met each other in a town called Plaything
And love seemed to be ringing on the chime

She said she was writing of her experiences
He told her that he was going to music school
So they planned to take some time to live together
And the law of love live by that golden rule

Cornelius and Rosalind are lovers
They live for you they live for me and tomorrow
Cornelius and Rosalind are lovers
They are my friends and I want the world to know

She said the town gave her a lot to write about
He told her that he was born there one time ago
So they kissed and loved and talked and whiled the time away
And dreamed about each other and tomorrow

They may be living together out of loneliness
But they keep each other up when things are down
So let them live the better part of happiness
And let's be happy in our part of town

Cornelius and Rosalind

Arnold Smith

Diana: The little house Pudding and I lived in at Stepney in Adelaide in 1982 was a workman's cottage with an outdoor loo at the end of a long, narrow garden. It was just big enough for the two of us, although Jimmy Chi stayed in the front verandah room for a while.

With Jimmy and the other Broome boys, Pudding went to music school every day at the Centre for Aboriginal Studies and Music, at the University of Adelaide. He learnt how to read music, play the drums, and all about traditional Aboriginal songs and music. Somehow, though, although he was a superb guitar player and singer, he ended up playing percussion in a reggae band.

I think the band members, especially the woman lead singer, thought I was the pushy girlfriend/manager. But thankfully, I never attempted to do a Linda McCartney or a Yoko Ono, and join the band myself.

I can't sing, anyway. But Pudding had a voice like an angel. He would sing to me all the time, songs like *Wonderful Tonight, Donna, Amazing Love*, Charlie Pride's *Special* and Kris Kristoffeson's *Christian Soldiers*. It rung out your heart strings. Made you want to cry. And I don't even like country music that much.

When we had been together for a few months, he stayed up really late one night writing a song. He was very excited about it and sang it to me in the morning. It was called *Submission Bells*.

In his own language, he'd done a brilliant job of summing up his life, and the pain and frustration he lived with. When he'd told me his life story I couldn't believe people could be so cruel to children, so unfeeling, and so blissfully unaware of the damage they were doing to another person's life. Another song he wrote, *Invisible Woman, Invisible Man,* expressed the control others had had over him and his life.

His was a life that hadn't been so happy—to put it mildly. He was moody, which Ollie never was.

But something made me follow him to Adelaide—his sense of humour, I reckon. When he was happy he was very funny. And I liked his acceptance of me, my own humour, my way of looking at the world.

In Adelaide, even though he was Aboriginal, he felt an outsider with the Nungas. I felt very much an outsider, though I caught up again with people like Frances Peters from Sydney. My friend, Jo Hawke, came to live in Adelaide, and stayed with us for a while. She got a job with AAP, which I hadn't applied to at the time.

The year before I'd lived in Darwin, after driving there from Broome via Borroloola with Dianne Williams. I'd had several jobs, including being the information officer for the Northern Land Council and editor for, of all things, a gardening and lifestyle magazine, *Tropical Gardening*. Now in Adelaide, I just wanted to settle down with a nine to five job that didn't involve travelling. I had thought it would be too difficult to hold down a job at AAP at that stage and maintain my relationship with Pudding.

So Pudding and I were pretty poor. I'd make Broome stews—a bit of meat strung out with potatoes and carrots. Apart from that, we seemed to exist on fishhead soup made with chicken noodle soup. (Everything Pudding made had this essential ingredient.) We'd horrify our visitors by giving them the soup still with the head in it and the eyes floating around. Pudding thought that was the best bit.

We'd also force them to listen to the silly tapes we made together, with me interviewing Pudding, the rising star. He'd speak in broken—Broome English. My cheeks are covered in tears of laughter when I now listen to these tapes, with Jimmy's high-pitched and totally infectious laughter in the background.

On explaining why he went to music school he'd say, 'Well, missus, long time when I was smaller—I bin seen everybody else play guitar and I think I better learn too.

I learnt chord and I bin think myself. But we never know the names of them chords.

We grow up and when we listen to them others they go nice, nice, and they play good and we play rubbish chords. Must be something wrong there. Must be man gotta learn properly, go gardiya teach them learn properly. They say, "You can't drink, drink, gotta go to school."

So I fill in all these forms—my age, what colour my shit, everything. I go school now. I go longa Perth. I look at all the old, old people of the school, don't tell me these old, old people are dumb like me? Young gardiya, they chuck him to teach us. But they wasn't dumb, liar dumb, only they gotta learn how you gotta do something nowadays. You gotta learn, proper, proper way. Gee.

I'd bin schoolin there, schoolin, next minute someone say you like playing guitar all the time, playtime, dung, dung, dung. Somebody said, "You gotta learn properly." Sent them forms away. Next minute letter came. I thought it was cheque coming, but nothing. I got happy for nothing. I open him up this letter, tell my sister, she's the brainy kind.

She says, "That's right, they said you can go there. You'll be famous now."'

Then Pudding would tell stories about drinking and life in Broome: 'Before when I used to be drinking I'd be working, working, working hard. Slack. Friday payday. Everybody smiling, joking. Line-up, sign your name, get your pay. Go home, give your missus money, go shop, buy shirt, trousers. Come home, shower, shave, shave, get ready for pub tonight. Everything look good. Start walking pub. Getting frightened cause I got money and all them countrymen might rob you.

You can't win with those kind people. Soon as you got money they'll drain you. Like flies round shit. Next day they won't even look at you. When you walk down you see that many hands, Jesus. Before you can hit the front door, you're half-broke already. As soon as you get inside you got to deal with those people drinking inside, let alone get to the bar. Soon as you get to the bar, that's it, you're cornered. You've got to fuckin be smart. I always get twenty dollars or ten dollars or something, go drive-in, change them to small money. I hide my money aways in my jeans, roll them up in my sleeves, got to be smart cause they sink the fangs into you.

My uncle Manny, he was telling me soon as he hit that pub in town, he reckon before he can hit the bar he sees six heads and twelve hands. If you could change one cents bit to half cents bit he would. No good trying to throw cigarette butt on the floor because it won't reach the floor, it won't touch the ground. So if you want to give up smoking, go there. Just go there for one month. And if you want to give up drinking, go there too.

I tell you, them mobs are real rogues over there. They must get a pleasure out of running people broke. "Hey, you're broke, you're too deadly, you're on our side now. You might as well join us."'

When asked about growing up in Beagle Bay he'd become suddenly serious: 'I can't say I enjoyed it. I just grew up there. Through a child's eyes you see things differently,' he'd say.

I was Pudding's 'right one proper'. We had wonderful sex, and a lot of it had to do with our mutual playfulness and laughter. I'd gone out with other Aboriginal men—my sister used to joke that, 'Aboriginal Affairs is Diana's specialty and she has plenty of them!' Oh ha ha. They were all different, and no better and no worse than white men, or any other type of men, in their libido. Pudding, however, was committed to me and I felt that in his lovemaking. He also had lots of energy. No wonder I lost lots of weight—and so did he. He grew very handsome at that time.

I felt so strongly that he had talent and I tried to help him, driving him everywhere, sitting in on boring band practices, recording sessions, play rehearsals, the whole bit. We did dance classes together and went to the gym. It all helped his self-esteem. But he seemed to always self-sabotage.

He joined a multicultural theatre group and got a main part in an Indonesian play by WS Rendra. He was going really well, considering he'd never had acting lessons. But then one night he went with a group from the music school and ended up in a pub. I got a call from the hospital and went to pick him up. He'd been in a fight with one of the guys and had his arm broken. I've a feeling the fight was something to do with me. He had to do the play with his arm in a sling. Once, I met a guy on the bus that I had a nice chat with, and when I mentioned it to Pudding he got insanely jealous. If I did favours for other people, but not for him, he would be furious with me.

After several weeks looking for work I found a job with the Department of Agriculture, editing fact sheets, writing press releases and making quarantine audio-visuals. I'd get my work done in the morning and do my own writing in the afternoon. I learnt all about the Giant African Snail, the Fruit Fly, and Foot and Mouth Disease from the resident quarantine expert. She'd stop you in the corridor and regale you with horror stories of these terrible foreign diseases and pests that were going to take over the country if we weren't more vigilant about quarantine. But the two journos I worked with were great. And it was a bit of security after all these months of wandering around.

I'd had an accident in my old station wagon in Broome, but managed to get the insurance money, and I bought a red Falcon ute from a depot for former government cars in Derby. It became known as The Red Terror. In South Australia, Pudding and I went on lots of trips in it. But I had trouble with the gears. They'd get stuck and I'd have to jump out of the car, undo the bonnet and wiggle them around. If I was at the top of a hill I'd have to be pretty quick to jump back in before the car took off (and wave to the people laughing at me).

During this time Pudding wrote a song about us— *Cornelius and Rosalind* (our middle names). It had a lovely calypso tune and I was touched. Nobody had ever written a song for me before.

But my parents didn't really approve of him. When we came to stay with them in Sydney, my mother said to me, 'He's a nice boy, but he's not for you.' I don't think it was the class difference or the racial differences, more that they just knew it wouldn't last. They'd never interfered in my love life, usually because I didn't tell them anything about it. Only when I was going out with Guy years before, Mum said something sort of similar: 'He's a nice enough fella, but you are bridging the generation gap.'

Maybe it was the confronting notion that Pudding and I were having sex together. They put us in separate bedrooms. My sister was about to have her third baby and she asked me to come over in the middle of the night when she went to hospital. I was bringing Pudding but she asked me not to. She is religious and didn't like the idea of us sleeping together. (I don't think this had anything to do with him being Aboriginal, she was just being moralistic about sex before marriage. Years later, she put my husband and me in separate bedrooms when we visited her before we got married!) I've always regretted that I didn't say no, I wasn't coming. Instead I took Pudding to stay at a mutual friend's place.

Once, when we stayed at my cousin's place, we had an enormous fight and he packed his bags. She got really angry with him and told him she didn't like him hurting me. I think he was surprised to have somebody defend me in that manner, so he stayed.

That year we drove with our friend Jo from Adelaide to Brisbane, for the protests at the Commonwealth Games against the Queensland government's draconian policies towards Aboriginal people and land. We all managed to get ourselves arrested there, Jo and Pudding and quite a few others, twice. The first time I dropped the gang off outside the stadium and went to park the car. By the time I got back they were all being hurled into paddy wagons. So I went to collect the bail money. With some of the others, we watched the TV news at a pub. When I came out somebody had stolen Pudding's guitar out of my car. There was tomato sauce smeared all over the steering wheel. It was all very strange and, of course, Pudding was furious with me later.

That night the police came driving through the park where the protesters were camped, allegedly chasing a stolen car. People had to roll out of the way in time to not be hit. We couldn't believe it.

So by the time of the final march, I'd really thought about it all, and I'd decided to go in it. Pudding and I held hands really tightly while the police tried to drag us away.

Jo and I and a whole bunch of women were thrown in a cell together after being searched by police women. We all laughed and joked, but behind the door somebody had scrawled: *Raped here, six cops* and the date. It didn't feel like fun any more. Eight or so hours later we were released. We were meant to be in court the next day but we took off, driving back to Adelaide, glad to see the Queensland/NSW border.

We'd been doing some voluntary work at a community radio station and put together a special on the Games protest. Jo and I found that not a single newspaper was interested in running our 'inside' story about the protests. Maybe they thought we were biased? One features editor told Jo: 'Diana Plater only ever writes about Aboriginal affairs, and we have plenty of others who can do that.' *But what about Tropical Gardening, the magazine I edited in Darwin?* I thought.

At the end of 1982 Pudding and I went back to Broome and the NT for a holiday, and stayed with his mother, Rita, at Pine Creek, south of Darwin. She was living there with her youngest son, Lesley, his girlfriend and their baby, Arthur. Mimi Dora was staying there too, from time to time.

I'd been to Pine Creek years before, when I was a child, with my mother and sisters. We always went on adventurous holidays with Mum. We'd been on a bus trip and got bogged on the way to Jim Jim Falls. We spent the night on the bus, then the next morning my older sister and some others walked off to get help. When we were rescued we only just had time to have a shower at the Pine Creek pub before making it to our plane home from Darwin. It would have been strange if Pudding and Ollie were there at the time. I remember I left my watch behind. But it seemed like time had stood still when I went there with Pudding.

We did go kangaroo shooting, but usually the routine of the day involved following the shade around the house. They'd get up in the morning, crack open the tinnies and sit in the front of the house. By the end of the day they'd be at the back verandah, and pretty full. This was fairly boring for Pudding and me as, at this stage, we weren't drinking. Despite that, Pudding and Rita got on really well. They had the same dry sense of humour.

Rita had her bank account at the local store. They even kept her bankbook for her, and took money out to pay for what she'd run up there. It didn't feel as if much had changed since Welfare days. When Pudding's cousin came to visit and his car hit a bullock on the way out of town, it was a good excuse for us to get away by driving him to Darwin.

Rita's husband had died several years earlier. But he'd left her the shack and the land it was on. Later Rita found out it wasn't their land, although the house was theirs. I don't know what happened, whether Lesley was the beneficiary or whether he sold it. We went to visit Rita's husband's grave one day and Pudding cried. I was surprised. Wasn't he the man who had sent him back to Beagle Bay when he couldn't handle the competition?

Ollie: The only other girlfriend of Pudding's I ever knew about was Lorraine, Adam's mother. I recall him going to Carnarvon to live with her. He used to stay at Kim's grandmother's place. He was working for Elders then. He was really reliable. Always got up and went to work.

When he came to Perth he got a job with King Edward Hospital, doing the grounds, a good job with uniforms and all, but it didn't last. When he used to come and stay with me I was feeding him and he was always asking for money. I was giving him pocket money.

In 1982 I was in Perth with the education department. In 1983 I went to work for the Department of Social Security. Pudding and Diana came over home to stay with us on the way through from Adelaide to Broome—must have been the end of 1983.

Pudding came to bring me back Dave's guitar, which he'd been carrying around with him. It was a beautiful twelve string guitar and Dave had lent it to him. When we took it out of the case you could see a huge bit like where it had been repaired. It took a while to prise the story out of him, but it seems he and Diana had had a big fight, and he'd been so angry he'd kicked a hole in the guitar. Diana told me she'd thrown chicken noodle soup all over the kitchen and bits of noodles had stuck to the wall. But she felt real guilty when she saw the guitar, and paid more than $100 to get it fixed. So nobody can claim that guitar now. It's got its own ID.

Later, my friend, Marky Bin Bakar, came to my home. Back in those days I used to leave the house unlocked. I had three sausage dogs then—Fifi, Sam and Kizzy, who used to bark a lot. When I got home there was a note from Marky, saying: *You should lock your doors or your dogs will get raped.*

After that visit the guitar went missing from my house. And for years I assumed that Marky had picked up the guitar. I used to ask him, 'You got my guitar?'

And he'd say, 'Ollie, I haven't got that guitar.' I used to laugh it off and think he was telling me stories.

Then one day Marky rang me up and said he went to this gig and there was my guitar. Apparently this girl had claimed it was hers, but Marky recognised it and said, 'That's Ollie's.'

She said, 'No, I bought it in Sydney.'

And Marky kept insisting. She eventually admitted it was my guitar. Apparently she said, 'I went round to a party at Ollie's and she was drunk, and said I could take it.' But that was bullshit, she stole it. So Marky took it for me.

I said, 'Hang on to it until I want it back.' So I finally got it back in 1994.

When Dave gave Pudding that guitar I told him not to sell it. And if he did, to give me first option. I did end up buying back the guitar from Pudding and finally gave it to Cindy. That guitar has done a complete circle.

Pudding was very, very talented, but he seemed to be into this country and western. I said to him before he went to Adelaide, 'Look, with country and western you've only got a very small audience. If you want to make it you've got to be versatile with rock-and-roll, reggae and all.' So it was really interesting to see when he came back from Adelaide on this trip that he was playing jazz, and I thought, *maybe it might have sunk in, what I said to him before he left.* I was really proud of him, he was expanding his music.

I had always felt sorry for Pudding. He had his father, who remarried, and then they kicked him out. Lorraine was telling me recently that when she and Pudding started going out together they were staying with Ambrose and Nancy Cox. They were the family who took him in and treated him like one of their own kids. When Cooney and Betty told him to leave he went from pillar to post, and I think the Coxes were one family that gave him some stability and security. They used to feed him and give him a bed, look after him. I never knew that before. I've developed a soft spot for this family.

But he gradually started to change. When he made his tape, *Submission Bells*, I was flabbergasted because he wouldn't give me one for free. I had to buy one off him. And another time I had these two boys from my street over. One was going with Cindy. Pudding was there. I was always proud of Pudding and his talent and I said, 'Pudding, play the guitar.'

Once upon a time, you didn't have to ask Pudding, he'd just pick up a guitar.

He said, 'No, I'll only do it for money—you boys give me two dollars.'

They were putting their hands in their pockets and I said, 'No, don't pay him.'

He started writing really simple songs like ones about band time and so on. That song he wrote, *Me Me My My*, I asked him what the meaning was. I wanted to know why he wrote it, the feeling behind it, because mimi means his grandma. He said he and Jimmy were just talking one day and it was just a nothing song, he wasn't writing about his mimi.

But then he graduated to much deeper ones about the Aboriginal situation, like *Hey Jacky*. He was becoming more and more angry at the world and his songs showed it. I think I may have liked him better when he was an innocent singer of country and western songs. But he had to grow up sometime.

When he's given opportunities he makes life difficult for himself. He was meant to play didgeridoo for a band and turned up with a vacuum cleaner hose. This was long before Ernie Dingo started doing that joke. Another time, Marky Bin Bakar offered to pay his fare to come to Broome to sing at a big festival, and he insisted on driving from Perth. But Marky couldn't give him money for petrol because the airfares had been donated by the airline. So he didn't turn up for the concert. I mean, what could you do to help him? Diana's right. He was into self-destruction.

Diana: After the Christmas holidays in 1983, Pudding started the second year at CASM. We'd given up our little house and moved into a caravan in the grounds of a crazy boarding house, run by a landlady straight out of a Lena Wertmuller movie. Everyday, her nephew would drive his Holden station wagon and trailer down the pebbled driveway, past chooks and statues of women covered in plastic flowers. He would unload second hand springless beds, cabinets, disused television sets and backless chairs. Then he would load another heap of ruined furniture onto his trailer and take it God knows where.

The bonfire was always burning and the mad landlady would cluck around it, throwing everything she could lay her hands on onto it. The black thick smoke choked the air and filled our grimy caravan, which was already regularly visited by the chooks.

At first I thought the place, inhabited by old men, young Aboriginal women, petty criminals, winos, and a guitarist who wrote poems based on astrology, was incredibly atmospheric. It didn't take too long of lining up for the bathroom where water dripped dangerously through the gas pipe, to realise we were all being ripped off by Senora Wertmuller.

To get away, we did quite a few trips around SA in the Red Terror—the Yorke Peninsula, the Barossa Valley, the Coorong, Port Pirie (to do a story on the controversy over lead poisoning). Always camping on the amazingly empty beaches and in the bush. Pudding was a very good artist and he would find bits of wood and bone and carve marvellous sculptures out of them. I have them today on my mantelpiece next to my carved boab nuts and boomerangs, and my kids are fascinated by them.

But I'd had enough of trying to make a living as a freelancer when I didn't even have a phone. It looked pretty bad doing interviews on a public phone from a busy street, with no number people could ring you back on. And things weren't really progressing with Pudding and me. I suggested I go to Sydney and find a job and a place to live, and he follow me there. He only had a few more months at CASM.

So I sold my ute for peanuts, bought a city car, a white Honda Civic, and drove to Sydney. I found a great little house in Redfern and started casual work at AAP. He arrived in Sydney a couple of months later.

He started meeting other Aboriginal musicians and jammed with them. One night he asked me to meet him at a dance. The place was packed with Aboriginal people. I think I was the only white person there. After I'd been in the Kimberley, I had felt strange if I went to a party and there were no Aboriginal people there. It was almost as if I was prejudiced against white people. But that night, I think for the first time, I understood how Pudding must have felt when we went to white 'dos' together. It wasn't so much that people were unfriendly towards me, they weren't. It's just I felt as if I was sticking out like a sore thumb.

In only a short time, Pudding decided he didn't like Sydney. He'd asked me to marry him, but he wanted to go back and live in Broome. I didn't want to. So we split up. But in the process Ollie and I became really good friends. So although the whole thing is sad, and when I listen to his music today I feel like crying, I gained something wonderful out of my relationship with Pudding—and that is my friendship with Ollie. But then Pudding might have a different view of all this. After all, he did take his song, *Cornelius and Rosalind*, off his tape when he made a new version of it.

Ollie: I remember Pudding as such as beautiful person, he was really fun to be with. Never said a harsh word about somebody. If you were having a bitch about somebody he'd never join in. But I've seen a change in him now. He might run down somebody, whereas he never used to do that before. He's stooped up. The shoulders are where you carry all your stuff. It looks like he's carrying all this stuff around.

He's funny too, though. He's got the real Smith family sense of humour. Dry as old bones. My mum is the same. The Smith family, they're great people to be with, they keep you in fits of laughter all the time. But when they get together they always fight as well. They've got this jealousy stuff happening. Aunty Monica had leprosy. She makes you weak. She always says, 'You don't like me cause I've got leprosy.' And Aunty Lena says, 'You don't like me cause I'm black, I'm a black Cinderella.' They have all these hangups.

Marky's got some good stories about Pudding. One of his mates, Lalga, has been living down in Perth. Pudding has been living in Perth for years, and sometimes I find the best way to find Pudding is to go to Fremantle markets, and any musos I see there busking, I ask them where Pudding is. They always know him and know where he is. Lalga, he moved down from Broome to Perth, and now a lot of the rules for busking in the Fremantle markets have changed. You can busk only there for an hour or so and then you have to move on. Marky was telling us a story—Lalga was there, and Pudding came along and said, 'What you doing in my spot?'

And Lalga reckoned, 'What you talking about?'

Pudding said, 'That's my corner.'

And Lalga said, 'But there's three other corners there, Pudding.'

But Pudding reckoned, 'No, this is my spot, and you have to move.'

Another time Lalga and Pudding were driving in a car and they heard all these sirens and realised that it was a fire engine. So Pudding moved to another lane and the fire engine moved across to that lane too. So Pudding decided to pull up and the fire engine behind him pulled up as well. When he got out he found out his car was on fire, and that's why the fire engine was following him, all sirens going.

Deaths in Custody, Public Service Racism and Partying with Sailors

7.

Deaths in Custody, Public Service Racism and Partying with Sailors

It's nearly band time now
I have to go out and play
All my friends will be there
Come! You don't have to pay
Hope I will see you there
Having fun in the night
So I'll see you at the Conti
And we'll hold each other tight

Band Time

Arnold Smith

Diana: I feel I will never look as good again as I did in that red dress I wore the night of the West Australian government's 1985 media Christmas party. I'd bought the '50s-style dress at a second hand shop, but it was a classy shop. And it looked good. I remember distinctly and clearly Brian Burke's eyes popping out when I walked past.

It wasn't the usual look the WA Premier would give me at those dreadful Monday afternoon Cabinet press conferences. That look was usually one of disdain. There was another unfortunate female reporter who was only about twenty. She worked for a university radio station, and always asked what you could see he considered silly questions. He would give witheringly sarcastic answers in response.

I usually didn't ask many questions—I left that to the boys. They were all in love with Burkie—that big round figure and balding head. He was an ex-journo himself—a good guy. He cracked jokes, and after years of conservative government and Charlie Court, he was a blessed relief. It didn't matter if he was doing deals with businessmen. As he explained, he was trying to use the West Australian taxpayers' money to the best advantage. At that stage, nobody dreamed it would all come crashing down on them in the form of WA Inc.

But back to that glorious summer evening when politicians and the media mixed happily, sipping wine and eating crayfish at outdoor tables down by the river. I was sitting next to a government minister, and another one, Peter Dowding, the Minister for Mines, was wandering around chatting to the journalists.

Peter and I had first met when he was just a lawyer. I'd been told to go and see him in his Perth office, high up in one of the skyscrapers in St George's Terrace. We arranged that we'd meet in Port Hedland and go down to a bush meeting at Yandeearra on my way to the Kimberley. He'd worked all that area when he'd been an Aboriginal Legal Service lawyer in the '70s. I was excited, as it was going to be a great introduction to the Pilbara—and Aboriginal politics. All went well until it rained and rained and rained. We'd gone there in my Falcon station wagon, which wasn't really a four-wheel drive. But we decided to treat it like one. In order to get across the swollen creek—or river, really—we just followed a four-wheel drive. The driver then used his winch to pull my car out of the creek.

At one point my car's exhaust had to be sawn off. All this took a few hours, while a carload of Aboriginal people coming towards Yandeearra sat patiently waiting. Peter drove as it kept pounding with rain, and mud splashed all over the car. I laughed all the way back to Port Hedland. Peter went back to Perth, leaving me a note and $50 to fix the car. That was a lot of money in 1979.

Well, Peter went on to fame, being elected the following year as a member of Parliament. When the WA Labor Party was falling apart, he got the not particularly popular job of Premier, only to be ousted by Carmen Lawrence not long after. These days he uses his considerable skills to represent Aboriginal people on native title claims and in other areas. Burke, as we all know, went to jail for stealing to pay for his stamp collection. How the mighty have fallen. But Burke's back now, still a major player behind the scenes in the Labor Party. WA is a very, very small world.

That Christmas party was like a sigh of relief after the past eighteen months of trying to survive as a journalist from the 'east' writing about the 'west'.

It was certainly no picnic covering the early deaths in custody stories in WA. Covering Aboriginal stories is not always a joyful experience, but this was particularly bad. I was torn apart watching people I care about die prematurely. I was also scared stiff seeing what the system does to people. The atmosphere during the October 1984 Federal election campaign was particularly tense. The then Prime Minister Bob Hawke and a band of Canberra press gallery followers were in Perth. Aboriginal land rights was on the agenda, as Burke persuaded Hawke about the damage the proposed national land rights was doing to the Labor Party in WA.

During lunch at a yacht club on the Swan River—it was the days just before the America's Cup, of course—talk came up about the state government's proposed land rights legislation, and its lack of the power of veto over mining for Aboriginal groups. I was asking questions, or more probably making comments about this, to Burke's press secretary, who was sitting opposite me. 'You're just a bleeding heart,' he sniped back.

It was the sort of comment I had become used to, although it still got to me. Anything to do with Aboriginal issues in those days was not popular with the WA media. And journalists who were seen to be sympathetic to the issue usually found they were outcast, not only by media management but often by their own colleagues. (Even members of the Labor Party were given a hard time and described as 'idealists' if they were seen to be sympathetic to 'soft' issues such as land rights.)

The attitude was partly an extension of the distrust Western Australians held for 'eastern staters'. Most of the journalists who wrote about this issue were working either as correspondents or freelancers for eastern states media. But some of them were from Perth. They included Jan Mayman, writing for *The Age*, and Duncan Graham for *The National Times*. Both Jan and Duncan received Walkley Awards for stories about Aboriginal issues. Jan received a gold Walkley Award for her coverage of the death of John Pat in Roebourne in 1983. Duncan worked with me for a while at AAP, and both he and Jan were a great source of information, support and help to me. A few journalists working for local media also showed interest in the issue, including Alison Fan from Channel Seven News and several from ABC Radio.

To us, the influence of Aboriginal issues on state politics was of national, and, it seemed, international interest.

The Federal election campaign came at a traumatic time for WA Aboriginal people. With the advent of Labor governments, and in the hope of gaining both state and national land rights, they had bared their souls and supplied intimate knowledge to land commissioners and lawyers. But yet again their time and effort had come to nothing.

And suggestions to Clyde Holding, who was then Federal Minister for Aboriginal Affairs in the Hawke government, that he needed to mount a public awareness campaign to counteract the extremely negative TV advertisements of black hands building walls across Western Australia, mounted by the Chamber of Mines, had not been accepted.

Then came a series of Aboriginal deaths in prisons, hotels and other places. The first case of an Aboriginal death in custody I reported on was that of Robert Walker, a young prisoner in Fremantle Jail, in August, 1984.

It was a brutal case, but what made it particularly meaningful to me was that I had met Robbie several years before, in Adelaide. He was a student at the Centre for Aboriginal Studies and Music, where Pudding had been studying.

Walker died at 4am on 28 August. At eight that morning, John Doohan, a civil rights activist and spokesman for the Human Rights and Civil Liberties Watch Committee, received the first of two phone calls from prisoners at the jail. The calls had been arranged by a social worker.

Later, in evidence before the coroner, those prisoners described being woken by horrifying screams, and climbing on top of their beds to look out their windows in order to see the action taking place in the quadrangle below. Walker, they said, was struggling with prison officers.

Other evidence before the coroner claimed that there was a depression in the grass where Walker's head had lain. It was alleged that there was blood in the hole where he died. Both the coroner, and later the Royal Commission into Aboriginal Deaths in Custody, rejected that evidence.

Other prisoners produced notes which they claimed were blow by blow descriptions of Walker's death.

The prison authorities and the officers on duty have always denied doing anything wrong.

Doohan then called Chris Falvey, a journalist on *The West Australian*, who he had been in contact with over other stories. And Falvey wrote a story quoting the prisoners' allegations.

Doohan, who had previously lived in the Soviet Union, had been trying to persuade local media for years about the issue, but believes he had been 'black banned' because of his radical views, and the fear of *The West Australian* newspaper management that he planned to sue them over what he says was a fabricated interview published in the newspaper. He tended to receive a better response from journalists representing the interstate media.

We spoke to each other often.

On the day of Walker's death, the Attorney General's office issued a statement saying the prisoner had committed suicide. I then spoke to Doohan and wrote a story questioning this.

The inquest was held in Perth Coroner's Court, but for several days it was transferred to the prison's chapel to take evidence from prisoners. That greatly limited the number of press and public who could attend, and at first Doohan was excluded, but finally he was admitted as correspondent for the West German newspaper, *Die Tageszeitung*.

I'll never forget the grim atmosphere at the inquest as we filed in across the quadrangle where Walker had died. Then more than 40 prisoners, one by one, gave evidence about what they saw or heard in the early hours of 28 August. Some claimed to have seen Walker repeatedly punched, kicked and struck with a baton during a struggle with five prison officers.

The officers deny that account of events. But the three officers said to have 'pressed down' on Walker as he lay in the grass, and their chief officer who was with them, did not give evidence at the inquest. Four other officers did give evidence.

As photos of Walker's corpse were passed around, I remember thinking that although Robbie was certainly no angel, nobody deserved to die the way he did, whichever account was true.

The coroner, David McCann, rejected the prisoners' allegations as 'unfounded' and was satisfied by the evidence that Walker died as a result of 'misadventure'. There was little doubt that the cause of death was asphyxiation, and the coroner found that this had occurred 'without brutal force'.

Walker's death was later investigated by the Royal Commission into Aboriginal Deaths in Custody, set up after much lobbying by the Committee to Defend Black Rights. The Royal Commission again rejected the prisoners' evidence, in part because they had discussed the events between themselves. The Royal Commissioner also visited the cells, and found that many of them had an obscured or partial view of the area where the events occurred. As a result, many of their accounts, he concluded, were 'seriously distorted'. But he found that the restraint applied by the officers had caused Walker's death, and that some aspects of the force used had been 'unnecessary and unreasonable'.

Doohan recalls it was *The Sydney Morning Herald* which first published photos he had obtained of another Aboriginal prisoner, Charles Michael, handcuffed and lying on the floor after he had died in September, 1984. The article was by Graham Williams, who had written about Aboriginal issues from Sydney for many years.

Doohan had received the photos of Michael, who had died as the result of a heart attack at Barton's Mill Prison, east of Perth, from his family, who in turn had been given them by a police source. The coroner later rejected an attempt to tender them as evidence at the inquest.

The deaths did not end there. In August the following year, 1985, the Aboriginal people of Mullewa, a wheat belt town east of Geraldton, rioted after 25-year-old Victor Simpson was killed when he was thrown out the door of a hotel.

The ruined hotel was a chilling sight as I drove into town. It was covered in railway dog spikes taken from a pile next to the tracks opposite the hotel and thrown by a production line of Aboriginal kids.

The 30 or so journalists who had come to Mullewa (some in the hope of seeing a South African-style funeral) were standing outside the only other hotel in town. Although the owners were probably pleased to receive the extra income they spent much of their time attacking the media for their 'biased' stories. Later I saw some people I knew in the black bar of the hotel and went to drink with them (where white journalists weren't supposed to go). It was good to get away from the other journos, all telling dramatic stories of the night's events. They seemed so out of place, up in the wheat belt, miles from Perth. They also seemed proud of the fact that nobody in town liked them and were going on and on about the colour bar, staying firmly in the white bar, of course.

When the situation started to become even more tense between the media and the Aboriginal people of the town, the Aboriginal actor, Ernie Dingo, who happened to be there to film a story for A Current Affair, was used as a go-between. Journalists were then permitted to attend the funeral if they agreed not to film it. Most agreed.

Although all of these stories received coverage in both WA and eastern states media, it took an interstate TV crew's visit to WA to awaken stronger national interest in Aboriginal deaths in custody in the west. The Four Corners program, *Black Death*, produced by Alan Hall and reported by David Marr in September, 1985, showed graphic re-enactments of the deaths of three Aboriginal people in custody in WA over the previous two years. It questioned the practices of police, prison officers and the coroner's court in relation to these deaths. Jan Mayman did the research and provided most of the contacts for this program.

As a response, the ABC was 'black banned' by the state's police and prison officers. At a press conference in Perth, a lawyer acting for the West Australian police and prison officers' unions called for an independent inquiry to investigate allegations of bias against the program.

The lawyer also personally attacked the team which made the program (which included Jan) and called for their suspension.

Jan and I used to talk to each other on the phone every day during this period. We really appreciated each other's support as we were both loners, normally working on our own without even the company of a photographer, and I'm telling you it could get pretty lonely—and scary.

For some reason, Ollie came to a Brian Burke press conference once, around this time. An Aboriginal radio journalist there, Marie Andrews, was asking all these confronting questions. Ollie said you could see Burkie going white.

The only time I really saw him change his smug expression was when I asked a rather impertinent question. I'd had a call from irate women Labor Party members, who were really annoyed about a certain woman's appointment to their advisory committee. She was an out and out blue ribbon Liberal, but the rumour was that a Labor minister had been having an affair with her. I said I'd ask Burkie a question about it. I wrote it down and I was nudged on by my colleague, Peter, from *The Australian* (another free spirit! He gave me a compass as my farewell present when I left Perth, to help me find my way back again). So taking in a big breath of air, I asked, 'Mr Burke, is it true that one of the women appointed to the advisory committee is having a close, personal relationship with one of your ministers?'

Burkie fudged an answer, although one of the pro-Burkie journalists yelled out the name of the alleged minister. When the press conference was over the former Premier walked round to my seat and asked me directly what minister I was talking about. I said I didn't want to say, and he said it didn't matter, he was pretty sure he knew who it was!

I got a bit of flak over that, comments like, 'Why is Diana giving ammunition to the Opposition?' I hadn't heard I worked for the Labor Party last time I checked.

So I'd go round to Ollie's place a few times a week to unwind. I'd let it all out over a bong or two.

Ollie: Just because I was Aboriginal didn't mean my non-Aboriginal colleagues discussed deaths in custody and these sorts of issues with me. I never talked about how they impacted on us. I was more likely to discuss it socially with my friends, or with Diana and with Dave, because they were both working in the media. It was particularly sad, because when there was a death in custody they did an investigation. But it always turned out that the prison officer was cleared, and you knew damn well that they contributed to the death. You could be in custody, institutionalised, and all the evidence would be against you. It was scary to know you were helpless.

Once, a group of us—mainly women—went to Fremantle Jail to talk to some of the male Aboriginal prisoners. The purpose of the visit was to expose to the prisoners that there were Aboriginal women in the work force. Their attitudes were really quite interesting. They said things like, 'If my missus was working I'd give her a flogging.' They didn't want their spouses to work, they wanted them to be at home. I guess seeing us who were in the work force, confident, strong women, was probably very threatening to them. We were supposed to be their role models.

When we went to Fremantle Jail they also had a concert. It was great, but I appreciate what prisoners went through, I felt really claustrophobic in there. I can remember the next day, going down to get my lunch and thinking about those prisoners, and here I was walking along the pavement, free. And I was thinking about them locked up. Every door you walked through you had a door locked behind you. For me that was very intimidating. Fremantle Jail is closed now. It's a museum now, with tours and all.

I used to envy Diana her job and all the knowledge and information with current affairs that she had access to. Even when she was doing those stories on the Filipino women in Port Hedland who were married to Aussie blokes, and so on,

I used to be envious of her having a job like that and being so knowledgeable and informed. I think I learnt a lot from her.

At the time I was working for the Department of Social Security in Midland. I'd left the education department in December, 1983. I had mixed feelings about going there, because I heard Midland was a racist office and I wasn't sure if there were any Aboriginal staff there. But when I started there it turned out there was one other Aboriginal person— Alan Ah Chee. He was in mainstream, and my position was the Aboriginal liaison officer. I had two lines of responsibility—to the Aboriginal services section in Social Security, because I was based in a regional office, and to my supervisor, who was the regional manager. I was a bit apprehensive because I knew Midland also had a high Aboriginal population, and knowing some of the attitudes in that office, and that many of their clients were Aboriginal, I was wondering, *how am I going to cope with this?*

After about a year or so I ended up having a fight with this girl. Every NAIDOC week they used to organise an Aboriginal sports carnival. And this particular time the carnival was in Geraldton, and we had all our clients coming in wanting to go to this carnival, so they were applying for counter cheques. And we had streams and streams of people coming through. The Midland region covered as far as Southern Cross, all the wheat belt areas, so we had people coming from all over the region, not just local.

What came out of that was the attitudes of some of the staff that were decision makers in the office, making racist comments and remarks about Aboriginal people. They were dismissing Aboriginal culture, but when it suited them, then they were saying, 'You know how they share? Why can't they just get one cheque and all jump in one car and go up?'—that sort of thing. One person came in and there was a racist comment made. And I thought, *no, I'll bite my tongue*. And another one, and then the third one I saw red and exploded at this woman. She was a Scottish descendant and had a broad Scottish accent. And I started, the gin came out in me, and I got really aggressive and angry and abusive, calling her 'cunt' and everything.

See, that mob never seen the other side of me, and I just exploded. She ended up crying and complaining to the manager about me. Then he called me in. I know I did the wrong thing, I should have handled it in a more professional manner and I should have been more assertive, rather than aggressive. I apologised to the manager for that and went out of his office.

And then I thought, *no, I'm not going to let it go*. And I went back to him and I said to him, 'From now on, any more racist comments, if you don't deal with them I'll be going outside, above your head. I'm not going to tolerate that any more.' After that the office was fine. But it took something like that to see the other side of me, and they didn't want to get on the other side. They may have learnt from that.

Diana: By the end of the first year in Perth I still wasn't breaking into the inner circle of Western Australian media. I was covering a lot of finance stories, which I wasn't used to. So I also had to get in with that clique. I'd ask the most general questions of people like Robert Holmes à Court, with three dots at the end for him to fill in, but surprisingly, he always remembered my name and was rather vague about some of my male colleagues' titles. I decided the only way to cut the ice was to throw a great AAP Christmas party.

I invited everybody! Nothing like grassroots contact in the pursuit of reconciliation. There were Liberal Party senators, Labor Party politicians, members of the Trades and Labour Council, veteran journalists, young journalists, stockbrokers and high finance people, AAP staff, Aboriginal musicians, old friends and fellow ragers.

It was held in the AAP office on the seventh floor of the Stock Exchange Building, where Laurie Connell (the disgraced stockbroker) also had an office. People would be ringing the doorbell downstairs and we had to send somebody down to let them in. AAP had given me some money towards it, but I paid for most of the food and grog myself.

I wore a lovely white lacy and slim-fitting dress, which made it difficult to rock-and-roll to Pudding's band, but we managed. Ollie and I were on the floor dancing most of the night.

I knew the party had gone well, because during the evening one of the veteran journalists turned to me and said, 'You've got style, Diana, you've got style.'

Ollie: Marky Bin Bakar and Kevin Dann were also playing in the band at Diana's party. Black Allan was in her office rolling joints all night. There was so much smoke you had to push your way into the room.

There was this white social worker there and Black Allan was touching up her tits. The poor girl didn't know what to do. So I said, 'Black Allan, leave her alone.' I could see she was really uncomfortable but she didn't want to say anything. Then I said, 'Fuck off, leave her alone.' But apart from that it was a great party.

Diana and my friendship really developed in '85–6. Diana came to Perth at the end of '84 and she started going out with Pudding again. He was living at the hostel next door to the Advancement Council. Diana and I went to see him there together once. It was a horrible place.

Diana: It must have been spring because I had really bad hay fever. Perth, with its dry winds coming in from the desert, is the place for hay fever. So I went to see an acupuncturist. He was such a sleaze. He had this giant statue of his head in his front garden. *Very strange*, I thought.

Pudding was waiting for me and I told him that old Needles had tried to touch me up (acupuncture needles and all, mind you). Pudding was really angry. 'They'll be more than his head in the garden if he tries that again,' he said.

When Pudding and I split up I was so upset and angry I had to go down and sit on the riverbank next to my flat and wait for him to go. A few weeks later he was playing in a band over at Fremantle one night. I was still really upset. He didn't want to talk to me. I was still jealous seeing him talking to other women. It was heartbreaking for him as well, I think. I hardly saw him after that. I started going to Ollie's place all the time. She'd split up with Dave by then.

Ollie: We were both ragers. Diana was the first person to take me to a gay bar, the Red Lion. I didn't even know gay bars existed. My jaw was touching the ground, seeing all these men together and women together. Diana knew where the bars were.

One night Diana said she was pissed off with blokes and said she was going to find a woman. We had a bowl of garlic mussels in Northbridge and then went to the Red Lion and then Connections. But nobody came near us the whole night. We were wondering if it was the garlic or whether they thought she and I were an item. When we got home I said to her, 'Diana, if you wanted to find a woman you should have gone out on your own. No wonder nobody came near us tonight.'

I never had a clue those bars existed. There was a young girl sitting next to me and there was another girl standing between her legs, rubbing and kissing. And I was trying not to be obvious, but I was fascinated by all of this. I was a very naive 30-year-old. Two friends of mine, who were both married, later told me they were gay. I tried to tell them it was okay, because I'd been to those places. They hadn't come out themselves. I thought, *here Diana is from Sydney, and she knows more about Perth than I do.*

Usually we'd go to straight nightclubs and bars. When the American ships were in port they'd be full of sailors. We all knew we'd get free drinks when the ships were in town. Some of my girlfriends liked them mullegas, but I didn't. I thought they were gammon men. If you drove down to Fremantle when the boats were leaving there'd be a line-up of girls kissing the sailors goodbye. Nine months later the maternity wards were full.

At the same time, there were all this anti-nuclear protests going on which Diana was covering.

One night Diana decided to write a story about Perth girls on the town, going after the American sailors. So she interviewed these guys—black ones, of course. She got talking to one guy. His name was Louis the something the third. He ended up getting really gurrajin and following us around all night, and we went back to his ritzy hotel room— just for coffee! Poor bastard had spent all his money on it, but reckoned it was worth it after three months sleeping in a bunk while his ship did circles around the Indian Ocean.

Diana said that when she sent the story she could only send six paragraphs at a time, and the subeditor in Sydney rang her to say hurry up and send the rest of the story. He couldn't wait to see what happened!

Diana: We'd get dressed up, then put on Tina Turner records to get us in the mood before going out nightclubbing.

Ollie always reminded me of a young and more beautiful Tina Turner. We'd frizz up our hair, wear tight pants and stilettos, put on a ton of makeup. I'd usually have some strange top that I'd bought in Japan or Thailand or somewhere. A leftover from my hippie days. Ollie liked big shirts over her pants. There'd be a few of us, Narelle and Leanne and Lynette, Ollie's cousin's girlfriend, when she was in town.

There were a few regular nightclubs we went to, and we'd usually end up at this Italian café in Northbridge for mussels and coffee around four in the morning. I was a free woman then, and met quite a few guys. I used to grill the sailors we met, using my friend Donna's advice to get the most information you could out of them.

One Saturday night 8,063 American sailors had landed in Fremantle, and true to tradition, the women were out in force to meet them. They were from the USS Callaghan, a guided missile destroyer, and six other ships from Carrier Group One. The music was piercing our eardrums in the disco, with a huge video screen flashing out images of black American singers. Black—when it's American—was beautiful in Perth.

Two white uniformed officers were standing in one corner. Another couple of sailors in uniforms walked in looking for some action. I was leaning against the bar talking to Ollie—when one rather short, but I guess you could describe him as cute, black sailor lurched up to me.

'Hi, how you doing?' he asked.

'Are you with them?' I asked, gesturing towards the sailors. He admitted that he was, but insisted he was not a 'squid'—a sailor or officer who wears his uniform on shore, probably to attract the women.

'You'll have to excuse me, but I'm rather intoxicated after 90 days at sea without a drink,' he says.

The conversation drifted towards the obvious question: 'Why did you join the navy?'

'Listen, I'm from Atlanta, Georgia. A poor black family. My uncle wanted me to get into his line of work. But I'm selfish and stubborn and I went off and joined the navy. Signed up for six years, one more to go.'

He told me he was 23, and asked if his age turned me off. I told him he never turned me on. 'That's what I call being dogged off,' he said.

'It's like you've been at sea for 90 days, and you haven't had a drink or seen a woman all that time, and you're trying to make it with a woman. And she's not interested. That's being dogged off. Like you've been put in the doghouse.'

Dial a Sailor may have been inundated with phone calls. But I wasn't one of the callers. I never went out with a sailor. It would have made it particularly difficult to have the right credentials to cover the women's anti-nuclear protests held by groups such as People for Nuclear Disarmament, which managed to force the US Navy to stop visits from one of the ships that weekend. 'We want to take the glory of war away,' explained one of the organisers, who said the most aggression they received was from fifteen-year-olds out to catch a guy, or older women whose husbands had been war veterans.

The women held a camp at a base south of Perth for about a week, and I managed to get permission to stay in one of the tents the night before the final assault on the gates. It was a mini Greenham Common. Women with crew cuts and wearing overalls were using bolt cutters to get through the wire. Others were climbing the gates and being thrown off by burly security men and police. Lots were arrested. It was chaotic, dirty and horrifying.

Around this time I went on a media visit to one of the American ships. They flew us over in a navy helicopter which landed on the ship. All the sailors were lined up saluting us as we walked down the gangway. So what did I do in front of all of them? Slipped over on my backside and slid right down to their feet. They were so well disciplined they didn't even smile.

All this didn't stop me asking the captain of the ship over lunch about his feelings on nuclear disarmament. 'No comment,' he said. The other journalists groaned, but probably at my question, not his answer.

I seemed to be making a reputation for making a fool of myself. At north-west base, where we went on a tour with

Burke, I'd been out sunbaking and swimming the day before and had the worst sunburn you've ever seen. As soon as we got inside, and just as I was about to ask my anti-nuclear warfare questions, I fainted. You'll be glad to know they revived me with Coca Cola.

Ollie: After I first separated from Dave, Diana used to say, 'Go and find yourself a man.' But I wasn't interested. It took me a long time. Well, I did have a little affair early on. I think I was still with Dave, but it was when we were just living under the same roof together, but weren't together. It was right up towards the very end and my friend, Paul, was the first person that I had an affair with. He and I have still got a really good relationship. We're friends. When he's in town he'll come and visit me.

Once, he came to see me at work and took me out to lunch. I said, 'We'll go up to Mango.' So lunchtime we got on the piss, and I came back to the office drunk, and I went to the boss and said, 'Can I have a lie down in your office?' He was a really great boss, and he could have said 'Ollie,' and started lecturing me—sacked me or whatever. I said, 'I have to have a little catnap.'

I didn't have a relationship for eighteen months after I split up with Dave, but once I got the taste... So the years 1986–8 was my unemployed musicians period. I was single again. I'd never had a single life prior to getting married to Dave, because I'd virtually come straight out of school, into work, met Dave, got pregnant, got married and had no single life. No dating or seeing other blokes. Now, after Dave and I separated, I was having my single life in my 'dirty thirties'.

At the same time, Diana introduced me to a whole other cultural world, which benefited me a lot personally. She had free tickets for the Festival of Perth and we went to see the African plays and other events together. We were exposed to other countries and cultures and people, people I would not have been exposed to otherwise.

We went to an African play and there was a nice spunk there that I fancied. The party after at the concert hall—the festival club—was really good. We also went to a party for the Africans and the other people in the festival. It was refreshing. The conversations were stimulating.

I was learning to have an appreciation for all this sort of stuff. It was something I wasn't used to. Like the modern dances, it was not normal, conventional stuff you'd see. It was really way out.

Diana and my relationship was both learning from each other. Arts and culture and other stuff. Dave used to get all the free tickets but we never used to go. Dave thought I wasn't interested, or he didn't want me to be interested. I realised after, that I could have had all those opportunities with Dave. And I could have had a better appreciation of the arts long before. Things like that I would never have been exposed to if it wasn't for Diana.

Diana: Covering the Perth Festival in 1986 was fun. Lots of acts came out from Africa and we saw some wonderful shows. I was really taken by this stunning white South African actor who did four one-person plays. I went to one which blew me away. The first half was about the Soweto riots and he did all the different parts. The second half was about an academic couple breaking up, and he did both parts in this too. It was hysterically funny, just as the first had been moving and serious. I instantly fell in love with him.

Now, being a journalist can be very handy at times, because you can use the excuse of doing an interview to get to know people better. So I organised an interview with him. He was to come round to my office and we'd go for lunch!

I was working away in my office, looking forward to the interview, when Mary, the office manager, came in looking worried. 'Diana, there's a deaf and dumb person waiting to see you,' she said.

'What?'

I went out to have a look and it was the actor! He'd lost his voice. He came into the office and typed out a message on my computer. *Can't talk. Must save my voice. Sorry, must cancel interview.* And much to my disappointment, he left. I mean, I wasn't that worried if he didn't talk.

In the meantime, Jan had arranged for me to do another interview with Avi, an Israeli conductor, who was in Perth to conduct the London Symphony Orchestra at a vineyard at Margaret River. She thought it would cheer me up, as I'd been so depressed after breaking up with Pudding. We all met in the cocktail lounge at one of the big hotels.

Well, he was very charming, but not really my type. But I said yes when he asked me out for dinner. The funny part was that he offered his invitation in front of the classical music writer from *The Herald Sun* who'd flown over from Melbourne especially to interview him. She knew every concert he'd conducted. I had to ask him how to spell his name. He complimented her on her intimate knowledge about him then excused himself to go upstairs to change for dinner with me.

'I'd say you'll find he's circumcised,' said one of my less than subtle male colleagues as he went to buy a round of drinks. The *Herald Sun* journalist looked miffed.

Before the vineyard concert Jan and I had private drinks with Avi and then muscled our way into the private area kept for Perth's nouveau riche. (They didn't appreciate classical music anyway.) We peered over the top of Alan Bond at Eileen Bond's enormous diamond ring as we listened to the most gloriously uplifting rendition of Beethoven's Ninth Symphony, made only more exciting by the call of kookaburras who joined in with the violins.

'That *Herald Sun* journo was worried sick you were going to scoop her with your inside story about Avi,' Jan told me.

I laughed out loud. Knowing how totally uninterested AAP would be in a story about an Israeli conductor, I hadn't written a word. The one I had wanted to write about was the South African actor. At a final festival party I heard the whole story about him. He was having an affair with another—female—actor and his voice had returned.

Ollie: Throughout my time working in Social Security, 1983–8, when we had full inductions for staff coming into the department, or any professional development or training, we also conducted cross-cultural training. I used to be involved and facilitate those. There's a woman in Broome who's at retiring age and every time I see her she always says, 'I met you years ago, you did that cross-cultural awareness.' I thought that was really nice. It must have had some impact, which is good.

DSS always had good training. I had training in session leading, public speaking and presentation skills, but I used to be apprehensive about the confrontation with people challenging you as an individual. When I first went to DSS it used to be non-Aboriginal people doing the cross-cultural training. That was quite interesting, because the racist comments were more prevalent when a non-Aboriginal person was presenting, because I think they assumed that that person had the same attitudes as them.

Outside in personal and social life, if you have got somebody that is racist and if you are white, they are quite open about their racism. But it's good, because then you know who is and who isn't. Other times when I have done courses, you always get one in the course that is loudmouthed or whatever, and they can be really disruptive and can be dominating over the audience. In my really inexperienced stages—you know how people try to test you out, challenge you, and it was good this particular time.

One woman was doing it, and it was her peers in the audience that were responding to her behaviour, and I stood back and let them go. In those cases and in those instances they take more notice from their peers. If it was something between me and that person, you know, it wouldn't have had that same impact.

In Midland Alan Ah Chee was the only other Aboriginal person with us in mainstream. We had upstairs and downstairs, he was upstairs. So on a day-to-day basis we didn't have a lot of contact, unless it was in our break time, having a cup of tea or something. But he and I ended up becoming really good friends and I think when you are in a situation where you are a minority you do tend to cling on to each other and support each other. Plus, he was from the Kimberley. He was a Derby boy.

When you had conferences you met all your Aboriginal peers from the other offices across the state, and then you had a lot of dealings with people from central office in Canberra. So you build up this network of support with other Aboriginal people, and it was good, because you could always pick up the phone.

Social Security did have an Aboriginal recruitment policy and their target was two percent, and that's fine, but I think in offices where you have a high Aboriginal clientele the numbers should have been more like 50/50. But at least it was something, you know. And at the time I think Social Security was one of the biggest employers of Aboriginal people nationally.

People would have been initially apprehensive about me. Initially, non-Aboriginal people have a bit of apprehension when you're working as their peers, because you're Aboriginal. They don't know how to behave, but then after a while because you don't fit the stereotype, they no longer see you as an Aboriginal person. They see you as an equal. I used to always get, 'Oh, but Ollie, you're different.'

And I'd say, 'I'm not different. I'm an Aboriginal person. I don't fit your stereotype of Aboriginal people.' They think we go walkabout, unwashed—all that sort of stuff. If there was any attitude problems they were never directly open about it to me.

Around this time we were also really interested in what was happening in South Africa with the protests over apartheid. It had so many similarities to WA. I even became a member of CARE (the Campaign Against Racial Exploitation).

We used to go to demos a lot, me and Diana. Land rights, anti-apartheid, all that sort of thing. We went to these African dances at Subiaco and at the Town Hall as well, dancing to reggae music.

I remember Diana interviewing Kim Hughes when there was all that fuss about cricketers going to South Africa. She interviewed a black South African she'd met at a CARE dance as well.

The story said that blacks played soccer because they couldn't play cricket. Cricket was a white man's sport, anyway. She called me and said how thrilled she was. The story made it to page one in one of the eastern states papers.

Another story she did that got a good run—even made it into a South African newspaper—was about a white South African woman then living in WA, whose son was involved with the ANC. Seemed he'd gone missing in South Africa, and she was real worried he'd been picked up by the security forces and tortured. She had some reason to be worried. He'd spent seven years in jail because of his association with the ANC.

'Whites have different motives for leaving—many to get away from the blacks,' this woman said. 'I came to get away from the whites. But some of the racism I've heard about here makes my hair stand on end.'

Diana said she felt really bad later, because the woman did hear from her son. He was perfectly safe and had called her after seeing the article. The woman said she cringed with embarrassment. But Diana thought she'd been doing the right thing.

What I liked about Diana was that she was extremely interested in politics and used her journalism to write about issues she really cared about. She found out that the local rags were recruiting white South African journalists, so she called some black South African journalists over there and asked them if they'd been recruited. Then she wrote a story saying they hadn't been. She was a stirrer, but she was a rager, too. She also loved going bush and would do anything she could to score a trip out of Perth.

In 1985, Diana, another friend, Barb, and I drove from Perth to Alice Springs, up through the desert and across the Gunbarrel Highway. We rented a Falcon station wagon and hit the trail. Diana had organised for AAP to pay for the trip. She took her little laptop computer and wrote stories as we travelled. We had a wonderful night in the pub at Leonora, being shouted by the local gold miners—a father and his son. They were multi-millionaires, but when they went to Perth they'd only wear jeans and T-shirts. One night they couldn't get into a Perth nightclub because the bouncer said they had to wear ties. So the father took out his wallet and paid these other people who were being let in hundreds of dollars for their ties.

All along the way, people warned us of the 'wild natives' we might encounter further up the track. At the Giles Meteorological Station, almost on the NT/WA border, they were blunt to the point of rudeness. 'Well, we did think driving a station wagon up this way was a bit unusual,' one man said. 'Especially being three girls alone. Women ain't exactly known for their driving skills.'

Diana and I together had probably driven on more outback roads than most, and we had just come 2000 kilometres without a single mishap, sandhills

In Sydney for the '88 Bicentennial protest: Diana and Ollie.

Ollie and a mate after the '88 march.

Ollie's family: sitting - Mimi Dora, l to r: Mona, Rita, Dick, Lena and Joy.

Ollie, Dianne Williams and Dotty Cox in Broome.

Ronny and Diana.

Rev JRB Love and Worora people outside the church at Kunmunya.
(Photo courtesy of Mortlock Library of South Australia, State Library of SA.)

Ollie and Angelco dancing at the wedding.

Drinking champagne before the wedding.
Diana's sister Antoinette is pouring.

Ollie's father, Wila Kale.

Ollie and her father in Sabu, wearing traditional dress.

Ollie, her daughter Cindy, and her family in Sabu.

The bride and dancers at the Galichnik wedding, Macedonia.

Diana at work on American ship off Perth, mid '80s.

Diana in Central America.

Ollie and Diana at Cable Beach.

and corrugated roads not withstanding. So it was a pretty dumb comment.

But those jokes and racist comments began to wear thin after a while. At Giles, on a board hanging near the bar were two pieces of string. Next to one, it said, *wet string, rain*, the other, *dry string, sunny weather*, and where there was meant to be a third, it said, *string missing, blackfellas around.*

I'd had enough by then. I just picked up my stuff and walked out. 'We'll camp up the road,' I told the others.

In Alice Springs we went off to the casino and had a good night there. I met a gardiya who was working for DAA. We picked up this lad there. The three of us were sitting down and then this bird come up. She must have been watching him, she knew him and she knew his girlfriend. I don't even remember his name—mustn't have left much of an impression. But anyway, she come up and says, 'How's Tracey? (or whatever her name was) When's she coming back from Bali?' It was for our benefit, not for his. She was telling us, 'Listen here, girls, he's got a girlfriend.'

But the heavy politics in Alice Springs especially, got me down. At every party or gathering—usually full of white people working for Aboriginal organisations—that we went to, it was 'land rights this, land rights that'.

If I hear those bloody words again I'll be sick, I thought. *Doesn't anybody around here know how to have fun?*

Diana: I couldn't help but be interested in land rights. I did write other stories—about finance, the north-west shelf, the America's Cup, TV licence scandals. WA had some of the best stories to cover. And although AAP were lousy payers, they gave me a great deal of freedom.

But land rights was definitely one of the top political stories going. I also had a personal interest, after seeing what living back on their own land meant to Aboriginal people, such as those I'd stayed with at Borroloola and Noonkanbah. So naturally, I had to ask a question about land rights at the end of an exclusive interview I did with the then WA Minister with Special Responsibilities for Aborigines, Ian Wilson. It was a pretty innocuous interview that his office had arranged to publicise a social welfare scheme, but his few comments on land rights was what made page one lead in The West Australian.

'Aboriginal land rights cannot be realised,' he told me. The next step in the debate was up to Aboriginal people.

'I believe that the issue at stake is that Aboriginal people have to see and accept that the major task before them is to commend themselves to the rest of the population,' he said.

Not long after, Dorothy Parker, the mother of David Parker, the then Minister for Minerals and Energy, resigned from the Labor Party, of which she'd been a member for 37 years because, she said, of her anger and disappointment over the land rights issue.

'The Labor Party should have spent money to educate people in WA about land rights, and what awful lies were being told,' she said.

⁂

Around this time I received a phone call from an Aboriginal man in Kununurra. He told me that Jimmy Bieundurry had died of a heart attack. He was only 44. A huge funeral was being held for him at Noonkanbah. I sat at my desk and cried. Then I wrote his obituary. I thought of all the good times we'd had when I first went to the Kimberley. Camping under the stars with this wise, fun-loving man, when he'd tell stories that belonged to his Walmajarri people. Once, he, another friend and I camped in the sandhills in Broome. When we woke in the morning he was laughing merrily to himself. A teetotaller, he was extremely amused that we had been drinking from a flagon.

But the funny part was that we hadn't finished it. 'If it had been my people there wouldn't be anything left,' he said.

Once, during the exciting days of Noonkanbah, we were all staying the night at the kindergarten teacher's house in Fitzroy Crossing. I had a bad dream and woke with a start. I must have called out, because Jimmy came over to see what was wrong. I told him I'd felt as if somebody was pushing me into the river. A few days later we heard that a Fitzroy man who'd killed a man down south had been followed back home by men from his victim's tribe. He had been killed and thrown in the river. When Jimmy was around I always felt as if I was closer to the elements—to a spirituality grounded in the earth—what it might be like to be Aboriginal, I guess.

Jimmy had given up his positions with the NAC and the KLC so that he could move back to his out-station, Jalyirr, in the desert south of Lake Gregory. But he was made WA Commissioner with the Aboriginal Development Commission, which meant he had to travel for meetings. All he really wanted was to live down in his country with his family.

Building up Jalyirr as a cattle station was a pilgrimage to the country of his youth—the country he roamed with his family, looking for food and carrying out tribal obligations. It was there he had wanted to finish writing his autobiography. For the sake of Australian history I desperately hoped his full story would one day be told.

Since then, his wife, Olive, has become a leader in her own right, and at one stage was chairperson of her community at Christmas Creek station. She also has worked with the KLC. She is related to Josie Ningali Lawford, the talented performer. As Ollie found out later, just by coincidence, she's also her relative—her aunty, traditionally.

Jan called me before Sorry Day. She was having a good laugh. A friend had rung her to say we both made an appearance in John Pilger's latest book, *Hidden Agendas*. So when Ollie was in Sydney she bought the book for me.

The reference was on page 245, if you're interested: *Among Australia's best journalists are those who have confronted bigotry and apathy in the newsroom: Jan Mayman and Diana Plater in Western Australia; Graham Williams, Tony Hewett and David Marr in Sydney, and others.*

What Jan, I and other like-minded journalists found most frightening were people who didn't find some of these attitudes and the violent deaths pretty unusual for Australia in the second half of the twentieth century. Jan, for one, had to put up with threats—even at a press conference in front of scores of media—because she was prepared to challenge the status quo. It wasn't strange, then, that we had had our beliefs about a fair society totally destroyed.

The last trip I did before I left WA was back up to the Kimberley. I was doing stories on Purnululu and that crazy white elephant—the Ord irrigation scheme. I was staying in Kununurra and the family of a young Aboriginal man who had died in Broome prison, allegedly of a heart attack, came to visit me in the motel. They were desperate. They did not believe the cause of death suggested by the prison, and suspected some foul play. For this reason they wanted an independent post mortem, but they could not afford it.

They had asked the local Aboriginal Legal Service to help but had been told they did not see the need for the second post mortem. So they asked me to write a story to help their case, which I subsequently wrote.

When they left my motel room they were stopped by the proprietors and asked what business they had speaking to a white woman reporter.

By this stage I was leaving WA to work in Central America. I had become very interested in what was happening in Nicaragua with the revolutionary Sandinista government. The year before in Sydney I'd interviewed one of the women ministers, who had fought in the revolution against the right-wing dictator Somoza, and was fascinated by the political changes they were attempting there. I wanted to spend some time in Latin America and then base myself in the US, where I was born. I planned to be away for a couple of years.

Ollie took me to the airport. I wasn't sad at leaving Perth at all, only sad that we wouldn't be seeing each other for a long time. She took me to the door to walk out on the tarmac to the plane and started crying. 'You're leaving me,' she said, and she seemed so frail and alone. But it was too late to change my mind.

Ollie: I picked Diana up from the airport when she came back from Broome. She was staying one night then leaving the next day for Sydney, where she was going to work for a couple of months before going to Latin America.

My house was full of visitors so Diana slept in my bed. I was pretty upset because I was really going to miss her.

Diana: Nothing I saw or heard in Latin America—as horrific as the war and death squad murders were—made me feel quite as sick as I had felt covering those gut wrenching stories in WA, although it is a part of Australia I care greatly for. Perhaps it was because it was my own country that I was reporting on.

Trendy Kooris,
Latin America, Losing Babies
and Finding Files

8.

Trendy Kooris, Latin America, Losing Babies and Finding Files

Once upon a time in my mind
There was a man reaching
Out to the sky
But he reached too high
And bumped his head on the moon

I saw him fall to the ground
He says his head was spinning around
I told him that he fell
Cause the stars were shining into his eyes
I told him that he fell
Cause the stars were shining into his eyes

Oh me me my my
My me me my my
You look so funny
Dressed up in your old clothes and shoes
Oh me me my my
My me me my my
You look so funny
Dressed up in your old clothes and shoes

He says he's going to try it again
The sky is the limit until then
He'll be dodging
Bar rooms, bullets, batons and balloons.
He says if I see him fall again
To know that I'm his best friend
So I smiled at him and said I will be singing songs of it all
I smiled at him and said I will be singing songs of it all

Chorus: *The god is reaching for the time*
The man is fitting in the rhyme
If he fits in good
The god will turn into the moon
So his body go back into the ground
Will his spirit go floating around
It's a story to be told to children
With tears in their eyes
It's a story to be told to children
With tears in their eyes

Chorus

Oh Me Me My My

Arnold Smith

Ollie: *Dear Diana,*

As I didn't hear from you I decided to call your parents. Your dad answered the phone, 10/11/86. Yes, I was starting to worry—lots has happened, I don't know where to start. Firstly, I was seconded to Aboriginal Employment and Training for six months, 7 April to 30 Sept. I was working with James Morrison on a special project looking at employment for Aboriginal people in the hospitality and tourism industry. While working there we held a function, the purpose was to promote Aboriginal potential. The function was in the form of a fashion parade. Boans sponsored us with their garments. Tony Barlow's, and of course the emu leather garments. There were sixteen models, eight males, eight females. It was great and very successful.

Since that function in August we had three other modelling jobs, two for the Perth Rotary Club and one for the ADC conference held in Perth. We have three fashion parades coming up this month, 22, 29 and 30 November, for the Fremantle Expo. Another ADC ball at the Sheraton Hotel, and we'll be doing a parade. It's all go, go, go.

So now I'm back at Social Security at Midland. Mind you, Employment wanted me to stay on. I declined. I wanted to *come back to my old job. I find this more rewarding and I do get job satisfaction.*

You know what?? You were right about black men. They ARE better lovers. I met this guy from Canberra. Uptown black, as we call them. Married. I met him here in Perth during the ALO conference. Unfortunately I was still at Employment, therefore I wasn't available to attend. Anyway, they arranged a dinner for the ALOs at the casino. I was invited. I was talking to this lad. Because he lived in Canberra and was married, I decided to go for it. No ties. No involvement. No commitments. This was on a Wednesday. Thursday I missed him. I went raging with the rest of the gang. Friday I saw the lad again. That was okay. I raced him home, as he was flying out that night at twelve. We sat talking, then I said, 'You gonna fuck me or what?'

He said, 'You're so direct.'

I told him, 'Being direct you get a direct answer, yes or no.' Raced him off again and took him to the airport. When we got there he'd missed his plane. I thought, this is good—however, there was another plane five minutes later. Since then he's been phoning here every day. He came over again for four days and stayed with me. It was beautiful. Cindy fell in love with him, they got on really well. He's still ringing, not as often. Unfortunately my plans backfired on me. We both feel the same way about each other. I suppose even though we don't want to admit it, we fell in love with each other. Like they say, time heals all wounds. Hope so. I have been trying to keep busy and to push him out of my mind, as I know I can't have him (being married). So I have tried to remedy the situation by seeing other guys.

I went over to Adelaide for a week, 6–10 October, to sit the test for SAIT Task Force. I was impressed with the institute and the lecturers. At this stage I still haven't heard if I've been accepted or not. If I do get accepted I shall decline. I met two nice guys, one from Darwin and the other a black from England. He was yummo.

When I came back from Adelaide I met up with an old friend I've known for years (white guy). Anyway, he's been wining and dining me, sending me flowers at work three days running. He tells me he's in love with me and I had to have an honest talk to him. I explained I don't want any commitment and I do not wish to change my lifestyle, and still want to see other male friends, and that I like my independence and freedom too much to get involved with one guy. He hears what I'm saying but refuses to believe me. I've never had a bloke who's madly in love with me. I told him I don't need him at this stage of my life, but maybe two years from now. I'm enjoying my life too much.

Cindy and I are going around Australia on a Kangaroo Pass by Ansett. Darwin for Christmas, leaving Perth 19 December, Cairns for New Year, down to Sydney, Canberra and Melbourne, return home 26 Jan.

Met up with Ronnie Ejai in Adelaide. We ran amok.

I'm writing this at work so I'd better do some work now.

Love
Merry Christmas
Happy New Year

Ollie

Diana: It was great to receive this letter from Ollie when I was away in Latin America and then New York. Ollie had included a photo of herself modelling the emu leather fashions. She looked gorgeous. She also put in a picture, and some background from a newspaper report, of the man in Canberra.

Based in Nicaragua, I covered stories about the effects of the revolution and the Sandinista/Contra war. I travelled throughout Latin America and also wrote on the political situation in Mexico, El Salvador, Guatemala, Honduras, Colombia, Paraguay and Peru.

After even only a short time in Latin America, I realised how little we foreign journalists really know or understand about the brutal conditions many people have to live under, so much more than we could ever experience. After all, most of us had plane tickets out.

Although I did a great deal of research and had background briefings before I went there, it was still a shock to see the situation first-hand.

I had started taking Spanish lessons from a wonderful Mexican teacher three months before I left. And in an attempt at becoming better informed I went down to Canberra to do an interview with Bill Hayden, then Minister for Foreign Affairs, who, by all accounts, was sympathetic to the Sandinista cause.

I borrowed my cousin's best Dress for Success suit but that didn't seem to help much with Hayden. He appeared bored with my questions and relieved when the interview was over. I was nervous and asked hesitant questions and his answers were suitably general.

'The Labor Party is a democratic socialist party, and by its nature is going to take a global overview of developments,' he said. 'It's going to be concerned about incidences of conflict—we've expressed concerns about developments in El Salvador, Nicaragua and between countries of Central America, largely on the basis of the fundamental sovereign rights of nations, and also issues of humans rights within nations.'

When I asked him how the US felt about Australia's largely pro-Sandinista stand, he said, 'If you want to know about American reactions (to Australia's position), you'd better ask them—it's understandable that they would have a preoccupation with that region.'

To me, Hayden pointed out that Australia's position on Nicaragua was as much as could be expected considering the distance we are from Central America, and the lack of trade and aid between the two countries. Also, there were 'very few Australian nationals' there.

'Those who go down there are usually idealistic young Australians like yourself,' he said.

It was not surprising that Hayden was careful in his wording to me. Apparently three years before, when he had spoken in favour of better relations with the Sandinistas, he had been rapped over the knuckles by the Americans, who told him to stop meddling in their backyard.

The head of Associated Press in Sydney had warned me before I left, 'You can't cover that part of the world without talking to the Americans.'

So before leaving Sydney I'd had a meeting with the US consul and his press attache. I had explained that because I was born in Boston (while Dad was undertaking a Neiman Fellow, a journalism scholarship, at Harvard) I had a US passport as well as an Australian one.

'Don't carry both of them together,' he warned. 'They may think you're a spy.' I kind of liked that idea!

I had some amazing briefings in Washington, one of which was with the so-called 'leader' of the Contras, based in the Pentagon. He was a short, dark Latino, possibly of Cuban background.

The morning of the interview I caught the subway a block or so from my hotel straight to the Pentagon. A soldier who was waiting to meet me marched me down a very long corridor. He was joined by at least three others, who kept grinning at me as I asked questions and took notes. (I wasn't allowed to use a tape recorder.) The 'leader' virtually told me nothing. No, of course there was no American aid to the Contras. No guns, no money, nothing. Well, perhaps only humanitarian aid. It was while I was in Nicaragua that the Ollie North story, that showed Congress's aid to the Contras, was finally unravelled.

While there (as in Australia) as a freelance print journalist, the one big advantage I had was my freedom, being able to get around the countryside and hear how people felt. I remember walking with a friend in the early hours of the morning outside a small town in northern Nicaragua. We were hoping to get a lift to a farming co-operative. My friend asked a woman standing in her doorway if we could have a cup of coffee. She agreed and invited us in. But when I went to pay—presuming she was a coffee seller—she wouldn't take the money. Probably thinking I was an American, she said, 'Your country is fighting our country, but that doesn't mean we are at war.'

I was hugely impressed by the bravery of the journalists of those countries—like the defiant Colombian journalists who held protest strikes when the drug barons murdered one of the country's most respected columnists.

In contrast to the neverending fear that they must have felt, my nerves were only tested when I hitched a ride on a coffee truck into a Contra camp in Honduras. There I met the commander of the camp, Commandant Invisible, whose name was embroidered on his shirt. I laughed to myself about how he wasn't living up to his name, as he showed me his 'museum' of landmines and other war memorabilia. It wasn't funny though, thinking about two sisters I'd interviewed from an orphanage in northern Nicaragua, on the other side of the mountains from the Honduran Contra camp. They had seen their parents massacred by the Contra. Yet they told me their story totally unemotionally. I have an image of them standing on the bridge outside their village waving to us, dry eyed. It gave me some sense of what it must have been like to be a survivor of the massacres in my own country.

As a journalist, my main worry was of being sucked into the potent messages and possible propaganda of the political groups I felt most sympathy for, where everywhere soldiers from both sides told you they were fighting for The Fatherland. I was worried that I was only believing what I wanted to believe, but not what was necessarily the truth.

I was concerned about going out on a limb against what others told me they thought was the truth; that maybe I was falling into a trap. I felt my beliefs were being challenged to the core, and I was left in doubt about what was reality and what the role of a journalist should be.

It was when I went on a hazardous journey to the Atlantic Coast of Nicaragua, involving a twelve hour overland and river journey to Bluefields, then a six hour ride up the coast on a confiscated Honduran fishing boat to some remote settlements, that the full extent of the war struck me. I was writing an article about the 'autonomy' movement that was calling for a form of independence for this half of the country. Local elections were being held by the Sandinistas, and there were rumours they were going to be sabotaged by the Contras. At one settlement only one woman came in to vote, because the rest of the people were either pro Contra, or scared that if they voted they would be killed by the Contras.

The bravery of the Nicaraguan people always amazed and encouraged me—the way they lived with fear and war and its devastating effects—physically, socially and psychologically. The way they coped with both an economic embargo and a war being waged against them, and yet still maintained their humanity. If the Contras set fire to the ferry to Bluefields it didn't stop people catching the next one. This is where all transport between settlements is by boat, so what else can you do when there is no other way to get from one side of the country to the other?

Back in Bluefields, the main town of the region, I felt as if I was in Broome again. It is a melting pot of Creoles, Mestizos (Latin/Indians) and Indians living in run down, picturesque houses, in suburbs with names like Old Bank, Beholden and Cotton Tree. The 'coast' is a land of jungles and rainforests, wide rivers and the Caribbean Sea, where in the wet season it rains relentlessly, and people speak their own version of English.

The interesting makeup of the Atlantic side of the country comes from the Indians of the Miskito, Sumo and

Rama tribes. And Africans, brought from Jamaica by the British to work in the settlements as overseers and clerical staff last century. Unusually, the British, who were more accustomed to using blacks as slaves, turned them in Nicaragua into a petite bourgeoisie. They also created kingdoms of Miskito Indians, using them as the dominant power over the other Indian tribes.

In Bluefields, I interviewed Ray Hodgson. For two months after the Sandinista revolution in 1979, he ruled the quaint former British outpost. Although he never fired a shot, he had his own private army. Anybody who didn't like the way things were done risked being jailed, and the key thrown away. The country was in chaos. The capital, Managua, had been bombed by the forces of Somoza, the former leader, and so the remote Atlantic Coast was not the top priority for those on the Pacific side.

'It was like a party,' Hodgson told me. 'I founded an army of 500 soldiers and we set up our own government. We had the arms that Somoza's National Guard had left behind.'

The new Sandinista government didn't know what to do with these Atlantic Coast people calling for autonomy (or land rights), and some were jailed. Some left to start their own Contra guerilla groups. But later the government reappointed these leaders and started to work with them to grant a form of self-government. These moves were thwarted, however, when the Sandinistas lost their first election, and now a conservative government again runs the country.

Bluefields in 1987 was a town—like Broome—that you visited for the people. It was a town where everybody knew each other, but addressed even their relatives as Miss Francie or Mr Joe. At the weekend, Creoles dressed their children like black angels in ringlets and dresses with puffed sleeves to go to church. It was a pretty sight to see them walking there with their bibles under their arms and carrying parasols to protect themselves from the sun. It was a town where Rastas—locals who have taken on the religion of Jamaica—talk about 'marijuana coming in from the sea'. This really meant dope had been thrown overboard by Colombian smugglers chased by the coastguard, and the strong tides had brought it into the port.

More than anything, Bluefields was music. Even the local radio station—next to the Bluefields Hotel—used a large loudspeaker to entertain passers by with reggae, ska, calypso and country and western songs. (I think I sent them a copy of Pudding's tape.) The local bands sing—in English, Creole and Spanish—of bananas, local places, love and politics.

When I got back to civilisation (Managua) I found out that an American had been shot down from a plane flying to Nicaragua while dropping supplies to the Contras. It was the best story for ages. I sent a telex: *On days like this I feel like giving up journalism, having been totally out of touch when Hasenfus dropped from the sky.* The foreign editor called and said he'd read my telex out to the news conference, and they had all had a good laugh. He then asked me to do a follow-up and cover the American's trial. Gradually the whole arms for Contras story unfolded.

Despite American aid to the Contras, it wasn't really the war so much as the economic embargo by the US, that finally brought down the Sandinistas. They were voted out in an election by people fed up with rationing, empty stores and lack of medical supplies. I was highly critical of them when I was in Nicaragua, but maybe my expectations of revolutionary governments were too high, and too much based on an Australian idea of democracy. When, after Hurricane Mitch, I saw on television the current president covered in gold chains and riding around in his big, black car, I felt sick to the stomach. Somebody said he looked like he'd been poured into it.

I often felt like Alice in Wonderland when I was in Nicaragua, and particularly when different people described the same scene or story to me in totally different ways, depending on where their political allegiances lay. When Paul Keating made that reference to Australia becoming a Banana Republic, for once I didn't laugh. And to anybody who did, I suggest a quick trip to Nicaragua, Guatemala or even Argentina for their next holiday.

Ollie: I was in Perth the whole time Diana was away. Most of the time I worked for Commonwealth was spent with Social Security. I did do a six month contract with DEET, that was back in '86. In '87 I did a twelve month contract with what is now called WA Department of Training. It was the state equivalent of the Commonwealth DEET.

My time at Social Security in Midland was really good and we ended up developing good relationships. There were mixed races of people including the Scottish woman, Koreans, Indians and Aborigines. I think you can turn things around to a positive way and change people's attitudes by the way you behave as an Aboriginal person. And I like to think that happened. I realise sometimes you can't change people's attitudes, but you can change people's behaviour in the workplace.

Around this time I started mainly going out with Aboriginal guys. I fell into the Diana trap of going for unemployed musicians. There were some nice ones—Les, from No Fixed Address, Merv, who I ran into again when I came to Sydney for Sorry Day. Me and Leanne were just cruising in Perth.

I went to Sydney in January 1988 for the protests to the Bicentenary. I had a really good feeling about that trip over there. In my opinion it was the first time Aboriginal people were united as a nation. The march was very moving. I felt choked up, my body was covered in goose bumps. All those sorts of feelings. It was like a reunion for Diana, Barb and I, of the Gunbarrel Highway trip.

We camped at the Aboriginal Tent Embassy at Lady Macquarie's chair, with the flag as a backdrop. That was amazing. We woke surrounded by picnickers waiting for the re-enactment of the First Fleet to come sailing down the harbour. They were taking photos of us.

There was all this chanting and it was like Zulu chanting, which we heard coming over the hill as people marched down towards the Tent Embassy. We drove to Redfern and joined the big march. What amazed me was, even though we got virtually no media coverage, there were so many ethnic groups that joined the march. There was thousands of people. And just looking up to the skyscrapers and on top of the buildings, there were Aboriginal flags flying. Coming through the tunnel the chanting just echoed and it gave you goose bumps. Everything echoed because of the overhead bridge near Central railway station. Everyone was singing out. The Aboriginal people went first, then the different migrant groups marched after.

We didn't see the others coming into the city from all over the country, but that was meant to be pretty spectacular. We watched the convoy on TV. All these Aboriginal people coming from across the nation, that was so moving.

Diana was still just the same Diana. It's always nice meeting up with her, especially because of her hospitality. She always made sure we had a good time. We went to a pub in Redfern. The three of us, with Barb, joined up again. We met the territory mob—my cousin, Georgie Smith, and Pudding's cousin, Marky Manolis. I think George was working for the NLC and he'd come down from Darwin on the convoy. There'd been a death on the way, so that was sad for them.

We went to La Perouse a lot. One night they had a great concert out there.

I caught up with Les when I was in Sydney. He came over to Diana's place and we had a big feed, cooking up all this seafood we'd bought from the Fish Markets.

Another night we went to see an old friend, Doug Parkinson, performing. We got pretty drunk that night. I had a ball.

Diana: When I got home in late 1987, Ollie told me she would be coming to Sydney for the Aboriginal protests planned against the Bicentenary celebrations for January 1988. People were planning to come from all over the country and it was going to be something really exciting. I knew we would be doing more than going in street marches. There was going to be a lot of partying, too.

My first impression that the mood of the country had changed was when I visited an Aboriginal art exhibition down at the Rocks. I went with a friend who had been working with Aboriginal people in the east Kimberley, and she seemed to be up on the latest stuff.

It seemed as if everybody was there—the Whitlams, Charlie Perkins, Pat O'Shane, politicians, artists and activists. All of a sudden, it seemed things Aboriginal—especially art—was the height of fashion. What a shock, after living in Western Australia during the height of the anti-land rights campaigns by the mining lobby, and the deaths in custody!

Everywhere you looked there were people wearing T-shirts with Aboriginal designs. On every wall there was a dot painting. The prices being paid were astronomical. Oh, why hadn't I bought some art when I lived in the NT, and went out to Arnhem Land and other communities reasonably regularly? I could have kicked myself. But I still had my fair share of treasures—most of which had been given to me or I'd bought directly from the artist. Each has a distinct memory attached to it.

I felt pretty alien being back in Australia. When we got together Ollie and I talked about what we'd been through over the past eighteen months. I didn't feel as if I was the same person any more.

I didn't think Ollie had changed, but I felt like I had changed from being in Latin America. Seeing the brutality there and knowing what an amazing country we have here, I felt strongly we could learn from Latin America's experiences.

But to be with her again was really refreshing—somebody who loved all the black, red and yellow paraphernalia, but wasn't at all concerned about being seen as trendy. She knew just how to have fun. My car seemed to know how to get from my little house in Ultimo to La Perouse, where a lot of the action was, on its own.

Being at La Perouse during this time made me realise why I had come home. This was still my country and my struggle, even if I wasn't Aboriginal. I had been determined to be back in Australia for the protests.

As more than two million people in Sydney celebrated 200 years of white history, a ceremony older than time itself was taking place in the original spot where the country was 'discovered' by the British.

Over on Sydney Harbour, Prince Charles and Princess Di joined politicians and the public to watch a spectacular display of fireworks. But at Botany Bay, to the south, the air was filled with the sound of clap sticks, the beat of bare feet on the earth and monotonous chanting as traditional people from the far north helped the Aboriginal people of Sydney renew their culture, so closely connected to the land.

It was a ceremony that very few of the white people of this 'great, south land' would have been the slightest bit aware of, or, in fact, even interested in. For despite the growing trendiness of things Aboriginal, there was still a huge gap in understanding between the world's oldest culture and one of the youngest western countries.

The 1988 protests were to let people know that Australia's got a black history.

Ollie: In September 1988, my single days came to an end—for ten years—when I married Kim Bin Amat. Gwen didn't say anything when I got married to Kim. But she was that kind of person. She'd say, 'This is your life.' They were a bit heartbroken about me and Dave finishing up. They were very fond of him. Kim had been my childhood sweetheart and Gwen had sent me to school in Perth, partly to get me away from him. He did an apprenticeship in boilermaking in Broome, then he left town. He came to visit me when he knew I was no longer with Dave and then he moved in.

It was my second time round, and I hadn't really wanted to get married in a church at Pallotines—my old school— but Kim wanted to. He was also separated—with grown-up twin daughters. We had a talk to the priest and he wasn't against us getting married in the church. I know Diana felt a bit strange though, standing up there near the altar, dressed in black.

We had the reception at Barb's place. My friends made the food—lots of curries. We didn't need catering at all. Pudding played in the band. Adrian Tolentino, my younger brother, was there. I told him, 'It's my wedding and you have to get drunk.' He was only a young fella. So he ended up getting on the drums and playing. Adrian was the only one there from my foster family.

Diana stayed for two weeks. She did an interview with Peter Dowding, who was Premier then. She said at the end of the interview, because she asked some questions about land rights and so on, he said, 'Just the same old Di. Still asking about land rights.' She went up to Broome as well, to do a story on Lord McAlpine.

Baamba came for the wedding and ended up staying for about twelve months altogether. He'd arrive home by taxi in the middle of the night. There'd be a knock on the door and he'd come to our bedroom cause he wanted money to pay the taxi. 'Sis, are you there?' One time Kim got up and he knew he had ten dollars and 50 dollars, so he pulled out this money to give to Baamba to pay for the taxi and apparently he heard the taxi leave. He found out in the morning that Baamba had taken off in the taxi, because he gave him 50 dollars, not the ten dollars. The lad had money so he cruised back to the casino.

Kim and I moved back to the Kimberley in December that year. Kim had been a road train and truck driver. He worked in all the pastoral stations across the Top End. He'd come in and pick up the cattle. The racism he's confronted there is terrible. Aboriginal people are the backbone of the industry—and they're not allowed to sit down and have a cup of tea. The cruelty on the stations is too much.

When Aboriginal stockmen started to get paid equal wages, a lot of stations got rid of them. The stations would rather pay a white man. Tourists are told that the white station owners looked after 'their' Aborigines, and that it was the Labor government that sold them out by forcing them to be paid equal wages. I reckon it should be compulsory for tourists to the north to read *The Unlucky Country*.

I really admired people like Jack Davis. You look at his life. He could have been a lot more bitter, but he got his message across in a subtle way. There's no bitterness. I don't know if I could have survived that era, working in stockcamps, droving. But the racism by the so-called sympathetic whites living in Aboriginal communities these days also leaves me cold.

We first went to live in Kununurra, where I was still working for Social Security. I worked in the Kununurra region, servicing the east Kimberley, so I went to all the communities in the east Kimberley to check on their needs and oversee the 'work for the dole' scheme (CDEP). I was the Aboriginal liaison manager.

Aboriginal people in those days were the only ones who worked for the dole. People with disabilities were employed on light duties. CDEP was administered by ATSIC, and Aboriginal people would be paid the equivalent of the dole, but they weren't counted in the statistics as being unemployed. So the unemployment figures were always false.

Once, I went out to Balgo (south of Halls Creek) on my own. I was a bit anxious, because the community adviser said the men there had just bought a whole lot of grog and there was going to be trouble—and I'd better get out. He said to go to Mulan. There was this back road to Mulan and I didn't know the road. He said he'd ring and let them know I was coming. His remark was, 'I'm going to lock my doors tonight, have a glass of wine and go to bed with my gun.' He told me I had to get out of Balgo. So I ended up driving off to Mulan.

The woman there was ropable. She said, 'I'm going to complain to the boss. How dare he send a woman out here on her own?'

Just before I started in Kununurra, ATSIC had pulled all their white staff out of Balgo. They had what they call 'riots'. Some of the men damaged one of the planes and they used to steal the cars and wreck them. They ran riot in the shop. Apparently one of the nurses got raped out there. Then after that they said, 'Make sure you lock your car.' When I started going out there, I thought, *no, I'm not going to lock the car. I'm not going to fight them for it. They can take it.* I never locked the car and I never ever had any problems when I went to Balgo. Cause I think if you show people respect, you get respect back. If I was a community person and I saw a stranger coming into my community and locking their car, I'd go and break into their car because I'd feel insulted. If they're going to steal it, they'll steal it. They'll just smash a window.

Okay, I went out one time and even the chairperson was drunk. But I never felt threatened by them and I used to enjoy going out there. All this wah, wah, wah, I got about the Balgo mob. I was there when they ran amok one night and I was staying out there. They never came and hassled us.

Some white people who work in those places are weird for starters. They're running from something, or they're drop-outs from their own society. Just look at all the rip-offs.

My colleague, Bob Marney, and I used to do all these trips into Purnululu. Diana came with us once on one trip. We went to Turkey Creek, where Ethel, a Beagle Bay orphanage girl, was the community adviser. It's good to see somebody from their own country working there. Then Argyle stopped us having access through that back country near Glen Hill. Another time me and Bob went down the highway, through Halls Creek, Nicholson and then up the Duncan Highway, and in all those communities the pumps weren't working and all the creeks were dry. They had no water, so me and Marney never had a bath for four days and we stunk. It was hot. That was typical of the lack of services to those communities.

After Kununurra I worked in Alice Springs for twelve months. I was the JET adviser—Jobs, Education and Training. It was a program specifically targeted to sole parents, getting sole parents to enter or re-enter the workforce, and being based in Alice Springs, we used to go to Queensland for training. We also used to go on DEET work information tours. If Aboriginal people were interested in an enterprise or whatever, this program was able to take them to where it was established and they could look at it for themselves, what would work or what wouldn't work.

All over the place were these terrible community advisers. It is hard enough for Aboriginal people in communities, but when you get non-Aboriginal people working and living there, and then you've got that division and friction between the whitefellas, it makes it even more difficult. So what hope is there for blackfellas?

And then, of course you, had all the hawkers that were ripping-off and making Aboriginal people dependent on them. For example, they'd buy stuff on credit—Aboriginal people were constantly indebted to them. What used to happen was that these hawkers would have all these clients' post going to their postal address, and even if these clients were in communities in the bush, their address was with this person in town. What they used to do was illegal. What he would do was cash their cheques for them, take what he was owed and give the balance. Sometimes that balance might have been forty dollars, and so then what would happen was he would give them more credit, as they did not have enough money and it was just an ongoing rip-off thing.

Even though I worked all these years for government I had always specialised in the Aboriginal area and services. Then I seriously started thinking of climbing the corporate ladder and getting into mainstream, because I thought I could be just as useful to my people in mainstream. (Even through the JET adviser was a mainstream position, the majority of my clients were Aboriginal.) Plus, I wanted to expand, and I also didn't want to be labelled that that's all I could do. I wanted to get into mainstream, to further develop myself, have more opportunities and to have transferable skills. If I was manager in mainstream I could go anywhere as a manager, in private or whatever.

So I did this middle management course while I was in Alice Springs. Part of that course was that you had to do a project. This meant you had to be placed in a management position for three months to consolidate that training. This is known as a placement. I always considered my boss, Peter

Doutre, as one of my mentors, and I suppose I was able to say to him, 'Look, regarding my application...'

He used to be very supportive and encouraging, and I said to him, 'What is going to stop me from getting the job as a manager?'

And he said, 'Experience.'

And I said, 'Okay, what are you going to do about it?'

And he said, 'I can put you into the RASU, which is the Remote Area Services Unit.' That was the Aboriginal Services Section then, for the remote areas. And even though it was an Aboriginal section, it also had non-Aboriginal people in that section as well, something like seventeen staff. He said, 'I can put you in there for three months.'

So I went in there, and with this legal stuff that was happening, I thought, *well, we are going to have to address it.* Then going into that section as a manager, I made a decision that we didn't change anybody's address. The hawkers used to come and say they wanted to change so and so's address, and I made the decision that we didn't change anybody's address unless that individual is there themselves, and comes in to tell us. I said that nobody is allowed to change an address unless that individual is with them and agrees to it. I was really glad, because my manager was very supportive too. He agreed with it.

So this hawker didn't like it and so he saw me. And we said, 'No, that is the rules. If you don't like the rules that's tough, we don't have a problem with you coming in, but you have to have that individual with you.' And he knew that was going to be impossible, because most of those people are in the bush. And that was the way he used to con those people. That bloke was really ropeable with us, he hated us. We couldn't prosecute him because we had to have the individual lodge a complaint. They weren't prepared to do that.

Those hawkers still con Aboriginal people. They get their cheques, and might only give them a ration like bread and meat, stuff like that. You know what kind some Aboriginal people, they think they're being looked after, but they are getting exploited and abused.

I've been really lucky in working in these departments because I've met some wonderful people. My manager in Alice was one of my mentors. He was a special person because he used to encourage me, believe in me. There were management jobs coming up. He'd say, 'Ollie, there's a management job in Hedland (or wherever), why don't you apply?'

I'd say, 'I'm not ready yet.' I didn't want to fail. I'd always make excuses. Then I thought, *if he believes in me, I must be able to do it.* I started believing that I could do a middle management job. He was a person who was very innovative, a lateral thinker. Every time I had a problem I'd go in and see him. I'd come out of his office thinking I never had a problem at all.

Diana: It wasn't long before I was back working on Aboriginal issues. In 1989 I got a job for a few months as a producer/trainer on an Aboriginal program, *First in Line*, at SBS TV. I worked mainly with one of the trainees, a Torres Strait Islander journalist, Constance Saveka. She sucked me right in the first day I met her, by telling me her husband-to-be would have to pay the bride price of a pig to her family when she got married. 'Oh really?' I said, and she burst out laughing.

Constance always called me Plater. On one program we did together, where we visited Thursday Island, we had such a long list of acknowledgements we decided to add in the name of my father's dog and give him both our surnames. Everybody was asking, 'Who the hell is Benny Plater Saveka?'

The program was fun to work on, if not frustrating, and others who worked on it too have gone on to fame.

One day I was waiting for the train at Edgecliff station when I saw Robert, who had just started on the program as a researcher, and naturally we started talking. He told me he lived at Palm Beach but was staying at Rose Bay. I was staying at my parents' place while they were overseas—the house where my cousins used to live as kids.

'What was your last name again?' he asked, the penny dropping.

'Not Geoff Plater's daughter?'

'No, Ron's.'

So we worked out we had a connection. His Aunty Amy had been my cousins' maid when they were kids. I remembered Amy really well. Of course, because she was the first Aboriginal person I ever met. And now here I was, training Aboriginal and Torres Strait Islander people to be TV journalists. Being a trendy, 'do-gooder' white and working with Robert. It was an extremely weird feeling. We laughed about it though.

Robert's mother was taken away when she was a small child. Taken off with Amy and her sisters to the home for Aboriginal girls at Cootamundra in south-west NSW. I'm not sure if they ever saw their mother again. But as a teenager Robert's mother went to work in the home of a disabled woman in Rose Bay. She lived there until the woman died.

After my stint at SBS I took a holiday in the Kimberley and went to stay with Ollie in Kununurra. She was working for the Department of Social Security. She had to visit some communities in the east Kimberley, including Purnululu, and we drove through that wild country together—to Glen Hill, on the back road behind the Argyle diamond mine. She and her work colleague would attend meetings while I read my book. Then we'd camp at night. It was great to be back in that country again. It was also great to see Ollie in the bush, as I'd always known her in Perth before that. She was a real bushie too, and a good driver!

Three months later I met my husband. We'd met at a party in Oxford Street but only pretty briefly. We really met at another birthday party. It was full of men standing next to a table overloaded with children's party food—cupcakes, fairy bread, potato chips. I thought they were going to offer us dark green lime cordial and give us a party bag full of teeth-wrenching lollies when we left.

I'd gone there with a friend and my brother. We'd been at a Christmas party for an Aboriginal women's organisation and I'd won—for the first time ever—the raffle, a stunning turquoise sarong. It must have been my lucky night. We ended up taking the whole of the party back to a photographer friend's party that we thought needed livening up. My now husband asked if he could come with us, and at the party we started kissing and didn't stop all night. From there we went on to Round Midnight in the Cross, where we got even drunker and danced and danced until four in the morning.

I took him to our farm at Foxground the first weekend after we met. I was waiting for him in the kitchen at home. I must have been doing the washing up because, looking out the window above the sink, I saw him coming through the gate. So brown and wearing white shorts and a singlet (just like we used to wear on the farm). He had long hair then. He was sort of whistling to himself as he knocked on the door. I guess he was looking forward to a weekend away. It was pretty idyllic, I must say.

I remember the farm as a kid as being golden-green, the creek's water icy, refreshing. Life was good. We had wonderful, healthy tans, wore cut-down jeans and tank tops and big straw hats. Had bits of grass clenched between our teeth as we wandered across the paddocks, climbing over rocks in the creek, scrambling through lantana and out to the other side of the overgrown bush. Finding cows even further back than I thought we could.

The farm was always a great place for parties. I had a farewell party there when I left Canberra to go to the Kimberley. We were marooned by rain and sat up all night playing cards. Finally we ran out of booze and cigarettes, and somebody walked across the swollen paddocks and hitched into town to replenish our supplies.

That weekend was like the ones of my childhood and my early days in journalism. We followed the creek up as far as we could, taking our clothes off and swimming through the deeper patches. Watching Amelia now as she plays in the creek, jumping from stone to stone, talking to herself in her imaginary games, it always takes me back to that weekend. The weather went cold on the Sunday and we made a fire. He moved into my house a month later. The only time we were apart was when I spent a night away at Bellingen for work.

We got married at the farm five months after we met. I'd finally met a man who really wanted to settle down with me, have children, and was totally responsible and independent. Not only that, he was a great handyman, so my mother approved. He was also Yugoslav, or Macedonian to be more correct. But that wasn't going to make any difference to multicultural me. And, of course, this was just before the Balkans blew up.

Our wedding was a sensational party. Yugoslavs and all the rest, dancing to a local rock-and-roll band. Lots of meat to keep them happy. Such a good mixture of family, old friends and his friends. Lots of kids. Ollie came to be my matron of honour and wore this beautiful light blue linen and chiffon suit that I'd bought in LA, on the way back from Cuba. With boots and a great navy hat my cousin, Jan, lent her. I have a fantastic photo of her dancing with one of the Yugoslavs, cigarette in one hand, the other on her hat.

I wore white! That was Mum's idea. I'd bought a floral cocktail dress. She hated it. So I succumbed, possibly for the last time. Well, it wasn't really white. More like ivory, really.

I've matured enough now to realise that it doesn't matter what colour my husband's skin is, he's the best for me.

Ollie: When I first met Diana's husband he and I hit it off straight away. Love the way he says her name—Diaarna!

Diana's wedding was great—the beautiful setting at the farm and then later on dancing at the reception. It was a mad mixture. I found with Diana's family that they always welcomed me—as her friend, but also as part of the family. That's what I liked about her family.

It was really nice to see Diana again. I was living in Kununurra then. We had champagne when we were getting dressed for the wedding, which put us in the right mood for the ceremony.

I got to meet all of Diana's family. I'd met her mum and dad, who everybody called Ron, before. I got on well with Diana's Uncle Geoff—with his scotch. We were the two smokers sitting out on the verandah together.

Ronny Ejai stayed too. He was living in Sydney then. He caught a train to Gerringong and then a taxi to the reception. He missed the ceremony but stayed for three days after the wedding. Like Baamba! We were there for a few days at the farm. We used to sit around the barbeque fire at night—Diana's older sister, Lindy, and her six kids. Her daughter, Mardi, and I got on well too. It was like blackfellas, all these people living in the house. Kids and all. Ronny got stuck out in the bedroom one day and was banging on the door. Alex, one of Diana's nephews, said, 'We got two Rons here, one black, one white.' We called one Ron and one Lateron.

I was happy for Diana that she'd found somebody. She'd gone through all that time alone, running amok for a while. I thought the relationship with Pudding would never work anyway, and I think I always told her that. I knew that at one time she did love him very much. I used to think she was mad! Like towards the end of their relationship he was into self-destruct. Kim couldn't make it to the wedding. It's funny how Diana and I settled down around the same time.

Her husband's always been happy that I'm coming over when I visit. I met his friends as well—two of them brought me down to the farm from Sydney. One night we went to the Sheraton for drinks with some other friends. Another time we went to listen to blues at a pub in Balmain.

Diana: Our honeymoon was more like a journey of discovery than the normal honeymoon of two weeks at a resort sipping cocktails by the pool. (That's what we do these days!) I was determined to find out more about Uncle Bob Love (the revolutionary missionary), and it was also a way to show my husband the country. He'd never been out of Sydney before, having only been in Australia since the end of 1987.

First we went to Darwin and the eastern fringes of Kakadu and Arnhem Land. Then on to Kununurra to stay with Ollie and Kim. I'd decided I wanted to visit Kunmunya, Uncle Bob's abandoned mission. It's about 240 kilometres north-east of Derby and only accessible by boat, and now part of an Aboriginal reserve.

For Christmas my father had given me a book, *Our Year in the Wilderness*, about Michael and Susan Cusack, who became known as the 'wilderness couple' after living alone in the bush for a year. Their experience—or ordeal—had been the brainwave of adventurer Dick Smith, who had chosen Kunmunya as the site for this experiment.

The couple had done the last leg of their journey from Koolan Island, BHP's big heap of iron ore which forms part of the Buccaneer Archipelago, on a ten-metre launch owned by Roland and Mulawai Long. I called Roland, who was the island's tugboat skipper, and he agreed to take us to Kunmunya as the family were going on a fishing trip anyway.

It wasn't long after we left the island that all we could see was blue sea meeting the horizon, and the occasional sea snake or turtle trying to hide under seaweed. It was deceptively peaceful, and hard to imagine why the maps were dotted with names like Rip Rock, Cascade Bay, Swirl Shoal, Tide Rip Islands and The Graveyard, where around 50 pearl divers have died in their quest for the jewel of the sea. But countless wrecked boats were a legacy to the maze of hidden reefs, uninhabited islands, wild seas and extreme tidal changes, the second highest in the world after Nova Scotia in Canada. Much of the area is still unsurveyed.

It took us about twelve hours to do the 85 nautical miles from Koolan Island to Kunmunya. The luggers carrying the early missionaries from Broome, including Uncle Bob, had to rely on trial and error with the tides, sometimes taking weeks to do the journey. It helped to have Aboriginal workers on board, such as Albert Barunga, who knew the tides and waters intimately. After seeing members of his family brutally rounded up by police, Barunga had spent his boyhood years working on the luggers before being taken back to Kunmunya by tribal elders, where he became a member of Uncle Bob's translation team and a widely respected community leader.

One of the difficulties we—and I suspect Uncle Bob—faced was timing our arrival at Kunmunya to coincide with the tides. We had to get into what was known as the 'Gutter', a slim finger of water and the closest 'port' to the former mission, around low tide, and come out again when the tide was dropping, before the mud was exposed.

We were too late for the tide the first day. So we anchored that night at Samson's Inlet, named after an infamous Aboriginal murderer who had hidden there. That evening we watched the sandstone cliffs of Kunmunya Hill change colour with the vivid sunset as a huge yellow moon rose in the sky. It was a strange country of steep hills, boab trees and straggly gums.

The next morning, when we walked into Kunmunya—a round trip of twelve kilometres—it was a good 38 degrees. Bloody hot. Our dinghy was pretty loaded down, with five of us including the Long's son, Roland, and their dog, Bullet, plus supplies. So I was glad that it wasn't until we were safely back on the boat that Mulawai told us that she had heard the crocodiles 'roaring'.

It was a rough walk in and we found that there was hardly anything left of the mission, except scores of wild donkeys. Bushfire had swept through many times. Long, yellow grass surrounded the remains of the buildings, disused wells, concrete water tanks and fence posts. We found the stone floor of the church under which a white child had been buried, and a tiny copper container for sail needles that probably had come off one of the luggers.

Like so many other white attempts to tame the north, the land and harsh climate had proven insurmountable. Water was the biggest problem. Deep pools left over from the wet season were deceiving, taking only days to dry up.

Ever since white man think they discovered it, there's always been grand plans for the north. Sir George Gray, the former South Australian Governor, explored the north-west between 1837 and 1839. He thought he could see the commercial advantages of the Kimberley, writing in his fascinating journals that it was best adapted for the cultivated production of cotton, sugar, indigo and rice.

Back in Derby, I went to Mowanjum, a few kilometres out of town, where the Worora, Ngarinyin and Wunambul people had been moved to in 1958, when the former missions were abandoned.

One of the last three Worora tribal elders, Patsy Lulpunda, heard that I was wanting to speak to people who remembered Uncle Bob. She was also one of the only people who remember the first missionaries coming to her country near the Prince Regent River at the turn of the century.

She watched while the missionaries built the first house at Port George IV, sleeping in their lugger until it was ready. When Uncle Bob arrived she was already a teenager.

'We were frightened the first time,' she said. 'They gave me biscuits, lolly. I'm thinking, *hey, what's this one?* I covered it up, never ate it. We never knew anything. They gave me bread. We chucked it to the fish. They put dress on me and I took it off. Thought they were trying to kill me. Me and David's mummy ran into the hills.'

The David she was referring to was David Mowaljarlai, an elder of the Ngarinyin people, whose mother had been Worora. He was a well known writer and subject of documentaries. Although independent and self-assured, with the voice of a poet, he was more than willing to show gratitude to Uncle Bob for his education.

'Mr Love taught us many things, like how to plant the vegetables, how to sew saddles and bridles, grease them up, keep them fresh, hobble strap out of bullock hide,' he said. 'He was a good bushman.'

Another colleague told me Uncle Bob was a man who put first things first, and that meant learning the Aboriginal languages of the area he was living in.

At Gosford, north of Sydney, I had spoken to Jim Duncan, who was also a missionary at Kunmunya. 'Pioneers like Love went into a pretty challenging situation,' Jim told me. 'At the time, other white people were blackbirding the Aborigines, taking them by force to act as divers in the pearl trade. The police patrols often had a fairly brutal way of collecting people. We'd see lepers being taken into Derby in chains.'

Another story I'd been told was about when the police came through the mission with a group of Aboriginal prisoners chained together around the neck. Uncle Bob told the police to unchain them, promising that they would be there in the morning. He believed in the law but not in cruelty. He told the prisoners, simply and plainly, that nobody was to run away. In the morning nobody was missing.

I felt really sad after visiting Mowanjum. Although it had been inspiring to hear about Uncle Bob, I had to wonder about the point of all those years of hardship and dedication by the early missionaries, who believed they were easing the 'civilising' of the natives. The Mowanjum people had been reasonably successful at 'integrating' themselves into the Derby community, particularly through sport, but at what cost?

Ollie: From Alice I came back to Broome. From 1992 I worked for the Commonwealth department called Health and Family Services. They changed the name three times when I worked for them over three years. They were Health, Housing, Community Services and Local Government, and then Human Services Department. They are now called Health and Family Services, and I think they are in the process of altering their name again because of all the changes. But the bulk of my time as a public servant has been with Social Security—I really enjoyed working for Social Security. I did extensive travel through my work, and saw a lot of places I would not otherwise have seen.

With Health and Family Services I was the Aboriginal Services project officer. We were looking after child care, aged care, disabilities and housing. Our department was the funding body for all these services. We'd go out to communities and frail aged hostels. We used to administer other programs as well—home and community care, emergency relief and Aboriginal health.

Working for government I have to be conscious that although I'm Aboriginal myself, I can't impose my standards and judgements. Government has been making all the decisions for too long. When I worked for Health and

Family Services I took the other approach. You empower people and ask them what they want, and they'll tell you. If they've got ownership, they won't allow it to fail—it's what they want. When you've been working as a bureaucrat you tend to lose focus, you start making the decisions for community people. You have to be mindful of that.

We do joke, though, about how some communities always want money for vehicles, which are always breaking down. This priority to have a vehicle, but not look after it, is known as 'Toyota Dreaming'.

Once, the Lotteries Commission held a meeting with local groups in Broome about their funding applications. All the public servants had a meeting at the end of the day with the commission. I was at that meeting.

'Well, thank God you fellas aren't asking for vehicles,' they told us.

We said, 'No, we're okay, we've got our government cars.'

Essential services are still the main problem in Aboriginal communities. At Mount Elizabeth, for example, in the north of the Kimberley, they had a bore put down, but they had no water for two years after it was put in. We went in just after the wet, and the creek was running. The community people were filling the water tank up from the creek. When we went to the community we were asking why they couldn't use this beautiful big ablution block. They said because there was no water. I said, 'Well, what do you do when the creek dries?' They said they go to the station and cart water from there.

So I spoke to the station wife there about it, as she had been doing the liaising for the community. She had been trying and trying and nothing had happened. When I came back to work in Broome I rang up the Water Authority and then ATSIC, and told them the problem. I told the community that they should go to the Opposition and get them to lobby about it. They didn't know how to go about fixing the problem. Eight months later they eventually got their water on. I reckon if I hadn't told the station wife who to go to and what to do, they'd probably still be waiting for their water.

Access to services is an equity issue. We take it for granted that it's basic human rights to have drinking water and so on. But being remote and isolated has an impact on accessing services.

Diana: At 9.15 pm on New Year's Day, 1991, I gave birth to our beautiful daughter, Amelia. I can still hear the sound of the commentary coming across the still air from the cricket ground near the hospital. It was an easy birth and she was a healthy baby. A card and money came for her signed from Aunty Ollie, and that's how the children have always known her.

Eight months later, in August, 1991, although I didn't really want to, I went back to work part time. For the next three years I was involved with an institution teaching journalism, the University of Technology in Sydney. Most of my work was related to improving the reporting of Aboriginal Affairs. In the end, my beliefs didn't change that much. I don't really believe that you can learn journalism from institutions.

Two years after Amelia was born, I was 22 weeks pregnant when I woke one morning with a stomach-ache that I'd had since the early hours. Something was wrong. Eventually I was taken by ambulance to hospital. The resident could not save the baby because I'd already started to give birth—he was breech, of course, at that stage—and his tiny lungs were still not ready to help him breath. At one point I felt as if I was dying, but the pain soon brought me back to reality.

My husband comforted me by reminding me we still had our wonderful daughter, and though I was grateful for that, we were totally destroyed by the loss of our little boy.

I had to face trying to pursue a normal life again and I felt an obligation to the students, so I went back to work after a week. Nobody really knew how to react. They were sorry, but they really had no idea what I'd been through. I remember trying to be brave, but finally, when I had lunch with two of the students, I started to cry. I felt like I'd never stop.

Ollie: Diana came to stay soon after losing her baby boy. She brought Amelia with her. Kim and I were living in a half-built house on the other side of the airport in Broome. It was unseasonal weather for the dry season and it rained almost the whole two weeks she was here.

Amelia was a very independent two-year-old. She was always saying, 'I do it,' or asking for apple juice. The strange thing for me for that reunion was seeing Diana as a mother. It's different when you've got another person in your life and you've got responsibilities as a parent. It was no longer that relationship where Diana was single, and plus, I was married. Both of us were different.

One night Dotty Cox babysat Amelia and we went out on the town, but the disco was dead. I don't think a single bloke talked to us. A change from our single days!

We couldn't go bush because of the rain, and the house was rough. Living with Gwen and Sid I came from a nice home, used to all my comforts, so I wasn't used to living rough. The toilet was just a hole in the ground. She kept Amelia in nappies while she stayed with us as it was easier than using the outdoor 'loo'.

Kim and I later bought a block outside of town and we put shack on it. But then I applied for a job in Derby as manager of DEETYA (the Department of Employment, Training and Youth Affairs). I left—and Kim stayed—but not only for my personal development. A major thing was, I was going to have a nice house.

Diana: Mum had had a spleen removed and had not been at all well in 1993. We'd all been terribly worried. But she was now in remission and looked pretty good. We'd had a post mortem done on the baby, who we had cremated and buried beneath a blueberry ash tree at the farm. He'd had an infection known as Streptococcus B, and the doctors said there was nothing more that I could do but try and get pregnant again. So by the end of the year I was five months pregnant and feeling pretty happy. Then in the early hours of Christmas Eve I realised that something was wrong—again.

That morning I went to the hospital to eventually be told that my membrane was ruptured and I would lose this baby too. When I developed a high temperature overnight the nurses and doctor suggested they induce the birth. We decided to go ahead with the birth, even knowing that because the baby was so young his lungs wouldn't be developed enough for him to live. We called the baby Nicholas. He lived, but only for a few minutes. His tiny eyes were closed tight as he struggled to breathe in my arms. He didn't have a chance.

After we lost the second baby there was no way that I was going to go through that again. So we did everything in our power to make sure I had a successful pregnancy. Eventually I wrote about this in my book, *Taking Control*, which is a medical self-help book. After finally finding a good doctor and getting pregnant I had a cervical stitch inserted and spent two months in hospital. All my frustrations and sadness came out while I was in hospital, although I kept myself busy enough working on the book. At one stage Ollie called me and I just burst into tears. I'd had enough of everything.

'You haven't been happy for a long time, Diana,' Ollie said. 'You have to do something about it.'

On 3 May, 1995, the day before my birthday, Marco was born. He is a wonderful little boy and everything we went through was worth it to have him. Some days I wonder what the personalities would have been like of the babies I lost. I'm sure they would have been gorgeous too, but they couldn't be sweeter than he is.

Ollie: I thought my father had abandoned me. Not knowing the whole story, I just thought he'd come over here to work in the pearling industry, had a good time and then fucked off. I thought he didn't care.

Then in the late 1980s I asked my mum what happened to my father and she told me he was deported about two weeks after I was born. In those days in the pearling industry you had Japanese, Chinese, Malays and all. But the Japanese used to get paid more than the Koepang and yet they were doing the same work. And because my father was outspoken and could speak English, people used to go to him. He was a bit of a stirrer, and that's why my mother thought he was deported.

This made me want to get my files. I wanted to find out my story. I'd always wanted to get my files, but I was putting it off, putting if off, and hadn't done anything about it. I can remember that move from the orphanage in Broome to Beagle Bay when I was about ten years old, and that's when I started to think about why my mum didn't come and take me out. But as I got older, I started to think, *where was my mother? Why did she put me in here?* There was all these questions.

I feel a lot of resentment and bitterness and anger towards my mother, but at the same time I feel this deep sense of guilt at the way I feel, because I can put myself in her shoes. As a mother, if I had my child taken away, I couldn't come to visit. It was too heartbreaking.

I think the state government has opened up the files for some years now. Initially you could have got your files through AAPA (the Aboriginal Affairs Planning Authority), and then you could also apply to Family and

Community Services in Perth. I don't know what the difference is, or whether both departments hold records on us. This was from Family and Community Services.

I found out through word of mouth that it was free of charge to obtain your file. I could also get the files of family members that are deceased. I'm still trying to get my files from the Catholics about my time in Beagle Bay. But I'm told it is difficult to access files from the Catholics. They say they sent them all back to Europe with the Pallotines.

I'd talked about getting my files for months and months and months. And then one particular day in 1993 I was going to Perth for work and I rang up the Welfare office in Perth. It was fortunate that there was a girl, Enid Blair, working in that section, she was a Derby girl. I told her that I was going to be in Perth on such and such a day, and that I was leaving on such and such a date, and I asked if I could have my file.

I really wanted to find out the real story, so I signed for my mother's Welfare file, as well as mine and my grandmother and grandfather's. I was able to get all those files in a week. I was quite surprised and shocked they did it.

My friend, Barb, took me out to pick them up. We went in her car to the department in the city. They had all my files ready. And I can remember driving home and I opened mine and started reading them, and saying, 'Listen to this, Barb. In my file, my mother is deemed as a native-in-law. But being born to a Koepang man, I was deemed a quadroon and that's why Child Welfare was responsible for me and not Native Welfare.'

I didn't even know what a quadroon was.

She felt really uncomfortable, she thought I should be reading my own file in my own privacy. But here I was feeling free to share it with her. She said, 'Shouldn't you be doing that on your own?' But I didn't have a problem with that.

And then from there I visited my foster mum, who was sick in Royal Perth Hospital. Gwen had been sick for a long time and had spent a lot of time in hospital. She had diabetes and was sent to hospital in Perth. She lost the circulation in her legs, and first they amputated one leg. They were going to take the second one but she refused to have it removed. She could tolerate a lot but it was awful to see her in such pain.

It was just fortunate for me in the job that I had that I was going to Perth quite regularly. So I was able to see her, and I guess out of the family I was the one who saw her suffering. And in a way it was good that the boys didn't see her like that.

This time when I went to visit her I took my files, because there was a lot of stuff written about her. I asked, 'Were you aware that this was happening, cause there's stuff about you in my files?'

She said, 'No.'

I asked her if she knew that there were all these letters back and forth between Child Welfare and Beagle Bay mission and other places, checking up on her and Sid to see if they would be appropriate as foster parents.

She said, 'No.'

Father Kearney was the superintendent then, and to his credit he described Sid and Gwen's house and garden as 'excellent' in a letter to the Director of Child Welfare. He wrote about Cooney, who, it seems, had told him that he could not care for me because I had 'no direct connection' with his family. *But all the time, even before Arnold went to his mother, he wanted his son to stay with him*, Father Kearney's letter said. Why hadn't Cooney done anything about seeking custody of his son?

Even the Shire Clerk had put in a good word for Gwen and Sid. Although it was agreed that Sid and Gwen could become my foster parents, they never received any money or child endowment to help them bring me up. And when

I went to Pallotines, Father Luemmen was still trying to get more money out of Gwen for the balance of my board there, although she'd paid for my uniform and books and so on. To his credit, though, he applied for more money from Child Welfare rather than continue to pressure Gwen for it.

I remember asking her about my mother. 'The whole time I was with you, did my mother send Christmas cards, did she write to you, did she ever send any money for me?'

She said, 'No, nothing.'

The only contact she had with my mother was when she and Sid went up to Pine Creek to see her, with the intention of asking if they could legally adopt me. Even at that stage I wasn't aware of their visit. I think it was a courtesy thing, going to ask her for permission. I'm not sure if she was able to give that okay, because I was a ward of the state, anyway. They were under the assumption they needed her permission. Anyway, they'd been friends years ago. With my mother having a relationship with Cooney before (and Sid being Cooney's brother) they were really close friends.

All my mother wanted to do was go out to the pub with them. Then she and her husband, Les, had an argument, and so they went to the pub and they were trying to talk to her about me, and she kept avoiding the subject. She was getting pissed and she insisted she was going to go back to Darwin with them and, of course, my foster parents were really uncomfortable with that, especially as my mum's husband wasn't aware of what she was planning to do. And so to get away they both pretended to go to the toilet. They slipped out and drove back to Darwin then.

Koepang, Sabu and Macedonia

9.

Koepang, Sabu and Macedonia

Invisible woman, invisible man
You touch me with your power
And touch me you can
You take away my freedom
And you take away my life
Now I could see your madness
You're as cold as ice
Cold as ice

Invisible woman, invisible man
You feed me with your poison
And poison you began
You rearrange the country
You rearrange my mind
But I could feel your gladness
You are as mean as kind
Mean as kind

Invisible woman, invisible man
You show me no mercy
And show me you can
You say that you love me
But you need me no more
You live on your emptiness
Die by your law
Die by your law

Invisible Woman

Arnold Smith

Ollie: Our files—those funny photocopied pieces of paper covered in handwritten scribble—held more secrets than I could have imagined.

From my file I found out what I had always wanted to know—my age when I was placed in the orphanage. I was three years old—that's what being up to my mother's knee meant. But my mother's file held the information I was really looking for more than anything. There in my mother's file I discovered the whole story about my father and why he'd left Broome. He had never abandoned us, as I had always thought. There it was in the file. It told me the real story. His name was Wila Kale and he was from Koepang in Timor. And he was deported because he was cohabiting with a native woman—my mother.

At this time, the late 1940s, the government was very concerned about the number of Aboriginal women mixing with Asian men, although the Asians had no women here anyway. (They weren't allowed in because of the White Australia Policy.) I think they were worried the Asian-Aboriginal children would take over the north, or something.

The first document regarding my father's deportation is dated 1 December, 1949, and is an urgent telegram from the police to Native Affairs in Perth: *Weela Kalle Koepanger arrested cohabitating Rita Smith half-caste over lengthy period stop will you authorise complaint magistrate leaving northern circuit this afternoon.*

The local sergeant would enforce the laws by conducting raids against Asian men cohabiting with Aboriginal women. Then the Asian men would be fined. In Mum's file it told about all the raids that were conducted. Usually under freedom of information they erase names, but in the files they listed the names of other people who were raided for cohabiting. It even mentioned Kim's mother and father, who was Malaysian. Kim remembers that his father, Mamid, was courting his mother, old Rosa. Mamid told Kim that the sergeant used to say, 'Stay home tonight.' This meant the police were going to conduct a raid to catch the Asian men going with Aboriginal women.

The complaint was authorised and my father was fined twenty pounds in Broome Court. My mother was about six months pregnant and my father admitted he was 'responsible for her condition'. The letter from the police said my father was: *a worthless type of coloured person*. The sergeant asked the Commissioner of Native Affairs in another letter what his views were about such relationships. He pointed out that: *These coloured men must have some sexual outlet, and the women referred to are, no doubt, quite prepared, and willing, to cohabit with them.*

The commissioner, SG Middleton, replied that his views were in line with Section 47(1)(b) of the Native Administration Act, 1905–47.

It is the function and duty of the Department of Native Affairs, inter alia, 'to exercise a general supervision and care over all matters affecting the interests and welfare of the natives, and to protect them, etc. Native women are not so much immoral as amoral, and therefore it must surely be our duty to protect them from themselves. Moreover, it is felt that the presence of many of them in Broome is probably due to a lack of foresight and thought of consequences on the part of official and mission authorities in the past, particularly since the recent war.

The letter concluded by saying a request had been sent to the sub-collector of Customs at Broome that my father be deported from the Commonwealth.

Letters started flying then.

The sergeant in Broome wrote back to the commissioner saying that he had noticed: *very little evidence on the part of his Department* to do what the commissioner had said in his letter. He sounded pretty pissed off, actually. He finished off by saying that: *Those female natives residing here who associate with coloured non-Australians, do so without much*

*encouragement from the latter, and in many instances are largely
to blame for the association.*

The sub-collector of Customs referred the matter to the
Commonwealth Migration Office in the Immigration
Department in Perth. Terry McDaniel, the pearling master,
then my father's employer, wrote to the Commissioner of
Native Affairs on my father's behalf, saying he was a
'most efficient diver'. He'd been a diver on one of
McDaniel's boats during the last season when it sank in bad
weather. But he was sure he would be absorbed in the
industry in the next season.

However, the letters fell on deaf ears, as the Immigration
Department agreed to have my father deported.

Then I was startled to find my mother had a little boy,
Richard, who was born on 4 January, 1950. In one letter
from a patrol officer, dated 1 February, 1950, it said my
mother was filing a complaint for the maintenance of her
child, which my father had agreed to pay for. There was a
handwritten note at the bottom saying: *If Kale is deported
then it looks as if Rita Smith and her child will be left high and
dry. However, perhaps this is preferable to a continuance of the
present position and it may act as a deterrent.*

Deterrent to what?

In March my father was signed back on board for work
in pearling, 'pending repatriation'. It seemed there was no
berth on a ship going to Timor for at least twelve months,
so the authorities felt it was better for him to be working
than hanging around town. (Mr McDaniel would have had
to pay for his berth at 'gigantic expense' to him, as well.)

After this, I found among the documents a letter saying
that Richard had died on 18 June. This really shocked me,
to know that my parents had had a little boy
who died before I was born. My mother had never told me.
He was five and a half months old when he died. He may
have had consumption.

In January, 1951, Senator Malcolm Scott wrote to the commissioner on behalf of Mr McDaniel, who now found it impossible to find a diver to take my father's place, owing to the shortage of divers in Broome. This might mean a boat would have to be laid up. He asked the commissioner to allow my father to stay on the understanding that if he again broke the law he would be repatriated. Senator Scott also received a letter from the officer in charge of the Native Hospital on my father's behalf, saying he was: *a very pleasant lad, always obedient and willing to assist in any way he can. In a capacity as a diver he has earnt many a much needed dollar for Australia.*

McDaniel also telegramed the commissioner. The Broome Shellers Association also put a word in for him with the Immigration Department.

The commissioner's memo to his minister said it all: *The question for decision is, I submit, whether the requirements of commerce are to take precedence over the state's responsibilities towards the Natives.*

When the point is made that the girls and women in Broome who are the subject of co-habitation with Asiatics are equally blameworthy, I must draw attention to the fact that many of them were taken away by Police and Departmental Officers in the past from the safe environment of Kimberley stations and placed in the Beagle Bay mission, or employment in Broome; that the Minister not only permitted but arranged the girls' employment in Broome, where they, the girls, subsequently became domiciled and have now become the chattels of the pearling industry's imported labour, and other depraved males who have brutalised and dragged them down to their own level. This being undoubtedly the case, my only reaction to any suggestion that encourages a continuance of this type of administration and treatment is one of hostility and disgust.

But by then the Minister for Native Affairs had passed the buck to the Immigration Department, saying it was: *unwise to intervene. You can see that leniency in Kalle's case would certainly have the effect of increasing the type of offence that has brought trouble upon Kalle.*

However, the Minister supported varying the date of my father's departure because of what McDaniel's and others had said, and because of his good behaviour.

It took a little over two years to deport my father, and in the meantime I was born—on 23 September, 1951. Father was repatriated to Koepang on the ship *Nicol Bay* on 30 December, 1951.

So why was my father singled out?

There's a lot of people in Broome with Asian parents. There were Asian men older than my mother, younger than my father, who stayed with their Aboriginal wives. My father was used as a scapegoat to enforce these laws because Native Affairs at the time wanted to set an example.

After I read these files, I felt relief. That's when I became determined that I had to meet my father, because it wasn't his fault. All throughout my life I had mixed feelings about meeting my father. It was, no I don't want to, yes I do. And then I found out the truth—that he didn't abandon me.

The other thing that had bothered me was that I was told my father could speak English and write English. And even knowing from what my mother told me that he was deported, I thought, *well, if he can speak English and write English, why hasn't he made some contact with me?* And at that time I still didn't want to meet him.

But seeing the documents about my brother, it was not as if it was a one-night stand relationship, it was a couple of years' relationship between them, having two children. And then I was really determined to meet him.

I came to meet my father in a roundabout way. If you believe in fate, that's what it was. I always believe when somebody dies, another door opens, something good happens. My niece, Mariah, was born just before Gwen died, just a few weeks before, so she was able to meet her. That kid was a baby but she talks about her all the time, about her nana. She looks up at the stars and says, 'Nana's watching us.'

Gwen grew up in Broome. Her mother was white but her stepfather was Indonesian. His name was Benardus Senge and he lives in Darwin. Gwen and her sister had the same mother and father. And then Benardus got together with her mum and they had a son, Uncle Johnny.

When Gwen was so sick we brought her back from hospital in Perth to Broome for Christmas. And then she stayed on in the hospital a bit longer. I think she died in May. She actually died in the Broome hospital. We had the usual rosary then we buried her. We had the wake, and Benardus and Uncle Johnny and some of his children came down from Darwin for the funeral.

At the wake Benardus and I were talking, having a conversation about my father. He's also a Koepang man and speaks the same language. He knew my father because he was working in the pearling industry himself. He told me my father lived on a little island off Timor called Sabu. I was just casually talking about it and, unbeknownst to me, when Bernardus returned to Darwin he took the initiative himself and wrote to my father. He sent a letter across to my father through this other woman called Pauline. She lives in Darwin, but she was going to Sabu and she delivered the letter to my father. I later met her.

I think it was about twelve months later that I got a letter. This time I was with Kim. I was in bed one Sunday morning and Kim came back from picking up the mail from our box. He said, 'There's a letter here from your father.'

I jumped out of bed and grabbed the letter and opened it. My father had written to Benardus and there was a separate envelope addressed to me that Benardus forwarded on to me. In the envelope there was a photograph of himself and a letter. The first thing I saw was the photo. I'd never seen a picture of him before. It was him in his sarong, and on the back of it, it had 'pearl diver'. Nothing else. It was an old photo. I just looked at the photograph and I burst into tears. It was the first time I'd actually seen my father, even though it was only a photograph.

I didn't read the letter until about fifteen minutes or half an hour later. I guess I was a bit scared. He was saying he was really happy that I wanted to contact him and meet him, happy that I was looking for him. Then I decided I would go over to meet him.

So I had my 44th birthday with him in September, 1995, over in Koepang. Kim and I flew to Darwin from Broome. From Darwin we flew to Koepang and my father came over to Koepang to meet us. I didn't have any expectations because I thought I mightn't even like the man, he was a stranger to me. We were there about two weeks, staying with some family there.

Fortunately we had a good reunion. My father was tall and he had a square face with high cheekbones. He must have been in his late eighties then. We just stayed there on our own. It was good, because we had our quality time together, no interruption from other family members.

I asked my father who gave me that awful name, Olive. He said, 'I named you Ollie, and that was after Ollie Radjah,' which was my grandmother's name. It's funny how I've always preferred to be called Ollie to Olive.

He started off straight away when I first met him, talking about my mother. He told me he loved my mother, they would have had more children and stayed together if he hadn't been deported.

My mum, she would have been 25 when she had me. My father was a lot older than her. I asked Sid and Gwen once, and they said he was about twenty years older than my mum. They would have met when my granny lived at the back of the picture show. The gambling house was there then. It wasn't far from where the Koepangers lived. He was scared of Granny, although he got on well with her. I guess he was scared of the way the women used to fight like men.

But he and Mum would sit in the back lane and talk. Because of the consorting laws they weren't allowed to associate. When they were courting they had to do it surreptitiously.

He used to buy Aboriginal people grog because they weren't allowed in the pubs. He said his only friends were the Binghis, the blackfellas. He'd go down to the mangroves and drink with the Binghis.

Before he came to Broome he travelled around on a ship. He went to the Torres Strait Islands and Sydney, working in a kitchen in a hotel in Sydney.

My father told me he was outspoken. He used to speak up for his people and that's why McDaniel's wanted to get rid of him, he said. He didn't mention the government and the legislation, although he was aware of some of it. Dad blamed McDaniel's for his deportation, but McDaniel's was actually very supportive. I was trying to explain to him that it wasn't McDaniel's, it was the government, the 1905 legislation. I tried to explain about my files and all the letters of support that McDaniel's wrote. It was really hard trying to get that across to him with the language barrier, even though he spoke quite good English. I felt frustrated that I couldn't get that message across to him.

After he got deported these schooners used to come over to Sabu to recruit Koepangers as pearl divers. My father threatened them and said no-one was going to work for them, because of the way he was treated. My father would have been sending money home to them so the Koepangers wouldn't go because they were more scared of my father. They would have had to come home to Sabu after working in Broome and face my father. The pearlers didn't get any more volunteers, and very few Koepangers came to Broome after that.

My father got into tourism when he went back to the island. Whenever they had tourists they'd call on him as the interpreter. Sometimes when there were ships going through, if tourists were sick, he'd be the interpreter for the doctor. He also used to entertain, because he was a really good singer. Interpreting wasn't an easy job, because where the ferries come into the island, and the airport, is 25 kilometres from where he lived. The port was the other side of the island from his village. And he used to have to walk that 25 kilometres when he was called upon for interpreting. He got paid a pittance.

When we were about to leave my father said to me, 'Don't come back unless you bring my granddaughter.'

We had a video with us, so I said, 'Have you got a message for her?'

So on the video he said, 'Cindy—come to see me.' Cindy didn't actually see the video until after she met him.

When I came back to Australia I decided that I'd go back in twelve months time. Cindy was living in Cairns at that time. I rang her and told her I'd met my father. I told her I was going back in September. 'Can you keep it free if you want to come?'

I didn't put any pressure on her. I left it entirely up to her. 'Just keep it free and we can go together.' So we did go together. The next year, 1996, Cindy went over to meet her grandfather for the first time. And the second time—for me—we actually went to Sabu, where my father lived.

I had the feeling of coming home. I was flying over Sabu, looking at this island, and from the plane I had this sense of belonging.

The island of Sabu is quite dry and arid. The terrain is very volcanic, very rocky. More semi-tropical. Every bit of land that had soil was used for growing food. There were traditional wall fences all round the country. Still a lot of traditional huts made out of grass, coconut walls, sticks. Then there's conventional brick houses with three bedrooms, a kitchen and lounge.

Over there they have markets, but you don't have to leave your home to go shopping. You get the vendors coming past your house selling fish, chickens, vegies. There's no frozen stuff. Our chickens are about three times the size of theirs. We had goat, chicken, pork. They eat anging (dog). I said, 'No, thanks.' I said I liked fish. So they brought me fish, cause I love my fish. When my cousin, who lives in Koepang, found out I like fish she sent somebody down to the markets. They've got that extended family, where people share and give.

Baabi means pig. In my father's village there were no toilets. You just had to go in the grounds and there was all these pigs running around—the baabis. The pigs used to eat the shit. Later I was telling the people in Koepang the story, and they were laughing at me feeling a bit strange about going to the toilet there.

My father spoke Indonesian as well as Sabunese. I was recalling when I was there that I knew some of the words—makan for food, slamat pagi for good morning, slamat siang—good afternoon, all the greetings, because I'd heard them in Broome.

There's big cross-cultural influences between the Koepangers and Broome people. The food in Broome is influenced from Sabu. In Broome we're also influenced by the Koepanger culture and customs. We say things like 'casi roko' which means give me a cigarette. Pudding knows a lot of the language.

We discovered the customs on Sabu are very similar to Aboriginal customs—you get that sharing thing. One of the things that always stood out for me was that they wanted to give you something, like a gift. Or they'd give you money. If they didn't have anything to give they'd feel really hurt.

They grew rice there and vegetables. We had baabi, goats, chicken. But the major thing was the rice fields. There was a couple of families there that were fishermen. Me and Cindy went to the beach once. They have nets, but they make all this noise and splashing, driving the fish towards their net.

I need to know where I fit. They tell you you're related to this and that one. In Koepang and Sabu it was really difficult, because you knew they were relations but you didn't know how they were related. Because of the language barrier it's really difficult.

My grandmother must have had more than one husband but it's difficult to pinpoint that. My father's brother, he looks totally different to my father. His name is Kale too. I don't think they have the same mother as his brother, Wei Kale, who I met—he was short, slightly built and had a oval-shaped face. So I suspect they would have had different mothers. Father said he had four brothers, never mentioned any sisters, but the third time I went, we met a sister who lived in Koepang who came over to Sabu while we were there. I think she was the sister of Wei Kale.

She looks like her brother, she looks nothing like my father. I'm assuming they had the same father and different mother. Every time I go back to Koepang I'm learning more.

My father had three children plus a stepdaughter over there. I've only met a brother and a stepsister. My brother doesn't speak highly of them. I asked if I could meet my sisters. My brother said, 'Loni and Kathy tidda buggas (no good). Ina Wila (me) and Ina Wope (Cindy) bugs (good).' Ina means daughter of, so they don't call me Ollie, they call me daughter of Wila.

In Koepang you have your elders. Elders make the decisions, like in Aboriginal society. There's the extended family but with a strong family structure. There's tight control. And they all live next door to each other, walled within the village. You have the village where all the family members live, they may only be separated by a wall. It's like a community within a community.

I think my brother, Adu, is like his father, who was adventurous, travelled and became worldly. But it's not acceptable for him to be that way. He's married and has three children. He had just decided to move to the village where his wife lives. For Adu to up and go, that was taboo. He was treated as an outcast. Maybe there was a bit of jealousy. From my observation Adu was like his father, and wanted to be adventurous and move around. But he was restricted. My father was more worldly than the others. They're poor people, and Adu wasn't able to travel like he had. And because he left that village and went to his wife's family he was an outcast. So they were always growling and running him down.

It appeared to me like they were waiting for my father to die, because even my father was a bit of an outcast. I think there was a lot of stuff put on to me. The jealousy came because Adu was the only son, so he'd be next in line to become a leader or be responsible. And they saw him as not suitable. And he was also very young. When I first met him he was 29. My father's other brothers' children were much, much older, but they still weren't next in the hierarchy. Initially they were quite open about their feelings to Adu, but I got sick of it, and I didn't want to get involved. I told them I loved my brother, I'm not going to be dragged into it. I found him to be a loving, beautiful, compassionate person. And after that there was no more nastiness about Adu.

Koepang is part of West Timor. There wasn't any evidence of violence when I was there. At that time they were celebrating 50 years of independence from the Portuguese. Our guide who spoke English said there was still a lot of tension. If they're seen to be buying books that were subversive they'd have a visit from the police. Everything was monitored there. You couldn't speak out publicly against the government. Some of the people I spoke with were worried about fundamentalist Moslems, as they're Christians. I didn't want to get into the politics.

When we went to Sabu we had to check into the police. We had to show them our passports and explain what we were there for, but we didn't have any problems. That was a compulsory thing that had to be done.

Cindy left a couple of days before I did, so we all went out to the airport to say goodbye to her. She couldn't stop crying. She was sobbing. She knew she wasn't going to see her grandfather again. At the airport you had all these people staring at this old Indonesian man and this young 'white' girl just crying and hugging each other. Everybody was staring, seeing this little 'white' girl crying with this old man at the airport.

Diana: While Ollie was getting to know her father and his family, I was finally able to discover more about my husband's country. We received word that my mother-in-law had died of cancer while I was in hospital for two months when I was pregnant with Marco. It was six months after my own mother's death. Her cancer had also got worse and she had been having chemotherapy. But the doctors couldn't stop the infection that was causing her high temperatures. They were both so young really. Cancer is the cruellest disease. I know it's a cliché to dedicate your first book to your mother, but I did, and to my mother-in-law. Mum was buried on the farm not far from my two baby boys.

We stayed in Skopje in the middle of the hot European summer. We had to keep the blinds down and the windows shut during the day to keep the 40 plus degrees temperatures out. But high up in the snow-capped mountains of west Macedonia, it was much cooler when we visited the stunning village of Galichnik. Famous for its stone houses, the village looks down on Lake Debar and on the other side of a series of crisscrossing paths, Albania. We were there for the Galichnik wedding, a real traditional wedding that is held every year to commemorate the traditions of the past.

As we stood at a graveside nestled among the wild cherry and pine trees in the overgrown cemetery, the silence of the alpine air was broken by the powerful beat of a drum. It was joined by the fierce, trumpet-like tones of the zurle as a group of musicians led the family of a young man about to be married around a precipitous path overlooking the gorge.

The music became more mournful as the groom, his mother, father and 'godfather' offered plum brandy and Turkish delight to their ancestors in a ritualistic offering that dated back to pre-Christian days. They had come that morning to invite their forefathers to their wedding.

This symbolic gesture was a way of re-awakening their history, their customs and their legends that had kept Macedonian culture alive, despite hundreds of years of occupation by the Ottoman Empire and countless other governments and peoples.

And that day perhaps, it was even more significant, as, with Macedonia managing its independence despite the shadow of war in neighbouring Kosovo—the largely Albanian former autonomous region of Serbia—its people were seeking to understand their identity and their past.

The Galichnik wedding, which we were celebrating that day, was born in a time when poverty sent the men of the village away from their sheep farming to be migrant workers in far flung cities and countries. In Belgrade, in Bulgaria, in Greece, even as far as Egypt, these former nomads from Slav tribes would know they must return home for St Peter's Day—12 July. Each year, that day would be celebrated with around 40 weddings. After the weddings the men would leave to work again and perhaps only return every year—or even less often—to sire their children.

At the graveyard we were inviting Macedonia's dead fathers to return to be at their sons' and daughters' weddings.

We were at the Galichnik wedding at the invitation of the young people who now run the town council. As we drank thick Turkish coffee made in copper pots at the village's only café, I learnt a little of these traditions.

In ancient times the women were said to have held more power, and so the wedding's symbolic rituals emphasise the need for harmony in the home and the village. When the mother-in-law hits the bride over the head with a cake, it signifies that the bride must leave behind her own family and accept her husband's mother as her new mother. (I was glad that never happened with me!)

As a fertility ritual it may have more meaning these days, as Macedonia's tiny population of two million people seem swamped by the events around it. While independence in 1991 was without bloodshed, and relatively painless compared to the other countries of the former Yugoslavia, the years since have been difficult for this country of legends. Not only have economic embargos imposed against Serbia hurt them, but Greece, too, upset by the use of the name Macedonia, closed its borders and slapped a trade embargo, which lasted until 1995, on the new country.

The most likely European nation to disappear either from migration or assimilation, Macedonians themselves are concerned that the birth rate of their largest minority, ethnic Albanians, who are mostly Moslem, may one day soon overtake them. Before the Kosovo crisis, they were also concerned about calls by some Albanians to annex part of west Macedonia in order to set up a separate state, which would include Kosovo.

Among the many stories I heard of Albanians were ones saying that even in the middle of winter they steal television sets and even cars, carrying them over their heads as they trudge waist-deep through the snow back to their side of the border.

When I first met my husband in 1989, two years after he arrived in Australia, he told me that although he came from Skopje, he was a Yugoslav. Then the war came, Yugoslavia broke up and people were forced to identify their nationality. There are around 250,000 Macedonians living in Australia.

He and his friends—a mixture of Serbs, Croats, Macedonians and Bosnians (both Bosnian Serb and Moslem)—had to watch as their country fell apart, wracked by a nightmare of hatred. As the saying goes, truth was the first casualty, and propaganda from all sides made it impossible to know what was really happening. When, following the lead of Slovenia and Croatia, Macedonian citizens voted for independence from Yugoslavia in a national referendum on 8 September, 1991, he wondered if he still had a country to go home to.

He found he did, even if it wasn't quite the one he had left. Preoccupied with preconceptions drawn from the Macedonians I had met here in Australia, the debate about the use of the name and the lingering images of the Bosnian war, my head was turned around with what I learnt and saw. From techno discos, to coffee bars, to remote mountain villages, nothing had prepared me for the deeper questions of cultural identity. As we grapple with issues of racism and multiculturalism, issues that have been close to my heart as a journalist for more than twenty years, I had to contend with similar issues in my husband's country without knowing what the real answer was. How can you be proud of your country without being dangerously nationalistic? And for a migrant, how do you accommodate your feelings towards your new country with feelings towards your former home?

'See how easy it is for racism to emerge in times of economic trouble?' my husband pointed out when we returned home to the race debate fuelled by the rise of One Nation. I could see why Hitler was elected in Germany, why international organisations were impotent in the face of the most bitter war in Europe in this part of the century, why 'ethnic cleansing', that most ludicrous of terms, which the Serb leader, Slobodan Milosevic, first used against Albanians in Kosovo, was again being used.

Despite the frightening spectre of war, most young Macedonians show their Mediterranean spirit by filling the coffee bars at night, talking about the latest music and fashion, rather than politics.

To my husband's maternal grandfather, Angele Velkovski, a landowner from Kosle, a village east of Skopje, whoever was in government during his 103 years of life was immaterial. He had seen the Turks expelled after the Balkan wars of 1912–13, Macedonia divided amongst Greece, Bulgaria and the Kingdom of Serbs, Croats and Slovenes, later to be known as Yugoslavia. And the First World War, the Second World War and occupation by fascist regimes, and Tito's Yugoslav Federation, then independence two years before he died.

Once, while he was running from the Turkish soldiers in one such skirmish, he dropped his hat. Sneaking back to get it, he realised he was risking his life in order to take the enemy's hat. It was a Turkish fez, the compulsory uniform of the Turks and those that lived under their rule.

It was 45 degrees the day we visited Kosle, and most of the men were sitting at the 'tap' or well, the coolest place in the village. My husband's uncle, Bogdan Bogoevski, was also visiting Kosle, and took us down to the cemetery where his grandparents were buried. Pointing down across the rolling hills to the road below, he explained that it originally was the Roman highway, which made Macedonia so strategically important for the later conquerors, including the Turks. He showed us the ruins where the Turks had waited to sack the village, betrayed by a Macedonian woman, or so the story goes. Later the Macedonian women would cut off a finger of their first born son's right hand to stop him being taken as 'blood tax' to be trained as special soldiers by the Turkish Army.

I had first heard about the fear of Albanians when we visited Tetovo, the eighty percent Albanian city, in the north-west. We had stayed with my in-laws in another monastery, where we feasted on barbequed pork and homemade wine. The monastery once stood on its own, but gradually it had been surrounded by Albanian homes and mosques built by people leaving Kosovo or Albania.

My in-laws held the key to the monastery but they were usually afraid to stay there at night 'because of the Albanians'. In the morning we were woken by the sound of the hodja calling the people to prayer in the nearby mosque.

These tensions came to a head in 1996 when amidst protests, the Macedonian government closed down a private Albanian language university in Tetovo, declaring it illegal. So when I made contact with an Albanian linguistics lecturer from there I was keen to travel back to meet him. Because of the difficult political situation, he preferred to remain anonymous.

We met at the bus station and the lecturer drove me to a café in the town. There, speaking extremely softly in order that people at neighbouring tables did not hear our conversation, he explained his family had lived in Macedonia for 'generations'. Although he spoke Albanian at home, he also spoke Macedonian as well as Serbo-Croat, the once official language. (Many Albanians say they do not speak Macedonian.)

The lecturer believed education was the key to a solution for this country—and perhaps the whole region. 'When I was 27, after doing my MA, I served in the former Yugoslav Army,' he explained. 'There was a Croatian doctor and a Serbian student of medicine who had not yet graduated, of the same age and educational status as me. The ethnicity was not the problem. We were the ones who sat together. This is something inborn of human beings, we want to be in the company of our equals. If the Albanian population remains uneducated, how can you integrate them?'

⁂

One day, quite a few months after we returned from Europe, there was a message on my answer machine from Ollie. She sounded quite cool at first, but then she broke up and was crying. Her father had died but she had only just heard. Although she was too late for the funeral, she was still going over there with Cindy to spend some time with the family. I felt so sorry for her. After more than 40 years she'd only had a couple of years of knowing her father, and only for a short time on both occasions. She'd been denied a father for so long. I started to cry myself, thinking about it.

I am so lucky. I still have a wonderful father, although he's given us a few scares. He has a heart condition and he has been close to death a few times. We—and he—never dreamed Mum would go first. He was a war hero, having fought in Papua New Guinea in the 39th Battalion and the 53rd Battalion in the Owen Stanley campaign. After the Australian forces were belted back to Port Moresby by the Japanese, he was transferred by the request of the commanding officer to the famous 39rd Battalion, which had born the brunt of the original Japanese attack at Kokoda. This battalion went back into action at Gona, on the opposite coast. His battalion captured Gona mission after fighting there for three months. Dad was wounded at Gona village a few days later. He was awarded the military cross for valour in the Gona campaign. But he always told me the war turned him into a pacifist.

After his last heart attack I went to see him in the intensive care ward in hospital. He was talking, almost in his sleep, about his army training in north Queensland. He spoke about how he had been to officer school at Duntroon, but that so many of the other soldiers were totally untrained and unprepared for the terrible fighting. The losses were huge, not only from wounds but also from tropical diseases and hardship in the mountainous jungle.

Dad became a journalist after the war then later went into PR. He has been my inspiration, although I must say my mother could write a very good letter!

Ollie: I received a telegram in January, 1998, to say my father had died. I think he died on the 21st. He was in his early nineties when he died. My mum was in her late sixties then. It was after he died—maybe a couple of days—that I received a telegram.

The traditional custom over there is that they spend three days with the body, they wash it and dress it. But because my father was a Christian they buried him the very next day.

I immediately rang Cindy and I said, 'I'm going over, do you want to come? We missed the funeral but I still want to go over.' She said yes. We had to fly over to Sabu. We spent two weeks over there. We were happy that we'd met him, we realised he was hanging on to meet us. One thing he had wanted to do, he wanted to get baptised. It was like he was preparing himself to die. He wanted to be baptised a Catholic, but his wife was Church of England. He asked me what to do.

Kim suggested, 'Then why don't you get baptised both, keep everybody happy.' He ended up Church of England. When I went back after he died we went to visit my father's stepdaughter and she pulled out this photo of my father being baptised. I just cried when I saw it, because that's what he wanted. The family members, they've got pictures of the sacred heart, icons and statues of Christianity.

You could see the similarities with Aboriginal culture and the way we grieve traditionally. We had all his family wailing over us. Cindy and I had to laugh, they started on me for what seemed like fifteen minutes then they were also talking. I didn't understand it. Then it was Cindy's turn. We was saying, 'When's this going to end?'

Before they took us to my father's grave they said to me, 'You have to cry now, you can't cry when you go to the graveside.'

And that was really hard. I ended up breaking down anyway. I thought, *well, that's their custom, that's not my custom.* They get all these white flowers, they cut them up and put perfume on them. Then we had to sprinkle it all over the grave, and then Adu, my brother, said I had to walk on the grave. They showed me. Over here we don't do that. I just couldn't help crying.

The second time we went to the grave was a lot happier, we were taking photos. I wanted to go to the graveside—just Cindy, me and Adu, but we couldn't do that. They were very protective of us. Even during the day, we had to go to the toilet at the neighbours, and every time you'd have the old boy, my father's brother, sing out for somebody. They'd come up, grab your hand, then wait outside for you.

There were times when you didn't need the language. My brother was constantly touching us. This time he was really sad, one, because his father was gone, and two, because he was ostracised by the rest of the family. I was asking Adu about his mum. He doesn't remember her name, she must have died when she was really young. I don't know for sure. That was sad. Adu wanted to come back to Australia with me. They kept saying, 'The old man said Adu can't go back to Australia with you.'

I said, 'That's his choice.'

It's been good for Cindy to find out about her Timorese side. She was saying to me last time we were there, 'Mum, you know how you always wear sarongs, is that the Indonesian side coming out?' I don't know. I lean to that thing too. Or maybe I just feel comfortable in them.

Cindy always grew up knowing she was Aboriginal. We used to go home to Broome every year. We're very close now, even though she's married and has her own life. She married a German man. We call him Jet.

We had a great time singing in the karaoke bars in Koepang. I told her it didn't matter how silly we looked because we didn't know anybody there.

'Don't be shamed. Nobody knows us, so we can run amok,' I said. 'I haven't got a deadly voice like Pudding but I'm still going to sing.'

Cindy had just been through Sydney when I came to stay with Diana in 1998. She and Jet stayed with Diana's father for a while then they drove on to Brisbane, where they lived for a few months before going to Europe to stay with Jet's family. She's been there before with him—to the Black Forest in Germany. It's good for us to see other countries and how people live.

It always impressed on me in Sabu, in Indonesia, how poor the people are and how hard their lives are. These people, if they don't work, they don't eat, they don't survive. Australians don't realise how lucky they are. They're getting the dole, around 300 bucks a fortnight. People over there get nothing—if they don't work, they don't eat. The contrast and the difference is incredible.

Once, I was walking across the fields and I saw a little hut. There was a man sitting in it moving some contraption to scare the birds away from the rice crop. He just sat there all day moving the contraption. It's a very important, if boring, job. There's no way they can afford to have the birds eat the seeds and destroy the crop.

Australians really need to travel to come back and realise. But at the same time, you look at Aboriginal people, and their circumstances still haven't changed—despite everything that's meant to have been done. My last job was with the WA State Department of Education. So with education, and me coming back into the system twenty years later, I've found that nothing's changed, Aboriginal kids still aren't achieving.

My work involved visiting all the schools in the Kimberley and helping them implement Aboriginal studies.

It's so sad to see that, despite the state and Commonwealth funding that's been pumped into Aboriginal education, our kids are still not achieving. They're under-achieving. There's both black and white kids coming out of our schools illiterate.

One good thing is that Aboriginal studies is going to be made compulsory. Another positive thing that's changed is that schools are now made to be accountable, and there's outcomes they have to achieve with quality assurance. Still, there's a lot of racism we need to change. We acknowledge there's a lot of good things happening in the Kimberley but our kids are still not achieving. At the end of the day we need results, that the kids are graduating.

In the past, too, the system tended to blame the victims, kids that were not achieving. They need to internalise and say, 'What are we doing wrong?' There were always fears—that you blame the teachers, you blame the kids. But it's not about blame. The system needs to say, we've been teaching this way, it's not working. Why not try other ways of teaching, and if that doesn't work, try something different. What they're currently doing is still not working and they continue to do the same bloody thing.

We need to promote education to our parents. Historically, Aboriginal people weren't allowed to have an education. I think it was in the '50s when they were allowed to go and have an education, but then that depended on the white parents. If they didn't want Aboriginal kids in the schools they could stop them going. So today education is undervalued because some Aboriginal parents don't see it as important for their kids. If parents are feeling that way then what chance have the kids got? Then the parents' attitude is if they don't go to school it doesn't matter. Lots of truancy. Kids may be living in poverty, no clean clothes, no tucker. Then they get lethargic, they don't perform. But even the breakfast program is another form of dependency. We need to educate the parents.

Before it was the churches and the missions that took on the responsibility of educating Aboriginal people. When I was in the orphanage going to primary school I went to a Catholic school. The state school was seen as being for white kids. Only one or two white kids were at the Catholic school. In Broome now, a lot of Aboriginal kids are leaving the Catholic schools and coming to the state school.

I was based in Broome. In the state system I was Level five, which is equivalent to ASO six in the Commonwealth system.

There's a few Aboriginal men and women working for the government departments I've been with. With DEETYA, who I went to work for in Derby, my supervisor was the regional manger when I started and he was Aboriginal. I think I was the only Aboriginal manager in WA. There were other Aboriginal managers—in the Territory, Queensland and eastern states.

With that job I achieved my personal and professional goals. I did two and a half years in Derby, managing the DEETYA office there. Then in 1998, with all the government changes, they closed the office down. But I was happy with achieving my personal goals. Those skills are always useful if you want to work for Aboriginal organisations or in the private sector.

Once upon a time, when I first worked with Social Security, in order to be a manager you had to go up the ranks. You also had to have technical knowledge of Social Security. But just before I left DSS you could be a manager anywhere, you could come from private into being a manager. This is the way, with the education department and their school principals, that it's heading now. The principals are actually managers.

The best part of the Kimberley education job, though, were the spunky young headmasters I got to meet. Diana asked me if they were Aboriginal, and I said, 'Nuh. I'm into white men again.'

Epilogue

10.

Epilogue

They watching us growing up
So much for mankind
They just don't care who we are
I used to be blind
Now that I am older
You know what I've found
Is that when we live our life
We go to the ground
Go back to the ground
Go back to the ground

Stop ringing the submission bells
Stop ringing the submission bells
Stop ringing the submission bells
Do we have to go through your hell?
Through your hell?

Verse two, *Submission Bells*

Arnold Smith

Diana: I don't feel particularly surprised at how things have turned out. Marriage, children, work, life. When I was young I vowed I'd never get married, but gradually as the years moved on, I hoped I would. Our kids are everything I could have ever hoped for, even if they are exhausting. Sometimes I feel like I just need to do it better.

It must be so hard for some mothers, particularly the ones who never really had a chance to grow up with their own mothers, like Ollie. I miss my own mother so much, and often think of calling her to ask her advice about the children, and then remember she's not around any more. Sometimes I see a woman in the street and think it's her. And it's similar with friends who are no longer here.

Once, when I called Ollie, she told me Ronny Ejai had died. He was in his early 30s, I guess. He was my first friend in the Kimberley. I have a photo of him cooking fish in his so called 'kitchen' on the rocks next to the beach in Broome. He was wearing a pink towel wrapped around him as an apron.

'Get out of my kitchen, I just mopped,' he joked as he waved his arms at us.

He and another friend and I had driven down from Derby, and after getting completely pissed at the pub, drove the car out near the sandhills to camp the night. We woke up in the morning to discover we were next to somebody's stable. So Ronny found some carrots and fed the horses as we boiled the billy for breakfast.

Ronny was a great dancer, a gorgeous guy, but so lost. He was gay, so although there was never any trouble finding boyfriends in the Kimberley—often the meat workers—he felt totally out of place there. That's why he moved to the city. Finally, after ten years in Sydney and talking about it all the time, he went home—all the way to the Kimberley by bus. On the way his father died, only a day or so before Ronny would have made it home to see him. The last I heard of him before his death was from Ollie, who said that he was sleeping in the street.

Sweet Ronny—I feel I failed him as a friend. But what could I have done to make up for 200 years of all of us being here? I don't feel guilty—really—just so terribly sad.

Dianne Williams, Ollie and I got together when I came to Broome in January, 1999. Dianne told me Ronny had come to stay with her not long before he died but he had been really, really thin. She remembered our good times in Darwin, where Ronny was also living, and the way people called her 'Jingo'. She was walking down the road in Broome one day and she heard somebody yell out of a car: 'Out, Jingo, out!' It was Neenyah.

But it was melancholy to think of all the people who were no longer around—Ronny, Nancy Francis, Dianne's dad, Frank, Peter, Mimi Dora, Jimmy Bieundurry. I never felt the Kimberley was the same after Jimmy died.

We used to have so much fun when I was in Broome in the late '70s. The fishing trips, the cooking up great feeds of fish and rice, the music, the trips to Beagle Bay, the football, dancing at the pub. Broome's white population has exploded now that the town has become the administrative centre for the Kimberley. Many Aboriginal people have moved to Derby. Perhaps they feel they have more control there.

In Broome there's new shopping malls, which, as Dotty said, keep the prices lower. But to me the place seemed suburban. The pubs and discos employ bands from Perth or play taped music, not local bands often. Marky's still involved in Radio Goolarri, though, and lots of initiatives are happening with music and film and the arts generally.

Almost as soon as I arrived at Ollie's house off the plane from Perth, we went through her files. I was pretty tired, as this 'incredibly experienced world traveller' had managed to get the tickets mixed up, and I was a day late. I'd stayed with my friend, Jac, in Perth, who had very kindly driven me to the airport at 5am in order to go standby.

Despite the tiredness, I couldn't stop reading the files. My heart was in the pit of my stomach, although as a journalist I found them fascinating. It's a story of how bureaucracy and government laws made it impossible for Aboriginal people to know what was happening to them. A story of control. Every little detail of their lives had a letter or document attached to it. It's a story of unemotional involvement in strangers' lives.

I think the authorities had a fear—and a fascination—of the idea of sex between Aboriginal women and Asian men. Amoral not immoral, huh! They talked of prostitution and venereal disease, but not about real relationships or love.

In the report of the inquiry, *Bringing Them Home*, it says

the Chief Protector's aim was to protect the children by taking them away. And to prevent the 'problem arising again in the future' there should be prohibitions against 'mixed marriages' and 'miscegenation' (interbreeding between races). As Ollie said, the early '50s was the time of the White Australia Policy. Arthur Calwell was no longer Immigration Minister, but Menzies was PM, and it wasn't until Harold Holt was PM in the mid '60s that the policy was changed. Apparently, even Timorese who had fought with Australians during World War II and had come here as refugees and married Australian women, were sent back. (This had nothing to do with Native Affairs, of course.)

Some say that the Immigration Department's 'siege mentality' still exists today. And sometimes I wonder if people's feelings about mixed relationships have changed that much.

※※. ※※. ※※.

We needed to walk on Cable Beach each evening to get this intense experience out of our system. Ollie played Shirley Bassey as we got ready to go out to drink cocktails watching the sunset from Cable Beach Club. A very kind man took our photo out there as the sky lit up all pink and orange. (It matched my dress.)

Ollie and I wanted to interview her mother, Rita. These are some of the questions we wanted to ask: How did Richard die? What happened when you went to Noonkanbah? Did you meet your relatives there? Were you brought up in the dormitories in Beagle Bay? What was your father like? Why was Pudding taken away? Why didn't you marry Cooney? Why were you arrested in Halls Creek? How did you meet Ollie's father? Did you love him? Why didn't you keep in contact with Ollie when she went to Gwen and Sid's? Why didn't you even send her a Christmas card?

But Ollie kept putting off calling her. She still blames

her, I think. But who wants confrontation? So these questions may never be answered. Ollie has changed from when I first met her. She's still outrageous and great fun, but perhaps not as carefree. She's still working through the pain of her life but she has come a long way.

⁂ ⁂ ⁂

During a job as a publicist with The Festival of the Dreaming, the first of the Olympic arts festivals, in 1997, I interviewed an Aboriginal dancer who'd devised a ballet based on the lyrebird's story, the totem of the Tharawal people. Their country stretches from the west of Sydney down to the Shoalhaven river, and so I believe our farm at Foxground was part of their country. Foxground is certainly lyrebird country. If you walk up in the escarpment and you're very quiet you'll hear them. They'll imitate anything—different animals, even the sound of chainsaws. You may see them scurrying across the path in front of you.

There's a path called Hoddle's Track that winds around the escarpment, past caves and over creeks. You'll find bits of cloth tied to tree branches that you can follow and make your way up out of the dark semi-rainforest onto the flat heathland of Barren Grounds Reserve. In spring it's covered in wildflowers and all year through there's Banksia trees full of 'Banksia men' as I call them from my childhood reading of *Snugglepot and Cuddlepie*. The first time I managed to get there I was on my own. I was breathless and excited by being so alone in this vast landscape. So I called my husband on my mobile. He was under a house laying the wiring somewhere in Sydney. It could have been an ad for mobile phones.

I thought about our wedding down here, the graves of our babies and my mother, and my time spent here with Ollie. I thought of that wonderful—and very witty—book, *The Songlines* by Bruce Chatwin, that I give to foreigners to help in an understanding of Australia. Ironic it was written by an Englishman! This is a country crossed by songlines, by connections, by feelings that run deep and strong, not always the best feelings—hatred, anger, resentment. But strong feelings for sure.

I've never felt NOT part of this country, even when I've lived overseas. And having lived and seen the effects of nationalism gone mad, like many others, I don't want that sort of nationalism here. I can't stand fake nationalism, either, that gets trotted out whenever there's anything to do with sport happening. The America's Cup and so on. It's as if it's compulsory to be ecstatic about holding international sporting events here. It's interesting how fake nationalism is often the big brother of petty corruption, isn't it?

I'm not against sport—I even cried when Mark Taylor sacrificed his chance to hold a cricket record for the sake of his team. But I don't need Olympic mascots to tell me to love my country. Silly, Milly and Dilly (as I call them) can go and get nicked. Anyway, they don't look anything like the real animals. We have echidnas on the farm, and I'm telling you, they can't walk upright.

I'm grateful that this is a country inhabited by an amazingly forgiving Indigenous people. Generous people. I thought of how my son, Marco, who does not take to grown-ups that easily, could nonetheless relate to Ollie. When she was staying with us after the 1998 Sorry Day in Sydney I had planned a really nice final day for us. We'd go into town by ferry and have lunch at the art gallery. But I got hit with tonsilitis and just couldn't move from the bed. I called out to her to ask her if she'd take Marco to kindy. He was playing up and wanting to climb all over me. She took him away and told him sternly not to bother his mother. When I got up in the afternoon he was curled up on her lap in front of the TV. He looked totally comfortable.

Amelia feels the same way about Ollie. She always says Aunty Ollie is very kind. 'She always gives us presents,' she said recently. 'She even gave me 50 dollars for Christmas.' And she never takes off a 'peace sign' ring Ollie gave her.

Ollie tends to wear rings on all her fingers. When I was last in Broome a jeweller friend of Ollie's made me a ring with a pearl in it. Ollie was trying on the stunning jewellery in his shop, and I said, 'You should just wear a few pieces of good jewellery, not all that rubbishy stuff you normally wear.'

The jeweller, who had only just met me, looked astonished. 'Nobody else would get away with saying something like that to Ollie!' But I think we're used to giving each other advice without taking offence.

I'm grateful for my friendships with Aboriginal people and how they've changed my life. This book, in a way, is dedicated to all my Aboriginal and Torres Strait Islander friends—particularly the women—who have tried to teach me to 'take it easy, sis'.

The scene has changed enormously since I first started work in this area in the late 1970s. There's a new, very smart and talented generation of Aboriginal and Torres Strait Islander people emerging. And there's also a healthy debate emerging about the role of non-Aboriginal people in Indigenous research.

Many Aboriginal people are sick of the growth industry and want to see some benefit for themselves, not just all the whitefella professionals involved. I still think, despite the growth of Indigenous media, there is a role for non-Aboriginal journalists writing about these issues in the mainstream media, and I guess at this stage I'm considering my future role.

I was thinking about all this as I walked across the Sydney Harbour Bridge holding Amelia's hand, with my husband and Marco and about 200,000 other people. I hadn't made it to bed until after 2am as I'd been at a friend's party. I was pretty burnt out again after working on the third Sorry Day/Journey of Healing, and so was enjoying letting my hair down. We hadn't had as much publicity this year because the media focus had been on the reconciliation walk and Corroboree 2000, but I couldn't help thinking it was the Stolen Generations who had led the whole thing in many ways. It was the stories of Ollie and others like her that had ignited the public's sympathy more than land rights or native title ever could.

As we walked with the Journey of Healing mob the first thing I noticed was how eerily quiet it was. I thought about Ollie and me going in the '88 march and how noisy and turbulent that had been. Every few seconds somebody would be yelling out, 'What do we want?' and the crowd would yell back, 'land rights now!' Then they'd yell, 'What have we got?' and the crowd would yell back, 'fuck all!' But this walk was all very polite—no four letter words, only one starting with S and written across the winter sky. We forced our way through the freezing wind and then my fellow walkers started to sing the Journey of Healing song. Although I felt happy—and amazed—at the number of people who came, I also felt a bit sad and a bit empty because Ollie wasn't there with us. She told me later she watched the whole thing on TV from her Perth home. I wondered if Perth could attract a similar crowd to an event like this, and I doubted it.

In the days afterwards there was much debate about how the walk, which had tried to be so apolitical, had been hijacked by those calling for a treaty. A treaty? Hadn't I heard that word somewhere before? A few history lessons might be in order. I was reminded that it was the government's Council for Aboriginal Reconciliation which had knocked off the whole treaty debate in the first place, when the Labor government was not prepared to follow through with Bob Hawke's promise to his son, Stephen. An Aboriginal journalist colleague put it very succinctly to me. She made me laugh as she described the non-Aboriginal reconciliation supporters as 'The People's Front of Judea', from the film *The Life of Brian*. They had crowed about their 'people's movement' and the success of the bridge walk, but how many of them were prepared to hand over assets, land and power to enable true reconciliation to occur, she asked.

It doesn't involve that much sacrifice to walk over the bridge on a Sunday morning, even with a hangover. And it's easier to say sorry than to really give up anything of your own. But I guess it's a start, and when governments see there is support for causes by a wide cross-section of people they're more likely to take notice.

For me, my work and friendships with Aboriginal people have involved an emotionally tough 25-year personal journey, but I don't regret it at all. And despite all the ups and downs, I greatly value and feel strongly about those friendships, especially Ollie's. We still love each other.

Ollie and I have often joked that if everything just got too bad in our lives, we'd head for Sabu. And I know she wants to spend more time with her family there. So if anybody has any complaints about this book—or our warped senses of humour—please don't try to find us. We'll be winging our way on a small plane to a tiny island off the west coast of Timor. We hope they serve cocktails there!

Ollie: Once upon a time I couldn't cry. In the early days of my marriage with Dave I used to honestly think there was something wrong with me. Even when I was with Gwen and Sid I couldn't cry. I didn't know the reasons then. I realise now that was my defence mechanism. I couldn't understand Gwenny. She used to cry at the drop of a hat.

I used to feel shamed for Gwenny. When we went to the pictures she'd start crying, or when she laughed everybody used to laugh at her laughing. When I was a kid that would be a shame job, I'd be cringing down in my chair. Or anything on the news, she'd just howl. I did think something was wrong with me for not crying.

Just before I left Derby in July, 1998, I was watching one of my favourite movies, *The Tale of Two Cities*. I saw that movie as a kid. I loved it because of the romance. It was a love story. It's set during the French revolution and the aristocrat's going to the guillotine. He was in love with this woman. She was in love with him too, but she married somebody else. Her husband was caught but this guy went and rescued him and went to the guillotine in his place. I just cried and cried and cried. I would always stop myself from crying in sad movies. But this time I felt really good. I just sobbed and sobbed. I was there on my own and I was just sobbing. He could have been a bastard, let him go to the guillotine and marry the one he loved. No, he did the right thing! I get all choked up now in sad movies. I couldn't understand why I didn't cry before, but now I can.

The Stolen Children's inquiry—it changed people. It certainly changed me. People are talking more now about the whole issue of taking children away. The first meeting I went to was in Derby. I went just for curiosity. I just wanted to know what it was all about. Initially, in the first meetings I still didn't want to talk about it. I put up my defence mechanisms. I didn't want to get hurt, didn't want to expose myself.

That first meeting there was hardly any people. I think there was only two of us who were directly affected. The rest of the people were the organisers and two people from Welfare. That's part of their work, I guess, representing their departments.

At that first meeting the organisers said, 'John Howard is not supporting this.' Straight off they said to the group, 'There's no way people will get compensation.' I was a bit annoyed about that because they were making assumptions about people in the group before it even commenced. So I raised a question.

I said, 'I don't think we should be pre-empting this. If people from the Stolen Generations are putting forth a recommendation that they want compensation then it should be documented and in the minutes. Whether Howard disagrees and there's no way he's going to pay compensation, it should still be recorded.'

And I said, 'I'd like to make a recommendation about these people from the Stolen Generations who want compensation, because these are people who have been taken away and can't go back to their homelands and they're caught in between. Now they're stuck in these towns and they're in Homeswest housing. I would like to put a recommendation that these people who have been dispossessed and who can't return to their homelands should be compensated. Their government houses that they're living in should be given back to them freehold, and then it's their choice what they want to do with it.'

I don't think that was ever minuted. I was angry that's that what they made out people were only there for—compensation.

In 1996 I gave evidence at a hearing in Broome held by the Human Rights Commission, who were conducting the Stolen Children's inquiry. I had been asked by the girls who had been in the Holy Child Orphanage to read our submission for the hearing. As I was living in Derby I was unable to attend the orphanage girls' meetings. Many of us were unsure why we were removed from our families and placed in the orphanage. But one thing is for sure—we weren't orphans. Unfortunately, there are many 'orphanage girls' who still believe what they were told as children—that their mothers neglected them and that's why they were taken away. It was what the government wanted us to believe. Even some of the mothers are still in denial. They'd say, 'I couldn't cope,' but that was just a cover up.

At the hearing before commissioner Mick Dodson, himself originally from Broome, there were many orphanage girls in the room. There were actually three generations of Stolen Generations people there, including my Aunty

Betty, who also gave evidence, and my grandmother, Mimi Dora. The Catholic bishop of Broome, Chris Saunders, and some nuns were also there. I think he was in tears. He told me after the hearing that he would discuss some of our recommendations with us later.

This is some of what I read to the hearing: *Today as adults, the impact of such legislation that effectively removed us from our family also varies from person to person and continues to impact on our lives today. Collectively, one question is asked from most of us and that is why? Why were we removed? Who authorised it and for what reasons? Since we became adults we have learnt why we were taken away, and some of us knew about the 1905 Aborigines Protection Act. There were a lot of girls, even though they were forcibly removed from their families, that are still not aware of that act. As a result of being made wards of the state and placed in the care of the nuns, many of us lost our family members. Physically and emotionally our relationships with mothers, fathers, sisters, brothers, are lost.*

The time spent in the orphanage, with no amount of best intentions, will ever replace those precious bonds which establish a sense of belonging. Esteem, identity and nurture, love, understanding and compassion were replaced with a regimented day to day existence. We were taught religion and education with a focus on domestics.

Our individuality as children was lost in the numbers to be fed, taught and accounted for. There were no hugs, pats on the head or kind words of encouragement. There was too much control. Every activity was a controlled event, up to any marriage proposal as approved by the nuns, which would see our departure from the orphanage. Because we were wards of the state, once you were eighteen you were no longer a ward and you were released. So you were just sent out into the world to survive in a lot of cases with no education, and importantly, with no sex education. I recall one aunty saying to me the extent of her sex education was to stay away from white men, and that was it.

As individuals there are memories we can recall with some fondness. The friendships that bonded us as orphanage kids, the weekends at Riddell Beach and other happy occasions. But as individuals also, each of us could pick out at least half a dozen grievances with the nuns as our caretakers, the discipline, the notes made on our records in relation to our intelligence, the removal of personal possessions, the removal of birth names, the denial of access to family members, the chores, and being locked up at night.

For some people to expose themselves at these hearings was very difficult. They had held it in tight and only some had the courage to come forward and talk about it. That's why for John Howard to dismiss our evidence is so unfair. But on the other hand, giving evidence was a chance to grow and heal. Even Lucy Marshall, who was in her 80s, was apprehensive about giving evidence. She said, 'I don't want to tell my story.' But once she started to talk about it she felt much better.

There's still a lot of people who don't want to talk about it still, and that should be respected. They'll take their stories to their graves. Some even say they're not really members of the Stolen Generations.

Myself, I had mixed feelings about the whole thing. I was apprehensive about giving evidence at that hearing. It was like exposing yourself—your weaknesses, your vulnerability. Throughout your life you put up your defence mechanism and you build walls and barriers so nobody can break through those barriers, so nobody can hurt you.

Not only that, but Broome's a small town and people bitch. Initially, I thought I didn't want to be exposed to that shit. In retrospect I'm glad I did it. I realised that giving evidence and finally talking about it is all part of my healing process. You can't live your life thinking I can't offend this one or that one, you have to do what you feel. There comes a time in everybody's life that you have to stand up and be counted.

This has all been part of my healing. It's changed me in the sense where now I can cry, whereas I wasn't able to. And that crying is all part of my healing and it's all part of getting it out. That's the only way you can heal—by getting it out.

When I was working in Midland I had work colleagues I made friends with. There were three girls and we used to go out to lunches. I considered them friends. I was going through my marriage breakup with Dave. I'd been separated from him for twelve months. These girls always asked about my family. 'How's Dave? How's Cindy?'

Finally I had to say to the three of them, 'Look, you've got to stop asking about Dave, we've been separated for twelve months.'

They were shocked. They said, 'We didn't know.'

I always kept my personal life separate to my work. I was able to hide that and not bring it to work. I get annoyed when people bring their personal life to work. I guess I'm making judgements, but I can keep it separate. You know, when people come to work grumpy and take it out on other staff, I get annoyed with that.

With the Stolen Generations stuff I was used to holding it in and not sharing it with anybody. I thought there was no big deal that I was in an orphanage. Like Diana, I knew about the Stolen Generations, but didn't really understand until I got older and found out about the laws. Like the laws regarding One Mile community, outside of Broome. We had kids in the school who lived out at One Mile. It was only later that I found out about the laws that stipulated that Aboriginal people had to live one mile out of town. Then I understood about the curfews and why Aboriginal people had to be out of town by six o'clock.

As adults we continued to be affected by the legislation imposed on us. We also had been removed from country, culture, language groups and traditional links. I don't think the government was trying to do the right thing. The policy of the day was 'assimilation'—genocide. They wanted to get rid of Aboriginal people. People talk about good intentions but I don't think that's what it was. Who's to say my mother wouldn't have been a good mother and different, had she been able to keep me, and my father had not been deported? One can only speculate. You can't say I would have been better off or worse off. For me personally, I thought I was robbed of two rich cultures and two languages that I could have been exposed to in that family unit.

At the inquiry in Broome I also gave evidence about my Asian background and about my father. We handed in some recommendations from the orphanage girls. We would have liked the Kimberley Land Council to negotiate with the bishop, the diocese for the orphanage land, including the land at Riddell Beach, to be handed over to the orphanage girls. This would not be for individual personal use. We would look at options for what we'd like to do. Some ideas are to place a plaque for the girls who are deceased.

We would also like all those who haven't already got it to have access to their files. We should have local archives where people can go and access those files. And we're talking about the Catholic church's files too.

I hope something comes out of all these inquiries and reports and not just more government departments and more acronyms.

When we were down at Diana's farm I finally had a chance to read her book, *Taking Control*. The introduction is her diary of what happened to her when she lost her babies and how she managed to have Marco. I'd never really heard the whole story before that, although we'd talked on the phone a lot. I read it in bed at night, but I couldn't finish reading because I was crying too much. It was really sad. I can see why people can relate to it. And when I got up in the morning I had red eyes. I told her sister, Anna, I'd cried. I hadn't realised exactly what she'd been through until then.

I guess there's now more of a connection. Diana said after losing the babies she understood even more about how my mother must have felt when Pudding and I were taken away from her. But she still reckoned she could never really know what that was like. It's like I said before, I was so scared when Cindy was a baby that Welfare or somebody would take her away.

Cindy stayed with me in Broome before going to Europe again, and we talked a lot about our lives. She told me that my father's last words to her at the airport that time in Sabu when she was crying were, 'I'll see you in my dreams.' He knew he wasn't going to see her again. Cindy didn't know exactly what he meant, but in her heart she knew she wouldn't see him again. That's why she was sobbing her heart out. She sent me a post card when she was away. It said, *I won't see you in my dreams. I'll see you in Perth.*

And now Diana and I have written a book together, so I guess it's the full circle. Writing this book has absolutely been part of my healing. I don't think I'd be able to do it if I hadn't got a lot of this stuff out.

As for me, I'm having a new start. I've left Broome and the Kimberley and gone back to Perth. Broome's a beautiful place but it's still a small town. I might even go and live in Sabu for a while. That narrow little world I grew up in has closed. That's another—in some ways, better forgotten—era. I may be in my late '40s but I'm not middle-aged yet! And neither's Diana. We went out on the town when she was in Broome and we were raging until three in the morning. You never know, I might even become a consultant.

Look at Tina Turner and Shirley Bassey (my heroines). They're not getting any younger but they look fantastic and have so much energy. The whole world worships them. Now the whole world is before me and I'm going to enjoy it. No tears. I promise. Well, maybe only in sad movies.